Is Bipartisanship Dead?

Policy Agreement and Agenda-Setting in the House of Representatives

Is Bipartisanship Dead? looks beyond (and considers the time before) roll call voting to examine the extent to which bipartisan agreement in the House of Representatives has declined since the 1970s. Despite voting coalitions showing a decline in bipartisan agreement between 1973 and 2004, members' bill cosponsorship coalitions show a much more stable level of bipartisanship. The declining bipartisanship over time in roll call voting reflects a shift in how party leaders structure the floor and roll call agendas. Party leaders in the House changed from prioritizing legislation with bipartisan agreement in the 1970s to prioritizing legislation with partisan disagreement by the 1990s. Laurel Harbridge argues that this shift reflects a changing political environment and an effort by leaders to balance members' electoral interests, governance goals, and partisan differentiation. The findings speak to questions of representation and governance. They also shed light on whether partisan conflict is insurmountable, and, ultimately, whether bipartisanship in congressional politics is dead.

Laurel Harbridge is an assistant professor of Political Science at Northwestern University and a faculty Fellow at the Institute for Policy Research. Her teaching and research focus on legislative politics, partisan conflict, and the lack of bipartisan agreement in American politics. She is a former Hoover Institution National Fellow. Her work has been published in the *American Journal of Political Science*, *Legislative Studies Quarterly*, and *American Politics Research*.

Is Bipartisanship Dead?

Policy Agreement and Agenda-Setting in the House of Representatives

LAUREL HARBRIDGE

Northwestern University

CAMBRIDGE
UNIVERSITY PRESS

32 Avenue of the Americas, New York, NY 10013-2473, USA

Cambridge University Press is part of the University of Cambridge.

It furthers the University's mission by disseminating knowledge in the pursuit of education, learning, and research at the highest international levels of excellence.

www.cambridge.org
Information on this title: www.cambridge.org/9781107439283

© Laurel Harbridge 2015

First published 2015

Printed in the United States of America

A catalog record for this publication is available from the British Library.

ISBN 978-1-107-07995-3 Hardback
ISBN 978-1-107-43928-3 Paperback

Contents

Figures and Tables

TABLES

Acknowledgments

The idea for this book developed after began research on what I thought would be a decline in bipartisan cooperation at all stages of policy making as party polarization has risen in Congress over the last 30 years. However, when I began analyzing the data on cosponsorship coalitions, the striking feature was the persistence of bipartisan cooperation rather than its decline. As a result, I altered my focus and turned to looking at why bipartisan agreement would be different in cosponsorship coalitions and in roll call votes. I narrowed my focus to changes in the composition of the legislative agenda to understand this puzzle. As this book comes to completion, I am thankful to all of those who have helped along the way.

This project began as my dissertation at Stanford University, where I could not have done without the advice and guidance of my chair, David Brady. He struck the perfect balance of allowing me the freedom to take my research ideas where I wanted, while nonetheless reminding me to keep the questions broad and relevant. His help in framing the research proved invaluable. I am also indebted to my other committee members – Morris Fiorina and Paul Sniderman – who helped me in the early stages by offering mentorship and advice on framing the research.

At Northwestern University, I found a wide group of colleagues who offered support and feedback throughout the process of completing the book. Colleagues in both the Political Science Department and the Institute for Policy Research offered suggestions, gave advice, and helped improve this book in many ways. In particular, Daniel Galvin and Anthony Chen were generous with their time, reading drafts and providing feedback; Benjamin Page and Jamie Druckman mentored me throughout the process of bringing this book to fruition; and Jason Seawright and Georgia Kernell offered suggestions on analysis and interpretation. I also found both undergraduate and graduate students who wanted to engage with this research and helped with research tasks, large and small. My thanks go out to Katherine Scovic, Sourav Bhowmick,

Leah Patterson, Nathan Abelman, Hanna Rutkowski, D. J. Flynn, Mara Suttmann-Lea, and Vijay Murganoor.

Other colleagues, near and far, also provided feedback and a sounding board throughout this project. Sarah Anderson, Margaret Peters, Alexander Tahk, Gregory Koger, Michael Neblo, and Daniel Diermeier all offered help along the way. I am particularly thankful for E. Scott Adler's guidance. He was my first academic mentor at the University of Colorado, and his guidance (and persistence), combined with the invitation to join him in research, led me to graduate school.

The editors and editorial team at Cambridge University Press have been very helpful. I thank Robert Dreesen and Elizabeth Janetschek in particular. I appreciate the suggestions from the reviewers for Cambridge (as well as anonymous reviewers for Oxford University Press), all of which helped to improve this book.

Opportunities to present portions of this research in seminars and a book manuscript workshop were invaluable. The Northwestern Political Parties Working Group, Institute for Policy Research, Cornell Government and Economics Workshop, Vanderbilt Center for the Study of Democratic Institutions, and Texas A&M Conference on Parties and Polarization in American Politics all provided feedback, suggestions, and advice that helped to improve this book. A book manuscript conference, with feedback from Barry Burden, Frances Lee, David Rohde, and Steven Smith, provided a critical angle on the project when I needed it most.

Support for this project came not only from my department and the Institute for Policy Research, but also from the Dirksen Congressional Center and the Carl Albert Center. I was able to spend time as a visiting scholar at Vanderbilt's Center for the Study of Democratic Institutions, where I not only presented this work but was able to brainstorm with Alan Wiseman, Joshua Clinton, and others. The final steps of this book could not have been completed without my time as a National Fellow at the Hoover Institution. This opportunity gave me time to finish this manuscript and the chance to engage with more scholars as I fine-tuned my arguments.

The analyses presented throughout the book would not be possible without the generosity of scholars who have shared their data. James Fowler's cosponsorship data, Adler and Wilkerson's Congressional Bills Project, the Policy Agendas Project, Rohde's roll call data, and Gary Jacobson's elections data offered treasure troves of information.

Finally, I am grateful for the support of family members and friends. In particular, I thank my parents, Bill and CD Harbridge, and my sister, Heather Harbridge, without whose support none of this would have been possible. I owe a special debt of gratitude to David Yong, whose support, encouragement, and listening ear helped propel me through the final steps of this book.

I

Introduction

> With both parties becoming more homogeneous and less diverse, the nation's political leaders have been freed to take harder positions, draw sharper lines and forsake the time-honored tradition of reaching across party lines to find common cause with the other side.
>
> (Westphal 2004)

This quote captures three key aspects of the conventional wisdom on rising partisanship in Congress: that members have become increasingly polarized into two separate and non-overlapping ideological camps, that bipartisan cooperation has fallen as a result, and that these changes work against desired and "time-honored" efforts to find common ground in the legislative process. Those most critical of partisanship go even further, arguing that it produces gridlock, stunts policy innovation, and diminishes responsiveness on any level. In essence, polarization damages effective democratic governance.

Just how well do we understand the roots of partisan conflict? Scholars have suggested that the existence of elite polarization is "largely noncontroversial" (Fiorina and Abrams 2008, 584). While there is controversy over the extent of polarization in the mass public, nearly all political observers agree that elected officials fall into two distinct camps, with few places of agreement between members of the two parties. Moreover, research clearly shows that party polarization in American politics, as measured by the ideal point estimates (i.e., ideological positions) of members in the two parties, has risen since the 1970s (e.g., McCarty et al. 2006; Theriault 2008). Rather than representing the full spectrum of the legislative process, however, these studies concentrate attention on just roll call voting. This book looks beyond (and before) roll call votes to explore the extent and timing of partisan conflict in the U.S. House of Representatives since the 1970s. Until we look beyond roll call votes, we cannot fully understand the roots of partisan conflict, separate the impact of individual members' positions from that of party influence and agenda-setting, or gauge whether bipartisanship is, in fact, dead. A better understanding of these issues is a necessary first step toward evaluating the normative concerns that discussions of partisan conflict typically provoke, ranging from issues of governance and legislative action (or inaction) to issue attention across policy areas and representation.

A focus on roll call votes can miss dynamics of policy agreement within House politics. For example, in the wake of the fallout from the collapse of the Enron Corporation in December 2001, the Republican House majority sought to address pension reform. Republicans proposed two separate reform bills: the Employment Retirement Savings Bill of Rights (H.R. 3669), introduced by Rep. Rob Portman (R-OH); and the Pension Security Act of 2002 (H.R. 3762), introduced by Rep. John Boehner (R-OH). Portman's bill, which was referred to the Ways and Means Committee, had bipartisan cosponsorship as it garnered the support of 15 Republicans and 6 Democrats. The bill was also reported from committee on a bipartisan vote of 36–2 (yea-nay) ("Pension Security Bills Falter" 2002). In contrast, Boehner's bill, which was referred to the Education and Workforce Committee, was highly partisan, having the support of 32 Republican cosponsors and only 1 Democratic cosponsor and a mostly partisan committee vote of 28–19 ("Pension Security Bills Falter" 2002). Both bills sought to address diversification and investment advice for employees, but demonstrated substantive differences in their approach to the problem. In particular, Portman's bill allowed employees to use some of their salary through a tax-free payroll deduction to purchase investment advice on their own, while Boehner's bill allowed employee-sponsored plans to give workers investment advice so long as they disclosed conflicts of interest (Swindell 2002).

Despite having the option of pursuing a bipartisan bill, House Speaker Dennis Hastert and Majority Leader Dick Armey decided to use Boehner's more partisan bill (H.R. 3762) as the vehicle for pension reform. A largely party-line vote on the House floor resulted, with 208 Republicans and 46 Democrats voting yea and 2 Republicans and 160 Democrats voting nay. During the floor debate, members emphasized that the Republican leadership had made a choice to put the more partisan bill on the agenda. Pete Stark (D-CA) noted that "this bill points out so clearly the differences between the Republicans and the Democrats" ("Congressional Record" 2002). Similarly, Bob Etheridge (D-NC) claimed that, "Earlier this year, the Ways and Means Committee passed a truly bipartisan pension reform bill. But, the Republican Majority chose ... a controversial bill passed by the Education and Workforce Committee" ("Congressional Record" 2002).

Although the partisan bill ultimately died in the Senate, this example highlights two important aspects of the argument presented in this book. First, even in recent decades when severe partisanship has been the story of Congressional politics, pieces of legislation with bipartisan support have remained. Second, even when there has been underlying bipartisan agreement on substantive policy matters, the majority party's leaders have been able to pursue partisan legislation on the floor. The resulting roll call votes give the appearance of two parties divided. If we looked only at the roll call vote on Boehner's partisan bill, we would have missed these two insights.

Throughout this book, I demonstrate continued levels of substantive policy agreement across the aisle, particularly in cosponsorship coalitions and bipartisan voice votes. Bipartisanship, in short, is not dead; it is just hidden from view. By focusing on the most visible legislative activity – casting roll call votes – we have obscured important stages of policymaking in which bipartisan agreement continued to exist. Roll call vote-based measures of polarization and partisan conflict show that Democrats and Republicans are voting differently from one another, but these measures are the end result of legislative agendas that can mask places of policy agreement. I develop new measures of bipartisan agreement by considering cosponsorship coalitions, and I use this data to shed light on how the House majority party uses its control over the legislative agenda to manufacture higher or lower levels partisan polarization. This approach demonstrates how the strategic nature of agenda-setting drives partisan conflict. The complex picture of governance that emerges reveals a latent but remarkably persistent level of substantive bipartisan agreement in the House between 1973 and 2004. This potential for bipartisanship has been overshadowed by growing partisanship in roll call votes.

WHY UNPACK THE ROOTS OF PARTISAN CONFLICT?

I argue that the distinction between partisan roll call voting behavior and bipartisan actions elsewhere in the House has significant consequences for our understanding of representative democracy and for our evaluations of Congress as a functioning governing body. Effective democratic governance is a concern of policymakers and citizens alike. According to the National Democratic Institute, "A capable and effective national legislature is a foundational pillar of democratic government"; the capacity of representative institutions to communicate with citizens and respond to their concerns, and to shape laws and policies that reflect national and constituent interests, is essential to an effective national legislature (National Democratic Institute 2013). When scholars and political commentators express concern over partisan disagreement, the implicit worry is that rising polarization, combined with institutional arrangements in the federal government, undermine Congress's ability to meet these requirements.

Scholars have characterized the institutional structures of government in the United States as both promoting and inhibiting democratic governance. In an effort to avoid the perceived pitfalls of a pure democracy, the Framers of the United States Constitution designed a complex constitutional system in which indirect mechanisms of representation, overlapping institutional prerogatives, and competing governing authorities altered prevailing notions of democratic sovereignty. Rather than translate the will of the people directly into public policies, the Framers ensured that the public voice would be mediated. It might be "refined and enlarged" by allowing the wisdom of representatives to "best discern the true interest of the country" (Madison 1787), or it might be corrupted or distorted. In either case, institutional arrangements would always be insinuated in the outputs of government (Burden 2005; Dahl 2003).

As the American polity and its mediating devices of representation further developed over the next two-hundred-plus years, political analysts reliably kept pace, identifying and evaluating perceived dysfunctions. Before becoming president, Woodrow Wilson (1900) argued against the separation of powers system on the grounds of inefficiency and corruption. He, like other scholars (e.g., APSA 1950; Schattschneider 1942), suggested that stronger parties with greater influence over their members would produce more effective governance. In recent years, however, attitudes on this topic have changed. Instead of viewing cohesive national parties as a vehicle for efficiency, scholars and political commentators since the 1970s have expressed alarm at the dramatic rise of party conflict (e.g., Gutmann and Thompson 2012; Mann and Ornstein 2006, 2012; McCarty et al. 2006; Sinclair 2006; Theriault 2008). Their worry is that party conflict exacerbates institutional inefficiencies (some say to the point of paralysis) and drowns out popular sovereignty.

Although some political scientists continue to defend partisanship and polarization (e.g., Muirhead 2006; Rosenblum 2008), in recent decades the more common refrain is that party polarization has replaced an idealized era of bipartisanship, producing negative consequences for governing and representation (e.g., Eilperin 2006). These complaints come in many forms. Some worry that "the policy process has been distorted, with deliberation and compromise replaced by a partisan steamroller" (Sinclair 2006, 344–5). Others tie polarization to legislative stalemate, suggesting that the parties find it harder to get things done in the public interest (Hacker and Pierson 2005, 5). In essence, critics claim that parties are focused on scoring political points rather than solving problems (Mann and Ornstein 2012, 101). Combined, these criticisms suggest that the outcome of policymaking in a partisan climate is undesirable, regardless of whether Congress passes partisan legislation or faces gridlock.

Political participants and observers share these concerns about the rise of partisanship. For instance, former House member Fred Grandy (R-IA) argued that "governing is about finding common ground, and liberals and conservatives must give up the automatic partisanship that has taken hold in order to truly solve large problems" (Grandy 1995). Ronald Brownstein, the editorial director of the *National Journal*, argued that "hyperpartisanship has unnecessarily inflamed our differences and impeded our progress against our most pressing challenges" (Brownstein 2007, 367). Even organizations like the Democracy Fund, which invests in social entrepreneurs to ensure that our political system is responsive to the public, are concerned about polarization. In a recent blog post about the organization's concerns and goals, Director Joe Goldman noted that "while polarization is not necessarily a bad thing (it clarifies choices and motivates participation), the checks and balances of the American political system require our two parties to work together in order for our system to function" (Goldman 2013). [In sum, partisan conflict appears at odds with effective governance.]

The assessments of the effect of polarization on representation are similarly pessimistic. Most of the current assessments of Congress herald bipartisanship and compromise as the normative good and see partisanship as a distortion of this ideal (e.g., Gutmann and Thompson 2012). From this perspective, the rise of partisanship reflects a failure in representative government, particularly at a collective level (Fiorina and Abrams 2009). Similarly, Hacker and Pierson (2005, 35) tie polarization to breakdowns in government responsiveness, as they question whether elections are playing the essential role of assuring responsiveness from those in power. Other scholars have pointed out that stalemate and partisan bickering erode the public's faith in Congress (Galston and Nivola 2006; Hibbing and Theiss-Morse 1995, 2002; Theriault 2008).

Polarization, then, has been linked to a breakdown in effective governance, in terms of both legislative compromise and constituent responsiveness (Rae 2007). But what exactly do we mean by polarization? Most discussions of the negative consequences of polarization assume that party members have moved so far apart ideologically since the 1970s that there is no room left for common ground on policy.[1] The result is partisan conflict.

"Polarization" remains an ambiguous concept, despite its common usage (Mayhew 2002, 98). First, polarization as a concept is not necessarily the same thing as polarization as a measure. As a concept, polarization often focuses on ideological disagreement, but, as a measure, polarization generally captures all votes that separate Democrats from Republicans, regardless of the reason (Lee 2009). Second, we know from existing research that party institutions affect nearly all of what we see in Congress, especially at the end-stages of the political process. These concerns are inter-related, and they suggest that we ought to specify the key features of polarization and ask how well our measures capture these features. Understanding the various facets of polarization has important consequences for how we understand partisan conflict as well as for how we evaluate congressional governance, assess representation, and, ultimately, seek to improve the political system.

The existing literature on political elites either defines polarization in terms of a roll call vote-based measure or not at all.[2] For instance, McCarty, Poole, and

---

[1] Some suggest that these ideological preferences are induced from members' constituencies. For instance, Cooper and Brady (1981) suggest that the source of partisan voting lies in the electorate, where cohesiveness in voting is driven by homogeneity of electoral coalitions and the resulting member preferences. Others suggest that member preferences are more extreme than those of their constituents (Fiorina and Abrams 2009; Fiorina et al. 2005). In either case, however, changes in members' preferences are often assumed to drive rising levels of partisanship in Congress.

[2] Scholars analyzing polarization among the mass public have paid somewhat more attention to the definition of polarization as they have debated whether the public has polarized or sorted (see Fiorina and Abrams 2008; Fiorina et al. 2005; Abramowitz 2010; Levendusky 2009).

Rosenthal (2006, 3) define polarization as "a separation of politics into liberal and conservative camps" based on voting patterns. Alternatively, neither Han and Brady (2007) nor Theriault (2008) offer explicit definitions of polarization, perhaps assuming, as many scholars do, that we have a clear understanding of this term.[3] Rohde (1991, 8–9) notes that polarization can be measured by the frequency of party voting, average party differences (absolute value of the difference in the proportion of each party voting yea), indexes of cohesion (absolute difference between the proportion of a party's members voting yea and voting nay on a vote), and party unity indexes (proportion of party unity votes that a member votes with the party). In general, there is little discussion of a conceptual definition of polarization beyond these measures, all of which focus on roll call voting.

Moreover, existing analyses equate roll call voting behavior (which occurs on one subset of bills at the end stage of the legislative process) with a broader inability of members to find common ground across party lines. The conventional wisdom, linking polarization to a lack of common ground, is summarized by a statement from Dodd and Oppenheimer: "Given the growing regional base of the two parties in the House and Senate, the decline in the number of moderates in both parties, the increased ideological polarization, [and] the strength of party voting, … finding common ground and room for the two parties in Congress to compromise on policy has become ever more difficult" (Dodd and Oppenheimer 2012, 480). Perhaps the best distinction between the grandiose claims and empirical measures is seen in a recent *Pacific Standard Magazine* story titled "There is No Common Ground Anymore" (Badger 2009). Despite the sweeping claims of the title, the text only discusses roll call voting and the resulting ideal point estimates. Quite often, then, while many use partisan roll call votes to imply the presence of disagreement across issues and across stages of the legislative process, they typically measure partisan disagreement on only the subset of bills that receive roll call votes.

Even though the extent to which policymakers want to find places of agreement is debatable, having common ground on legislation is the first step to reaching cross-party agreement. If our current take on polarization and partisan conflict is correct, it would appear that these ideological partisan differences are insurmountable. If, however, there are places of common ground, bipartisan agreement may be possible if politicians are incentivized to pursue these places of agreement rather than their places of disagreement. Senator Susan Collins of Maine suggested as much in an interview with Norah O'Donnell for *CBS in the Morning* in 2013. Collins said, "Women span the ideological spectrum, just as men do. We don't all agree. But what I do think we

---

[3] Theriault (2008) does provide a number of statements in the opening chapters of his book that hint at various components of polarization, including "disagreement about procedures" (3), "members who cast increasingly ideological votes" (4), greater differences between the parties and increased party voting (7), and the division of parties into separate camps on vote-based measures (16). Nearly all of these comments tie polarization to vote-based measures.

bring to this issue [gun control] and so many others, is a more collaborative approach and a willingness to find where the common ground is" (O'Donnell 2013). Page (2009, 50) also notes that, despite ideological differences, members of both parties support subsidies for businesses and spending for programs back home. There would appear to be some places where even a polarized Congress could find policy agreement and where voting could be bipartisan. If leaders have incentives to pursue these types of policies on the floor, bipartisanship could be more common.

Understanding the potential for bipartisanship and common ground on policy, and why that agreement might not be picked up in roll call votes, is important for understanding the normative consequences of partisanship and the appropriate solutions to current levels of partisan conflict. There are different implications for the evaluation of governance,[4] representation, and other pressing normative questions depending on whether polarization is largely restricted to differences in voting behavior or whether it indicates a broader inability to work across the aisle. Working from the premise that polarization is undesirable, a number of scholars have proposed potential solutions (e.g., Brownstein 2007; Galston and Nivola 2006; Mann and Ornstein 2012). But whether we want to dramatically overhaul the composition of members of Congress, change the incentive structure for members through different primary election or fundraising structures, or make internal reforms in Congress hinges on how we understand the basis of partisan conflict. If members of Congress do share common ground, but are embedded in a legislative process that increasingly favors partisan disagreement, solutions should focus on this process and on the majority party's incentives to pursue partisan legislation, and not on simply instigating legislative turnover.

AN EMPIRICAL STRATEGY FOR UNTANGLING THE ROOTS OF PARTISAN CONFLICT

Focusing on bipartisan cooperation in a variety of legislative circumstances provides a useful starting point for examining the extent of partisan conflict in the House of Representatives. The term "bipartisan" can be used to characterize legislation, the behavior of members, and the strategies of parties. If political commentators are correct in asserting that partisan differences have become insurmountable, we should see instances of bipartisan agreement falling similarly over time across all stages of the legislative process, including – but not limited to – members' cosponsorship coalitions and roll call votes. If, instead, we observe differences in the patterns of bipartisanship between early and late stages of the legislative process, we ought to consider how institutional

---

[4] A multi-faceted topic like governance is necessarily simplified in this discussion. Throughout the book, I focus on the extent of government activity (i.e., public laws) and the degree to which outputs are bipartisan.

arrangements, including political parties and agenda control, act as a filter on the legislative process. The belief that political parties affect policy outcomes through agenda control is widespread (Aldrich 1995; Cox and McCubbins 1993, 2005; Rohde 1991), but the connection to partisan conflict is less well established. As such, this book seeks to understand both the potential for bipartisan agreement and the role that political parties play in manufacturing partisan conflict.

In order to gauge the extent of common ground between members of the two parties, we must look beyond – and in this case *before* – roll call votes. Without doing so, we risk attributing changes in the floor agenda and party strategy to changes in member ideology alone. Gaining any traction in separating the degree to which partisanship in voting reflects the preferences of members, as opposed to the strategy of the party, hinges on an ability to look at the behavior of members absent the agenda-setting decisions of the majority party. To put this another way, we need to somehow distinguish between at least three possibilities: that increased polarization in roll call voting results from members' preferences; that legislative agenda-setting has changed while members' preferences have remained unchanged; or that both processes, in part, explain polarization (Clinton 2012). Roll call votes are an excellent source of data, but can only reveal legislative behavior, coalitions, and policy content after the agenda has already been set (and only on a subset of bills receiving votes). This insight suggests that we ought to consider the behavior of members and the extent of bipartisan agreement earlier in the legislative process.

In this book, I examine patterns of bipartisan agreement over time and look at how party influence affects later legislative stages and resulting policy outcomes by examining the distribution of coalitions on cosponsored bills before and after the party sets the floor and roll call agendas. That is, I assess the frequency of bipartisan coalitions pre- and post-agenda formation. Throughout this book, I use the term "coalition" to describe a group of legislators who sign on as cosponsors on a piece of legislation. I note, however, that this does not necessarily assume that members have communicated or coordinated their activity.

The pre-agenda measures of legislative behavior and common ground between members are based on cosponsorship coalitions. The frequency of bipartisan coalitions on all cosponsored bills speaks to the potential for bipartisan agreement. Like voting behavior, cosponsorship provides a quantifiable metric of coalitions based on public position taking by members. But unlike voting behavior, cosponsorship coalitions occur prior to the leadership winnowing down bills for floor attention. The distribution of support from members of the two parties in these coalitions captures the extent of bipartisan agreement on policy.

Members appear to use their cosponsorship records to signal their political views to their constituencies. Anecdotal evidence from member newsletters to constituents as well as from responses to newspaper editorial boards point to cosponsorship, and bipartisan cosponsorship in particular, as important means of position taking and credit claiming, allowing members to convey their records and demonstrate that they are willing to work across the aisle. In a sample of newsletters from the 105th Congress (1997–98), 55 percent mentioned either members' sponsorship or cosponsorship of legislation, as compared to 20 percent that mentioned members' votes.[5] This illustrates the emphasis members place on these non-vote-based actions. In 2004, Representative John Kline (R-MN), for example, sent out a newsletter titled "Creating Jobs and Growing Minnesota's Rural Economy: A Report from John Kline." In this newsletter, he detailed four different bills on which he was a cosponsor – encouraging ethanol production, reducing small business expenses, providing access to health care for the self-employed, and expanding health coverage for the uninsured. He also noted (and even underlined) that he had "joined a bipartisan group of Members of Congress and Senators" to represent the concerns of grain producers and the domestic grain industry. The content of his newsletter, like many others, attempted to portray him as bipartisan and working on behalf of constituent interests, efforts which include the cosponsorship of legislation (Kline 2004).

Recent examples suggest that members of Congress communicate their records of cosponsorship, including bipartisan cosponsorship, through the media as well. Prior to endorsing candidates in 2010, the *Chicago Tribune* editorial board asked both incumbents and challengers a number of questions about policy and, for incumbents, questions about their actions while serving in office. Many of the members' responses emphasized cosponsorship and their efforts to work with bipartisan coalitions. For instance, Donald Manzullo, Republican incumbent for Illinois' 16th District, highlighted his bipartisan efforts, including his cosponsorship of the National Manufacturing Strategy Act of 2010 (H.R. 4692), authored by Democrat Dan Lipinski (D-IL) (Manzullo 2010). Likewise, Democratic incumbent Melissa Bean, in Illinois' 8th Congressional district, discussed her cosponsorship of the bipartisan SAFE Commission Act (H.R. 1557) (Bean 2010).

Members of Congress also know that journalists pay attention to their cosponsorship activities. For instance, western New York's local newspaper *The Leader* provided a report card for Representative Tom Reed (R-NY). The report drew on Reed's sponsorship and cosponsorship record, noting the frequency with which his bills garnered support from across the aisle and how often he cosponsored bills sponsored by Democrats (Post 2014). Ultimately, cosponsorship coalitions point to the policies legislators support and how often they work across the aisle, and these records are seen in members' own communication and that of the media.

---

[5] To explore how members manage their image and convey records of bipartisanship to their constituents, I examined a subset of majority member newsletters to constituents from the 105th Congress (1997–1998). Like Lipinski (2004), I drew on newsletters from the franking archives of the Legislative Resource Center in the House of Representatives. Given the exploratory nature of the analysis, members were stratified on the most and least competitive third of districts for the 105th Congress and a random sample of 35 members in each group were selected. For each of these members, all newsletters and constituent questionnaires sent in either 1997 or 1998 were gathered.

The post-agenda measures of legislative coalitions come from roll call voting and the cosponsorship coalitions of bills receiving roll call votes (or other floor attention). The frequency of bipartisan coalitions on bills receiving floor attention or roll call votes speaks to the degree of post-agenda-setting bipartisan agreement. By knowing the cosponsorship coalitions of bills that receive roll call votes in each Congress, I am able to classify the roll call agenda as primarily bipartisan or partisan, and explore changes in the agenda over time. The same is true for measures of broader floor attention, including both roll call votes and voice votes. Throughout the book, I focus on these legislative agendas, which I define as bipartisan or partisan depending on whether the selection of bills for floor attention (and for roll call votes in particular) focuses on bills that were able to garner bipartisan or partisan support at the cosponsorship stage. The content of the agenda is important because it is controlled by the majority party and shows which bills are receiving serious attention (Kingdon 1995, 3). Moreover, the content of the agenda affects the degree of partisanship in floor voting.

Methodologically, this work draws on the insights of scholars who have pointed to the ways in which vote-based estimates of ideology may overstate polarization (Crespin et al. 2013; Stiglitz and Weingast 2011), to instances in which partisanship goes beyond ideology (Lee 2009; Noel 2013), and to the limited ability of roll call analyses to separate members' preferences from party effects (Krehbiel 1993, 2006). I also build on the work of scholars who have utilized cosponsorship coalitions to assess legislative behavior (e.g., Aleman et al. 2009; Zhang et al. 2008).

Cosponsorship coalitions provide an excellent complement to roll call votes as they are another avenue for members to take positions, signal support for legislation, and join a coalition, but they occur prior to party influence over agenda-setting.[6] By examining bipartisan agreement in these coalitions across different stages of the legislative process, I explore how party strategy combines with the preferences of members to produce an increasingly partisan Congress, thereby limiting opportunities for bipartisan cooperation among members.

The Importance of Considering the Legislative Agenda

Consider a parallel to studies of polarization in the electorate as a means of understanding how the congressional roll call agenda can artificially inflate members' enthusiasm for partisan politics. Using evidence from presidential and congressional elections, some scholars have argued that the American public

---

[6] Although cosponsorship occurs before floor agenda-setting (since bills can be cosponsored any time between their sponsorship and committee reporting), this does not rule out forethought by members or coordination between members and party leaders. Members can anticipate floor action on legislation and this may affect their behavior at earlier legislative stages, particularly through the selection of which bills to consider for cosponsorship. However, it does not change the key assertion that members support the policies to which they attach their name.

has become increasingly polarized and that voters in blue states and red states – or Democrats and Republicans – have opposing and polarized views (Abramowitz 2010; Abramowitz and Saunders 2008, 1998). In contrast, Fiorina and his co-authors (Fiorina et al. 2009; 2005) argue that the public has seen relatively little polarization. Fiorina notes that the electorate is not expressing its true positions when voting; rather, its citizens are forced to choose between candidates representing relatively extreme views, therefore giving the appearance of polarization. Thus, when choices are polarized, voting appears polarized as well. The same choices apply to members of Congress in roll call voting. Like Cox and McCubbins, I argue that "Parties matter ... because the majority party controls which bills their (and other) members have an opportunity to vote on to begin with" (Cox and McCubbins 2005, 221). Even if members of Congress have become more ideologically polarized along party lines, the roll call agenda can exacerbate these differences.

The importance of the agenda is also seen in the case of voting on the impeachment of President Bill Clinton in 1998. Although a large number of members, particularly Democrats, would have liked to vote on censuring the president, the Republican leadership did not allow that option to come to vote. Rather, the only choice up for a vote was impeachment or no punishment. The result was a party unity vote, with only five Democrats voting to impeach and five Republicans voting to acquit ("House of Representatives Casts Historic Vote To Impeach Clinton" 1999). Despite scholars' acknowledgment that this type of agenda-setting occurs, little work has systematically assessed the consequences of this on ideology estimates or subsequent inferences about the common ground between members, policy formation, and representation.

A brief overview of some of the changes in Congress in the last several decades further highlights the importance of separating the influence of the agenda from claims about the ideological homogeneity of members. Whereas the roll call agenda in the 1970s prioritized bills that had bipartisan support, by the early 1990s the roll call agenda prioritized partisan bills. After the Republican Revolution in the 104th Congress and subsequent legislative gridlock and electoral losses in 1996, the Republican majority backtracked on its partisan strategy, somewhat increasing the number of bipartisan bills on the House floor. Few would argue that the ideological make-up of the House became less polarized between the 104th and 105th Congresses, but the roll call record is clear: the percentage of roll call votes that were bipartisan (i.e., were not party unity votes) increased by a third, from less than 30 percent in 1995 to more than 40 percent in 1997. These changes demonstrate that the floor agenda is a strategically manipulated area that does not automatically reflect the degree of underlying substantive policy agreement between members.

Throughout this book, I look at how the institutional structures of parties and agenda control affect what legislation is pursued and passed by the House of Representatives. I show that institutional arrangements play a significant role in manufacturing partisan conflict. Examining bipartisan agreement across different stages of the legislative process – cosponsorship coalitions, floor attention, and roll call votes – demonstrates how party strategy has combined with the preferences of members to produce an increasingly partisan House, and limit opportunities for bipartisan cooperation. The primary analyses of the book focus on the period from 1973–2004[7] – a period seen by conventional wisdom as encompassing a nearly linear increase in polarization[8] – but the final chapter presents comparisons to the post-2004 period, particularly the post-2008 period under the Obama administration. The period from 1973 to 2004 offers critical insights about changes in American politics over the last quarter-century – a time where "normal" politics shifted from bipartisanship to partisanship, at least in standard vote-based measures.

Throughout, I emphasize two important themes: first, that changes in the content of the agenda are important for understanding the decline of bipartisanship in roll call voting; and second, that bipartisanship persists over time to a greater extent than the roll call record alone indicates. Although agenda-setting plays an important role in the decline of bipartisanship in the House of Representatives, particularly as seen in roll call voting, the findings of this book suggest that the agenda does not stifle bipartisanship altogether. Governing demands require that leaders pursue bipartisan legislation, particularly in periods of divided government or small majority seats shares. Even when conditions are more favorable for the pursuit of partisanship, bipartisan legislation remains part of the roll call agenda and dominant in voice votes. Ultimately, those bills that become public law overwhelmingly originate as bills with bipartisan support. Moreover, both the amending process on the House floor and reconciliation with Senate legislation offer opportunities for compromise that can make policy outputs more bipartisan. Although the latter two routes of using compromise to achieve bipartisanship are beyond the scope of the book, I emphasize them here as another means for tempering partisanship in Congress.

This book asks whether partisan conflict is insurmountable, and, ultimately, whether bipartisanship in congressional politics is dead. The findings of this book speak to questions of how party institutions mediate the representative relationship and affect both dyadic and collective representation.[9] Party

---

[7] See Table A1.1 for a reference of years, Congresses, House majority control, and presidency.

[8] Whether measured as the difference in party means (or medians) of Poole and Rosenthal's DW-NOMINATE scores or interest group scores like Americans for Democratic Action (ADA), polarization between Democratic and Republican members increased substantially over the 1973–2004 period. For DW-NOMINATE scores, the difference in party means increased from roughly 0.5 to over 0.9 on a 2 point scale and the correlation with time is 0.97. For ADA scores, the difference in party means nearly doubled, from less than 40 to over 70 on a 100 point scale, and the correlation with time is 0.96.

[9] Dyadic representation refers to a correspondence between the actions of an elected official and his or her constituency, whereas collective representation refers to the correspondence between what the institution produces and what the public wants (Weissberg 1978).

institutions in the House narrow the choices for members, often in ways that overstate either bipartisan agreement or partisan disagreement in voting. As a result of agenda-setting power, when partisan voting is common, members' responsiveness to their districts may be seen in their cosponsorship behavior, rather than their roll call votes. At a collective level, party control of the agenda can skew policy outputs toward either bipartisan or partisan outcomes. Ultimately, the findings presented here suggest that there *is* common ground between members, but that the roll call agenda has increasingly exploited places of partisan division. Bipartisanship is not dead – but neither is it being actively resuscitated by our political parties.

findings

PARTY POWER AND THE IMPLICATIONS FOR PARTISAN CONFLICT

Theories of congressional organization and party influence provide important insights about agenda-setting and when members will cede power to party leaders. However, the connections between the ability of party leaders to block legislation or pursue favored proposals (negative and positive agenda control) (Cox and McCubbins 2005),[10] the conditional nature of party influence (Aldrich and Rohde 2001; Rohde 1991), and the extent of partisan conflict is not obvious. This is particularly true when thinking about what various theories suggest for the relationship between partisanship in voting and partisanship in other steps of the legislative process, including cosponsorship coalitions.

my research differs

Although consistent with the key insights of many scholars of political parties, my theoretical framework (termed *strategic partisan agenda-setting*) and approach differs from the broader party influence literature in a number of ways. First, this book focuses explicitly on the majority party's indirect influence of agenda-setting. Scholars who have critiqued the use of roll call votes for assessing party influence often focus on evidence of direct party pressure, looking at whether parties convince members to vote in ways contrary to their preferences (e.g., Krehbiel 1993). The evidence for direct party influence is relatively weak (see Smith 2007). In contrast, this book focuses on how indirect party influence, via agenda-setting, contributes to floor partisanship.

Second, this book directly considers the consequences of agenda-setting for partisan conflict in voting. Although many scholars have noted the important role of the floor agenda, researchers continue to rely predominantly on roll call voting patterns in their empirical tests of party influence. The idea that agenda-setting – either in the selection of bills for votes or in the manipulation of special rules – affects voting appears throughout the congressional literature (e.g., Bach and Smith 1998; Lebo et al. 2007; Sinclair 2006, 1983; Smith 1989). Rohde

---

[10] Negative agenda control refers to the ability to prevent legislative attention on bills that are opposed by the majority party, while positive agenda control refers to the ability to pursue legislative attention on bills supported by the party.

(1991, 43), for instance, points out that the goals or preferences of members are not the only things that matter for voting patterns, as "the nature of the agendas from which choices are made is also important." However, these considerations are often omitted or sidelined in empirical analyses that rely on voting patterns. Even those analyses that do directly consider the implications of agenda-setting – the assumption that agenda-setting should minimize the number of votes on which the majority party is rolled[11] (Cox and McCubbins 2005, 2002) or the expectation of how votes should split members for and against the legislation under various theories of party influence (Clinton 2007) – typically treat the pre-agenda pool of bills as a black box. This project focuses on early stages of the legislative process to assess the pool of available bills that *could be used* in the floor agenda, and then examines which bills *actually* receive subsequent legislative attention.

Third, this book focuses on the conditions under which parties pursue more partisan agendas and considers why members support this strategy even as they continue to engage in bipartisan cosponsorship coalitions. Both conditional party government (e.g., Rohde 1991) and cartel agenda theories (Cox and McCubbins 2005) argue that parties have more influence over agenda-setting when their members are more homogenous. Conditional party government argues that when members of a party have similar preferences (and have distinctly different preferences from members of the opposing party) they will cede greater power to party leaders (Aldrich and Rohde 2001, 2000; Rohde 1991). The cartel agenda theory proposes that the majority party is always able to block legislation (via negative agenda control) and is only dependent on the similarity of member preferences to pursue legislation (via positive agenda control). The puzzle in both of these theories is why an individual member would cede power to the party if his decision might result in less optimal policy outcomes for that member (Krehbiel 1998, 1993), or put him at electoral risk. In addition to the collective benefits from pursuing partisan legislation, I note that members can pair bipartisan cosponsorship *at an earlier stage* with support for partisan legislative agendas *at a later stage* to balance the costs and benefits of each.

Fourth, this book considers the trade-offs that leaders face when setting the agenda. These include individual versus collective goals and policy versus electoral interests. Many scholars gloss over these trade-offs in their discussion of party goals.[12] Cartel models of political parties suggest that parties will use their negative agenda power to avoid floor losses, but do not sufficiently account for the need of parties to put something on the floor to fulfill the requirements of governance – whether appropriations bills, reoccurring issues, or a more general

---

[11] Majority party "rolls" occur when the majority of the party votes against a bill but the bill passes anyway.
[12] There are, of course, exceptions to this critique. For instance, Lebo et al. (2007, 464) suggest that parties "choose a level of party influence to maximize electoral gains of legislative victory while minimizing the electoral costs of partisan influence."

electoral need for problem solving (Adler and Wilkerson 2013). As Smith notes in his critique of the cartel theory, it reduces the party to an inflexible machine: "It remains mum when it cannot succeed on the floor and it remains inert in devising strategies that may facilitate tradeoffs in building a record of legislative accomplishment" (Smith 2007, 135). In contrast, I focus on these trade-offs, suggesting that party leaders consider the joint interests of policy and reelection and are flexible in setting the agenda. They pursue partisan bills when they can and bipartisan bills when necessary.

This book therefore provides a theoretical framework that is consistent with many key insights of existing theories of party influence, but that challenges scholars to take seriously the content of the agenda and its effects on policy formation. It does so by examining how the agenda is fleshed out in terms of bipartisan or partisan content, and by explicating what theories of party influence mean in the context of efforts to pursue bipartisan agreement. The results offer value not only to scholars of Congress, but also to those who worry that the political parties have grown too far apart to find common ground.

PLAN OF THE BOOK

The remainder of this book focuses on assessing whether bipartisanship in the House of Representatives is, in fact, dead, and whether agenda-setting exacerbates partisan disagreement. I begin with an empirical strategy for assessing patterns of bipartisan agreement. The goal of Chapter 2 is to provide a justification for looking beyond roll call votes, and toward cosponsorship coalitions, in order to assess substantive agreement between members. Moreover, it presents an empirical puzzle of declining bipartisanship that is dependent on the legislative stage at which we assess coalitions. This decline of bipartisanship in voting, despite the persistence of bipartisanship in cosponsorship coalitions, is the puzzle that motivates the remainder of the book.

Chapter 3 presents the theoretical framework of *strategic partisan agenda-setting*. Drawing on insights from literature on legislative behavior, party influence, and elections, I focus on four key guiding insights. First, the content of the agenda affects the voting behavior of members. Second, members and parties must balance individual and collective goals. Third, parties, and especially the majority party, care about legislative success and a record of effective governance. Fourth, party conflict, particularly on roll call votes, offers opportunities for signaling to external audiences. Building on these insights, I argue that party leaders strategically choose whether to pursue bipartisan or partisan legislation on the floor and roll call agendas depending on whether the political environment makes bipartisan or partisan bills the more effective choice for balancing the electoral risks to members, legislative success, and partisan differentiation. In some environments these pressures push in the same direction (e.g., toward partisan legislation), while in other environments these pressures push in opposing directions.

To reconcile the puzzle of persistent bipartisan policy agreement in cosponsorship coalitions despite declining bipartisanship in roll call votes, Chapter 4 examines shifts over time in the selection of bills that reach later stages in the legislative process. Beginning with the premise that cosponsorship reflects pre-agenda-setting coalitions on legislation, this chapter provides the first evidence that strategic partisan agenda-setting explains this puzzling divergence in bipartisanship. The primary aim of this chapter is to demonstrate that there is variation in the *selection* of bills for votes, and that this variation parallels patterns of party conflict in roll call votes.

Chapter 5 empirically tests my theoretical framework of strategic partisan agenda-setting by looking at the conditions under which the majority leadership pursues a bipartisan or partisan strategy. My primary focus is on the relationship between the political environment – extent of cross-pressured members, divided government, and majority seat share – and the pursuit of bipartisan or partisan cosponsored legislation, but I also consider some of the other bill-level variables that affect legislative attention.

Strategic partisan agenda-setting occurs not just at the aggregate level, as bills are selected for roll call votes, but within and between policy areas as well. The evidence in Chapter 6 suggests that the largest shifts from bipartisan to partisan agenda-setting occur within those policy areas that are the most partisan, consistent with expectations from literature on issue ownership and the desire to differentiate the two parties on these policies (Gilmour 1995). Chapter 6 also examines the first implication of strategic partisan agenda-setting: that a bipartisan agenda strategy provides legislative attention to issues that are different from those under a partisan agenda strategy.

If leaders pursue partisanship as a legislative strategy and members increasingly vote with their party, does this mean that members are increasingly unresponsive to the public? Chapter 7 explores this question by focusing on the implications of partisan agenda-setting for legislator responsiveness and, ultimately, for members' electoral concerns. While it does not offer a comprehensive account of member-party relationships, this chapter focuses on some of the possible trade-offs members may face when choosing to support a partisan legislative strategy.

Chapter 8 summarizes the findings for the 1973–2004 period, considering broad implications about the way institutions alter the relationship between constituents, members, and policy outcomes in the House of Representatives. With these conclusions in mind for this period, I consider recent developments in bipartisanship. Examples from the congressional terms since the election of Barack Obama suggest that we are in an era of politics in which substantive policy agreement has declined dramatically in comparison with the previous four decades, and where partisan agenda-setting has dominated despite its tension with legislative success during divided government. By exploring these patterns and the conditions that foster this partisanship, I offer some speculation on the likelihood of a return to greater bipartisanship in future.

Throughout its analysis of strategic partisan agenda-setting, this book draws on quantitative evidence of roll call votes and bill cosponsorship coalitions. I buttress my analysis with qualitative evidence from the papers of party leaders and party organizations. The quantitative evidence draws on voting data compiled by David Rohde (2004) and the Policy Agendas Project (Baumgartner and Jones 2000), combined with bill-level data from James Fowler (2006b, 2006a) and the Congressional Bills Project (Adler and Wilkerson 2008) and electoral data from Gary Jacobson (2010). The qualitative work draws on the archives of Carl Albert, Robert Michel, Richard Armey, the House Democratic Caucus, and the House Democratic Study Group, newsletters from the House Legislative Resource Center, as well as interviews with former members and congressional staff (a complete list of these interviews is located in the Appendix).

Having established the aims of this book and emphasized the need to move beyond roll call vote-based analyses, I begin to explore the patterns of bipartisanship over time in the next chapter. Chapter 2 justifies the use of cosponsorship coalitions as a secondary measure of bipartisan agreement, and then considers the extent to which bipartisanship declines over time in roll call and cosponsorship coalitions.

2

A Puzzle of Declining Bipartisanship

Popular belief holds that bipartisan policy agreement in the House has declined dramatically since the 1970s. How accurate is this depiction? No one who follows politics should be surprised to find that the prevalence of party unity in House voting has increased, that bipartisan patterns of voting have declined, and that the resulting estimates of legislator ideology show evidence of increased polarization. As noted in the introductory chapter, estimates of legislator ideology show increasing differences between members of the two parties, indicating that polarization has nearly doubled between 1973 and 2004. But while vote-based measures reveal many insights about partisan conflict, they are not the only way to assess cross-party agreement on policy. As this chapter demonstrates, an alternative measure of bipartisan coalitions based on bill cosponsorship behavior shows much greater stability in bipartisan agreement. Declining bipartisanship in roll call votes over time, despite continuing bipartisanship in cosponsorship coalitions, creates a puzzle. The lasting evidence of bipartisanship in cosponsorship coalitions over this period should caution us against assuming that members of Congress are so polarized that there is no common ground left between the two parties by the 2000s.

This chapter begins with a brief discussion of the concept of bipartisanship that will pave the way for its primary aims, which are to justify the research design of this book and to dig in to the first empirical analyses. The research design leverages roll call votes in conjunction with bill cosponsorship coalitions to better understand the underlying degree of common ground between House members. It also highlights the weaknesses of traditional roll call vote-based measures for understanding bipartisan agreement. The empirical analyses presented in this chapter compare the trends in bipartisanship in voting and cosponsorship coalitions over the period 1973–2004.

THE CONCEPT OF BIPARTISANSHIP

In the previous chapter, I suggested that "bipartisan" and "partisan" are useful terms for categorizing legislation. These terms point to the degree to which members work across the aisle and reach agreement with the other side. This approach acknowledges the complicated reality that not all of politics necessarily maps onto a one-dimensional line running from liberal to conservative. Being able to describe all pieces of legislation as either partisan or bipartisan is particularly important since I consider the broad range of bills that are introduced and cosponsored in Congress, not just those that receive roll call votes. As Talbert and Potoski (2002) have noted, the floor agenda-setting process creates the one-dimensional policy space observed in voting. I have therefore attempted to identify a common concept for characterizing policy agreement at both the cosponsorship and roll call voting stages.

The term "bipartisan cooperation" includes many different meanings. First, bipartisanship may refer to places of common agreement between members of opposing parties. This agreement can occur on issues that have a broad basis of support, that are non-ideological, that cut across parties, or that have regional (but not party-specific) support. In all of these cases, bipartisan agreement can be achieved without compromise. Second, bipartisanship may refer to compromise on issues where members of the two parties have distinct and different positions. Despite being the ideal policy of neither group, each side compromises and the resulting policy garners support from members of both sides of the aisle. Third, bipartisanship may refer to wanting the "other" side to compromise "their" positions and come closer to "your" positions. While the third concept of bipartisanship is similar to the second because it involves compromise, the idea that compromise will come from all sides or predominantly one side makes it distinct. This use of bipartisanship, based on unequal compromise, is often found in political rhetoric. For instance, Republican Richard Mourdock, who defeated Dick Lugar in the 2012 Republican Senate primary election in Indiana (but ultimately lost the general election), was quoted as saying, "I have a mindset that says bipartisanship ought to consist of Democrats coming to the Republican point of view" (Weinger 2012). Likewise, an Associated Press writer summed up the political use of the third definition as follows: "We're ready to cooperate right now. All you need to do is go along with what we want" (Babington 2010).

The approach to measuring bipartisanship presented in this book draws primarily on the first definition, in that it focuses on the degree of common ground between members. I acknowledge, but do not explicitly measure, the degree of compromise of the second or third definitions. Bill cosponsorship coalitions reveal information about the underlying degree of bipartisan agreement on the initial policy proposals. Likewise, voting coalitions reveal additional information about the degree of bipartisan agreement on policy outputs. Clearly, in moving from the time of original sponsorship and cosponsorship to roll call voting on the floor, bills may undergo changes that involve further compromise. These compromises may occur in committee, via amendments on the floor, or in reconciling House and Senate versions of legislation. Although systematically assessing these compromises is beyond the scope of this project, I do consider how intermediate steps in the legislative process encourage or constrain the ability to reach bipartisan compromises.

Defining bipartisan agreement in terms of the supporting coalitions from each party is no easy task. Anyone who follows political news coverage knows that both politicians and political commentators use the term "bipartisan" to describe many different things, including votes, proposals, groups, meetings, and commissions, to name just a few. The term, however, is very rarely quantified. When it is, the definition varies dramatically and may shift over time or depending on who is making the assessment. For instance, the media has hailed everything from the single crossover vote of Olympia Snowe (R-ME) on the committee vote for health-care reform in 2009 (e.g., Hulse 2009) to unanimous votes (e.g., Morgan 1995) as garnering bipartisan support. Given the variability in how the term bipartisan is used, the empirical analyses in this book focus on specific quantifiable metrics for both roll call voting and cosponsorship coalitions.

HOW SHOULD WE ASSESS BIPARTISAN POLICY AGREEMENT?

My measurement of bipartisan agreement focuses on the coalitions that members form in roll call voting and bill cosponsorship. For both types of measures, I assume that members' actions in support of a particular bill, either by voting for it or cosponsoring it, indicate common ground between the members of the supporting coalition. What we can infer from these supporting coalitions and from changes in the frequency of these coalitions over time, however, differs for roll call votes and cosponsorship coalitions. While the former captures common ground on the policy proposals that happen to get subsequent floor attention, this subset of legislative proposals may not be representative of all bills. In contrast, the latter better captures the common ground on all policy proposals, or what I refer to as the underlying level of policy agreement. This section further considers the inferences we can (or cannot) make from these two measures and why combining the analysis of roll call votes with cosponsorship coalitions is fruitful for understanding the extent of common ground between House members of opposing parties over time.

What Roll Call Analyses (Cannot) Tell Us

Students of American politics are likely to think that there has been a partisan tidal wave in the House in recent decades, as vote-based measures have shown dramatic increases in ideological polarization and an upsurge in party voting. NOMINATE, Poole and Rosenthal's (1997) summary measure of legislator ideology, is the most common approach for measuring these differences. Based on the observed roll call voting behavior of members, NOMINATE extracts an estimated ideal point, which is often used to infer the ideological positions of members on a scale of liberalism versus conservatism.[1] Using this measure, the difference in mean values between the two parties does show increasingly large differences over time (e.g., McCarty et al. 2006).

Alternate measures of voting coalitions also show dramatic increases in partisanship since the 1970s. These measures of coalitions, dating back to Rice (1925), include what *Congressional Quarterly Almanac* (CQ) terms bipartisan votes and party unity votes. First included in their summary of legislative behavior in 1963, CQ defines bipartisan votes as "Roll-call votes on which a majority of voting Democrats and a majority of voting Republicans agreed" ("CQ Fact Sheet Bipartisan Voting" 1963, 735). The percentage of votes that are bipartisan by CQ's measure is the complement of the percentage of party unity votes. The latter are "votes that split the parties, with a majority of voting Democrats opposing a majority of voting Republicans" ("CQ Fact Sheet Bipartisan Voting" 1970, 1139). Though scholars have also considered other definitions of bipartisanship (see, for example, Cooper and Young 1997), all of these definitions use roll call votes to create measures and make comparisons. Using the voting record of individual members, scholars draw on party unity support scores to show how often each member has voted with the majority of his party on party unity votes. Like ideology estimates from NOMINATE and others, both party unity votes and party unity support scores show increasing partisanship since the 1970s.

While all of these roll call vote-based metrics capture an important part of the rise of partisan conflict, they may conflate changes over time in policy agreement and agenda-setting. Since understanding the decline in bipartisanship over time hinges on being able to assess the potential for cross-party agreement, it is worth pausing to consider the limitations of roll call votes. First, the roll call agenda is not a random sample of legislation in Congress (e.g., Aldrich 1995; Carrubba et al. 2008; Cox and McCubbins 2005; Heller and Mershon 2008; Loewenberg 2008; Poole 2004; Snyder 1992). As Aldrich (1995, 196) puts it, "Roll call voting patterns do not tell us what did *not* make it to the floor or show whether the content of a bill that did make it was shaped by strong party control ... They tell us little about agenda control and coalition formation."

Because only a small fraction of legislative decisions are subject to roll call votes and this subset is not random, inferences from roll call votes can only be generalized to the broader congressional environment if the processes that govern decisions in the various environments are similar (Vandoren 1990, 313). We know, however, that the processes that drive decisions on sponsorship, committee votes, voice votes, and roll call votes are likely to be different. Moreover, estimates

---

[1] Although many refer to NOMINATE scores as estimates of ideology, these scores measure everything that separates the votes of members, including party pressures, constituent interests, and ideology (Noel 2013, 187).

from roll call votes fail to consider whether factors that explain why a bill receives a vote at all are related to the ultimate voting coalition on the bill (Vandoren 1990, 313). For instance, partisan conflict on a vote may be correlated with the decision to have a roll call vote on an expectedly partisan bill (for instance, one shifting the tax burden from lower- to higher-income individuals). This may be particularly true if the party leadership has the incentive and ability to construct agendas that maximize within-party agreement and emphasize between-party disagreement (Aleman et al. 2009; Carrubba et al. 2008).

Nor do roll call vote-based measures account for changes in the form of voting for various types of legislation over time. Since the type of vote – including roll call versus voice votes, or regular order versus suspension of the rules – is correlated with the likelihood of bipartisan agreement on the vote, the frequency of each type of voting over time can affect the overall frequency of bipartisan coalitions. Lynch and Madonna (2008), for instance, find that the prevalence of voice votes relative to roll call votes on significant legislation varies both across time and across issues. Similarly, Crespin et al. (2013) find that the degree of party divisiveness in voting is driven, in part, by what types of votes – final passage, suspension of the rules, amendments, or procedural – make up the agenda.

Moreover, inferences about changes in bipartisan agreement over time based on roll call voting are contaminated by the degree to which congressional leaders construct legislative agendas that purposefully pursue partisan or bipartisan legislation. For instance, theories of House agenda-setting suggest that the majority party only pursues bills on the floor when a majority of its members are expected to support the bill and the bill is expected to pass (Cox and McCubbins 2005; Rohde 1991). As a result, variation over time in the similarity of electoral coalitions within a party and the differences between the parties is likely to affect whether bipartisan or partisan bills are pursued for votes. Without first considering the agreement in pre-agenda stages and then considering the composition of the agenda itself, we do not know how accurate the roll call agenda is in assessing underlying levels of agreement between members of the two parties.

In order to understand how bipartisan cooperation has changed, and ultimately to answer questions about governing efforts and representation, we need to be able to disentangle individual-level efforts at bipartisan cooperation from the limitations to bipartisan agreement imposed by the roll call agenda and party strategy. Cosponsorship coalitions provide one avenue for doing this.

The Value of Looking at Cosponsorship Coalitions

In order to overcome the limitations of roll call votes as a post-agenda measure of coalitions, I consider the use of bill cosponsorship coalitions as a second measure of bipartisanship in Congress. Bill cosponsorship occurs when a member formally adds his or her name in support of another member's bill. In the House, a member can cosponsor a bill anytime between its introduction and the time of committee reporting. While the resulting coalitions need not require coordination or further communication between members, they point to policy agreement between participating members and provide a metric of bipartisan agreement at the bill level. In particular, cosponsorship coalitions offer an opportunity to assess legislative agreement prior to agenda-setting, provide public information about the policy positions of members, and capture positions that are not merely cheap talk. Thus, cosponsorship coalitions offer an important opportunity to assess policy agreement between members and measure the frequency of bipartisanship in legislative coalitions.

Like bill sponsorship, cosponsorship provides a relatively easy way for members of Congress to become involved in the policy process, and may be driven by efforts to promote good public policy and by reelection considerations (Schiller 1995). In 1967, the House passed a resolution allowing up to 25 cosponsors on a bill ("Congressional Record" 1967, 10708–12). Since it was first allowed in the House, cosponsorship has largely replaced the use of duplicate bills (Thomas and Grofman 1993), suggesting that members view cosponsorship in much the same way they do sponsorship because they can make the same claims back in their constituencies. In the 95th Congress (1977–78), the House passed H. Resolution 86, which allowed unlimited numbers of cosponsors and allowed cosponsorship up until bills were reported from committee (Thomas and Grofman 1993).[2] Since the early 1970s, members have used cosponsorship frequently.

Although congressional observers debate the reasons why members cosponsor, the assumption in this book is that members cosponsor legislation that they genuinely favor. Desposato and his colleagues sum this up nicely, saying, "Why assume that cosponsorship is sincere? Because cosponsorship is a form of public position taking. Taking the 'wrong' position is very risky" (Desposato et al. 2011, 536). While members may differ in terms of the legislative priority they place on a bill that they cosponsor, their decision to cosponsor nevertheless reflects their support for the underlying bill at hand. Since members cosponsor only a fraction of the entire number of bills that they might favor, their selection of which bills to cosponsor may reflect aims of signaling or reciprocity, in addition to a more or less random consideration of bills. Regardless of how they narrow the pool of bills to consider for cosponsorship, however, signing on as a cosponsor indicates support for the legislation.

---

[2] With the change in cosponsorship rule from a cap at 25 to unlimited cosponsors, a potential concern is whether bills "filled up" on cosponsors in the 93rd and 94th Congresses in ways that might affect measures of bipartisanship in subsequent analyses. For example, if a large number of bills in these years had exactly 25 cosponsors, there may have been more members who wanted to cosponsor, but whose partisanship would have changed the coalition from partisan to bipartisan (or vice versa). However, the evidence indicates that "filling up" was not a substantial problem. Of all cosponsored House bills in the 93rd Congress, 0.14 percent had exactly 25 cosponsors; while in the 94th Congress 0.19 percent had exactly 25 cosponsors.

Cosponsorship coalitions are useful for gauging bipartisan policy agreement for a number of reasons. Perhaps the most important is that these coalitions occur prior to agenda-setting by the majority party.[3] Moreover, cosponsorship is unlikely to be subject to agenda control or leadership interference (Kessler and Krehbiel 1996; Krehbiel 1995). Conversations with House staffers support this assumption. For instance, Eric Lausten, Chief of Staff to Representative Daniel Lipinski (D-IL), noted that it is uncommon for party leaders to get involved with members' cosponsorship decisions. A committee chair or ranking minority member might, on rare occasions, suggest that a member not cosponsor a bill, but only if the bill is not as innocuous as it may seem (Lausten 2011). There are some reports that Nancy Pelosi discouraged bipartisan cosponsorship by Democratic members in the lead up to the 2006 election (Brownstein 2007, 342), but these reports are seen as notable precisely because this has traditionally been an area free from leadership interference.

Like roll call votes, bill cosponsorship coalitions provide members the opportunity to take a position and indicate policy agreement with a coalition of other members. Which bills a member cosponsors, and with whom he cosponsors, allows that member to send signals about his policy positions to constituents, congressional members, challengers, and interest groups. "Cosponsoring helps clarify your message. That way people know where you are ... and that trickles down to constituents" (Koger 2003, 232). In addition, cosponsoring legislation provides information to constituents that roll call votes cannot because cosponsoring allows members to claim credit for helping bring legislation to the floor in a way that merely voting for a bill cannot (Koger 2003). Cosponsoring also allows members to take positions on more issues than just those that receive roll call votes. Sulkin (2011) finds that members' campaign promises (particularly in the House) can be seen in their sponsorship and cosponsorship issue priorities. Ultimately, members' campaign promises and subsequent legislative activity are driven by their interest in these issues. In other words, cosponsorship of legislation reflects underlying issue priorities and expertise (Gilligan and Krehbiel 1987; Wawro 2000).

A recurring point across accounts of cosponsorship is that members' preferences or those of their constituents determine whether or not they choose to

---

[3] While cosponsorship must occur before bills reach the floor, it is not necessarily exogenous to agenda-setting as members may foresee future attention for bills. While the lack of exogeneity means that we cannot know the precise distribution of cosponsors if the agenda were completely unknown in advance, there is also uncertainty about the agenda for members when they are making decisions to cosponsor. As a result, members are unlikely to be driven purely by their judgment of what will or will not make it to the agenda, particularly since they can be held accountable by challengers, interest groups, or the media for their cosponsorship regardless of whether the bill receives a vote. Empirically, bipartisan cosponsored bills that do and do not receive roll call votes have similar distributions on key observable features (e.g., extremity of sponsor ideology, the percentage of cosponsors from the opposite party of the sponsor), suggesting that these coalitions are similar in many ways.

cosponsor a bill (e.g., Koger 2003; Swers 2002; Wilson and Young 1997). Strategic considerations may affect which subset of bills members cosponsor, but will not induce them to cosponsor bills that their constituents oppose. Since members are accountable for their cosponsorship, they will not cosponsor just anything. They must be "concerned with protecting their endorsements from becoming a devalued currency" (Campbell 1982, 417). Thus, cosponsorship coalitions speak to policy agreement among the signing members.[4]

My use of cosponsorship coalitions to measure the support that members have for various legislative initiatives is not novel. For instance, Swers (2002) uses bill cosponsorship to assess differences between male and female members' attention to women's issues in Congress. She describes cosponsorship as "loud voting because legislators are not forced to take positions as they are with roll call votes but they can choose to register their views on an issue by signing their name as cosponsors" (Swers 2002, 57). Similarly, Schickler (2001, 205) uses cosponsorship to show that junior members of Congress were more likely than senior members to support the Stevenson Committee reforms in 1977. Most similar to my approach, Binder (2003) uses cosponsorship to gauge the degree of partisanship on a bill. Journalists also use cosponsorship to signal policy agreement between members of the two sides, with recent examples covering immigration reform (Preston 2013) and one aspect of gun control – cracking down on so-called straw buyers (Geiger 2013).

Although cosponsorship may be viewed as less costly for members than voting, it is not merely cheap talk, or what might be viewed as costless and therefore meaningless action. Members do not casually attach their names to legislation, only to regularly vote against the bill or remove their name later. Moreover, the uptake of issues from challengers has similar consequences for sponsorship, cosponsorship, and floor statements, suggesting that members utilize cosponsorship in similar ways to these other more time-intensive legislative tools (Sulkin 2005). Sulkin's (2011) work, which ties together members' campaign promises and cosponsorship behavior, strongly rejects the claim of cheap talk since members focus campaigns on the issues they care about, and follow through with promises for further action. She concludes her work by stating, "Thus, the argument that introductions and cosponsorships are just symbolic or epiphenomenal no longer has much traction" (Sulkin 2011, 201). While members certainly cosponsor legislation for a number of reasons – substantive, symbolic, or *both* (Hall 1996, 25; Sulkin 2005, 151) – there is mounting evidence that members are sincere in their support when they cosponsor. Cosponsorship can provide members with both individual electoral payoffs and policy payoffs. Members open themselves to a number of risks by attaching

---

[4] Of course, members of a coalition can differ in terms of the priority they place on a particular component of a bill or whether they like some components more than others. However, the public nature of cosponsorship (like voting) suggests that members are willing to offer general support for the legislation they cosponsor.

their names to legislation that they do not support on policy grounds, or that they would not support in a vote.

One way to consider the sincerity of cosponsorship is to examine the rates at which cosponsorship agreements are withdrawn. Although we cannot know the reason for withdrawal in each case, a high rate of withdrawn cosponsorships would be concerning. Drawing on Library of Congress summary information for each Congress about the number of bills cosponsored and withdrawn for each member, I find that withdrawn cosponsorships are very uncommon. Between the 93rd and 112th Congress, the average percentage of cosponsorship agreements that were withdrawn by members is 0.14 percent. Even at its maximum in the 105th Congress, only 0.55 percent of cosponsorships were withdrawn. This finding supports the contention that cosponsorship coalitions provide a meaningful measure of substantive agreement between members.

The most conclusive evidence against cosponsorship as cheap talk comes from recent work by Bernhard and Sulkin (2013), who find that reneging on cosponsorships – cosponsoring but then voting against the bill – is rare and costly. Although nearly all members renege at some point, these negative actions constitute a very small percentage of total cosponsorship agreements. Approximately 1.5 percent of cosponsorship decisions are reneged on when members cast roll call votes. When members do renege, it is costly, leading to a decreased likelihood of cosponsorship support in subsequent interactions. Of course, studies of reneging can only occur on the subset of bills that receive votes. Nonetheless, there are few reasons to believe that cosponsorship on bills that do not reach votes is a less meaningful indicator of policy support as journalists, challengers, or interest groups could attack members for their records of cosponsorship regardless of how far in the legislative process a bill progressed (since cosponsorship reflects a public pronouncement of position taking).

As with any measure, cosponsorship has weaknesses. First, analyses using cosponsorship must make inferences from a small number of coalition members. Unlike roll call votes that require members to vote yea or nay (unless they are absent or abstain), the frequency of cosponsorship is an individual decision. As a result, the median number of cosponsors on a bill has rarely been above ten. Second, members attach their names to bills of varying policy importance. At the bill level, analyses treat each bill and each cosponsorship decision as equal, regardless of whether that bill seeks a major policy overhaul or a more minor legislative initiative. While failing to differentiate major and minor legislative initiatives is a weakness of this approach, the same is true of vote-based studies. Very rarely are votes weighted by the importance of the policy change at hand. Third, members may foresee the likelihood of floor attention for some bills, which could affect their cosponsorship decisions. Fourth, cosponsored bills may not be representative of all introduced bills, thereby limiting the ability of researchers to make inferences from the patterns of bipartisan cosponsorship to the overall level of bipartisan agreement in the House. While it is impossible to remove these weaknesses, and not every issue can be sufficiently addressed in this book, I seek to minimize these concerns through the analyses that follow in this chapter, in subsequent chapters, and in numerous robustness checks presented in the Appendix.

In sum, cosponsorship can provide a useful measure of cross-party policy agreement. It can more accurately assess the potential for substantive policy agreement than roll call votes because it is largely in the full purview of members and is not dependent on agenda-setting or other party influence.[5] Moreover, it can be a costly action, both in terms of the repercussions for reneging, and in terms of a member being open to attacks from challengers and opposing interest groups if he cosponsors the "wrong" legislation relative to constituent preferences. While cosponsorship can occur for policy, symbolic, or strategic reasons, the most important feature of cosponsorship for my analysis is that the decision to sign on as a cosponsor indicates substantive agreement with the legislation and with others in the cosponsorship coalition.

BIPARTISANSHIP IN ROLL CALL VOTING AND IN BILL COSPONSORSHIP COALITIONS

The following analyses explore trends in bipartisan cooperation in the House of Representatives over time, using roll call votes and bill cosponsorship coalitions for the period 1973 to 2004.[6] The roll call measure from *Congressional Quarterly Almanac* (CQ) shows a decline in bipartisanship during that period. As mentioned previously, CQ defines bipartisan votes as those on which a majority of voting Democrats and a majority of voting

---

[5] The argument that it is the more accurate assessment of positions refers to the cosponsorship of legislation (i.e., the equivalent of yea votes), and not necessarily the failure to cosponsor, as the latter cannot be assumed to be equivalent to a nay vote (Desposato et al. 2011). Given the difficulties of how to treat failures to cosponsor, this book focuses only on describing the supporting coalitions as bipartisan or partisan and does not seek to offer an alternative estimate of legislator ideology, either pre- or post-agenda formation.

[6] The analyses are restricted to this period because it encompasses the modern (post-reform) House and has coverage of the data necessary for assessing agenda-setting. In terms of assessing patterns of bipartisanship over time at different stages of the policy-making process, I am restricted to this period because bill cosponsorship was not allowed in the House until 1967 and did not become common until the early 1970s. Moreover, party and ideology were better aligned in Congress during this period compared to earlier eras (Noel 2013). The end date is truncated at 2004 because of data availability for measures of issue content and data for matching bills to roll call votes. However, these start and end dates capture theoretically relevant and substantively interesting years. They capture a period of transition in the House of Representatives, wherein the conventional measures of polarization show a dramatic rise in party conflict and discussions of polarization focus on ideological conflict. Moreover, they capture variation in the electoral environment, party control, divided government, and other variables that allow me to examine the factors that influence bipartisanship and agenda-setting processes. Although I forego systematic analysis after 2004, I return to recent developments in bipartisan agreement during the Obama administration in Chapter 8.

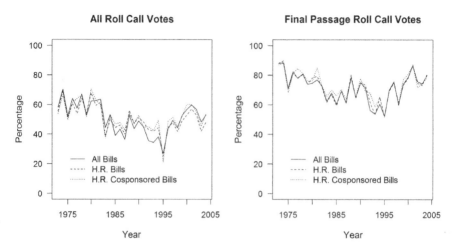

FIGURE 2.1 Bipartisanship in House Roll Call Voting

Republicans agree. Beginning with an analysis of all House roll call votes, this measure (see Figure 2.1, left-hand panel, solid line) shows a fairly steady decline in cross-party agreement from 1973 to 1995, with a subsequent increase after the 104th Congress (post-1996) and another decline in the early 2000s.[7] Although many congressional observers recall the "Republican Revolution" as a time of increasing partisanship, this rise in bipartisan voting in the late 1990s is noted by other scholars (e.g., Crespin et al. 2013). The rise in bipartisanship is related, in part, to an increase in the number of votes under suspension of the rules, which require super-majority support.

For the purpose of comparing patterns of bipartisanship in roll call voting and cosponsorship coalitions, it is important that the patterns of bipartisanship in roll call voting are similar on all bills, House bills (H.R.), and cosponsored House bills.[8] The thick dashed line in Figure 2.1 (left-hand panel) captures the percentage of votes that are bipartisan when the votes are restricted to House bills, and the thin dashed line restricts the analysis to votes on House bills that are cosponsored. Both trends are very similar to the overall trend of bipartisanship

---

[7] Note that even as the percentage of bipartisan votes increased after the 104th Congress, party unity support scores (measuring the degree to which members vote with their party on party unity votes) increased over this period. Thus, the party unity votes increasingly reflected one party voting against the other party.

[8] Votes on all bills include House and Senate bills as well as amendments and resolutions. The further subsets of votes are important because subsequent analyses comparing cosponsorship coalitions, voting, and the selection of bills for votes will focus on cosponsored House bills. The assignment of votes as occurring on House bills utilizes the Policy Agenda Project roll call data for determining the relevant bill for each vote. Following their coding, votes on passage (and amendments) are included if the underlying bill was a House bill (H.R.).

on all votes.[9] Clearly, bipartisan agreement in House roll call voting declined between the 1970s and 1990s.

A number of scholars note that partisan conflict is particularly pronounced on procedural and amendment votes, either due to party pressure or good "teamsmanship" among members (Lee 2009; Roberts and Smith 2003; Theriault 2006). Among final passage votes that omit these procedural issues,[10] the percentage of roll call votes that are bipartisan (using the CQ definition) declines from approximately 90 percent in 1973 to 52 percent by 1995 (see Figure 2.1, right-hand panel).[11] Not surprisingly, the level of bipartisanship is higher on final passage votes than on all votes, which includes amendment voting and other procedural votes. More important for this analysis, however, is the trend over time. Measures focused on all votes and those focused on the subset of final passage votes both show that bipartisan agreement in voting declined between the 1970s and 1990s, and that members of the two parties were finding fewer places to agree.

Regression analysis further highlights the decline of bipartisanship in House voting over time. Table 2.1 presents the results of regressions where the dependent variable is the percentage of bipartisan votes, first calculated for all House votes, then for final passage votes, for votes on only House bills (H.R.), and finally, for votes on only cosponsored House bills. For each dependent variable, the first column includes time as a linear predictor and the second column includes a quadratic term on time to capture the increase in bipartisanship in the late 1990s. The results of the models illustrate the decline in bipartisanship over time. In all cases, the point estimate on time as a linear predictor is negative, and it is statistically significant for all but the final passage analysis. When the quadratic term is added, time has a significant negative effect in all analyses, and the quadratic term is positive and smaller in magnitude. This model captures the overall shape of the data over time, allowing bipartisanship to decrease and then increase. For instance, estimates from the second model tell us that the percentage of bipartisan votes dropped by half between 1973 and 1993 (from 58 percent to 29 percent) but then rose again to 41 percent by 2004. The roll call vote-based measures result in patterns that many congressional observers would expect – bipartisanship in the House declines substantially from the 1970s, until it reaches a low point in the mid-1990s. Over this time period, members found

---

[9] The correlation between the percentage of bipartisan votes among all House votes and just H.R. bills is 0.95 and the correlation among all votes and just H.R. cosponsored bills is 0.90.

[10] I draw on data from Rohde (2004) to assess the frequency of bipartisanship on final passage decisions that omit these procedural votes. The analysis of final passage votes uses Rohde's vote type classifications of 11, 12, and 15. These refer to final passage/adoption of a bill, final passage/adoption of a conference report, and final passage/adoption of a bill under suspension of the rules.

[11] As with the previous measure, voting patterns for all final passage votes, final passage votes on House bills (H.R.), and final passage votes on cosponsored House bills are similar. The correlation between bipartisanship on all final passage votes and H.R. bills is 0.98 and the correlation between all final passage votes and H.R. cosponsored bills is 0.94.

TABLE 2.1 *Regression of Percentage of Bipartisan Votes on Time (1973–2004)*

	All Votes	All Votes	Final Passage Votes	Final Passage Votes	All Votes (H.R. Bills)	All Votes (H.R. Bills)	All Votes (Cosponsored H.R. Bills)	All Votes (Cosponsored H.R. Bills)
Intercept	58***	72.1***	75.7***	90.8***	58.3***	66.2***	58.1***	67.1***
	(3.53)	(4.46)	(3.42)	(4.01)	(2.94)	(4.26)	(3.35)	(4.85)
Time	-0.453*	-2.94***	-0.240	-2.91***	-0.485**	-1.88**	-0.367*	-1.96**
	(0.187)	(0.624)	(0.181)	(0.56)	(0.155)	(0.595)	(0.177)	(0.678)
Time Squared	—	0.0753***	—	0.081***	—	0.0422*	—	0.0482*
		(0.0183)		(0.0165)		(0.0175)		(0.0199)
N	32	32	32	32	32	32	32	32
R^2	0.164	0.471	0.0556	0.486	0.245	0.371	0.125	0.272
Adjusted R^2	0.136	0.435	0.0241	0.450	0.220	0.328	0.0961	0.222

Standard errors in parentheses. ^$p < 0.1$, *$p < 0.05$, **$p < 0.01$, ***$p < 0.001$.
Note: Dependent variable is the percentage of bipartisan votes.

themselves voting more and more with their own party and less with majorities of the other party.

There are a number of potential explanations for declining bipartisanship in roll call votes, including the conventional wisdom that it reflects a lack of substantive policy agreement between members. To explore whether declining bipartisanship is driven by something more than a lack of policy agreement between members of opposing parties, I look further back in the legislative process and examine bipartisanship in bill cosponsorship coalitions.[12] If the patterns of bipartisan agreement in cosponsorship coalitions differ from those in roll call voting, then this suggests that declining bipartisanship in voting is driven by more than just a lack of common ground between members.

Before focusing on bipartisan cosponsorship, it is important to understand the trends of cosponsorship more generally. Throughout all analyses of cosponsorship coalitions, I focus on House bills, omitting resolutions and amendments.[13] On the whole, the use of cosponsorship increased in the House from the 93rd Congress onward (see Table 2.2).[14] Whereas only one-third of public House bills were cosponsored in the 93rd Congress, more than half of all bills were cosponsored by the 98th Congress. In the 108th Congress, nearly three-quarters of bills were cosponsored. The median number of cosponsors on a House bill (including those bills that are not cosponsored) also rose over time. Among bills that are cosponsored, the median number of cosponsors nearly doubled in the period of analysis, from six in the 93rd Congress to 11 in the 105th through 107th Congresses. However, members are selective in their cosponsorship. No more than 6 percent of all cosponsored bills had more than a hundred cosponsors.

To date, there is no standard way to classify cosponsorship coalitions as either bipartisan or partisan. I therefore use a threshold of cross-party support to create

---

[12] To measure bipartisan cosponsorship, I utilize cosponsor data initially collected from the Library of Congress by James Fowler (2006a, 2006b). From Fowler's matrices of bills for each Congress, I create bill-level data on the party of the bill sponsor and cosponsors, and then add data on issue areas, legislative attention, and roll call voting from the Congressional Bills Project, the Policy Agendas Project, and David Rohde's roll call data.

[13] The analysis of all House bills can include private bills. Private bills provide benefits to specified individuals or corporate entities. In contrast, public bills (the bulk of House bills) apply to everyone within their jurisdiction. The frequency of private bills ranges from 1.7 percent of bills in the 108th to 9.7 percent of bills in the 96th Congress. However, private bills are rarely cosponsored – none of the private bills in the 93rd, 94th, or 101st–108th Congresses were cosponsored and only between 1 and 9 private bills were cosponsored in the remaining Congresses. Nearly all subsequent analyses will be focused on cosponsored bills only, thus making the effect of private bills negligible. For those analyses that compare cosponsored and non-cosponsored bills, as well as analyses in subsequent chapters of agenda-setting, private bills are excluded. Of all roll call votes on House bills, only 16 occurred on private bills.

[14] These measures exclude private bills, of which there are 6,780 in total across all Congresses, with only 29 being cosponsored. When private bills are included, the proportion of bills with cosponsors drops slightly (e.g., 0.28 in the 93rd Congress, 0.72 in the 108th Congress).

TABLE 2.2 *House Cosponsorship Summary Statistics*

Congress	Number of House Bills	Proportion of Bills Cosponsored	Median # Cosponsors (all bills)	Median # Cosponsors (> 0 cosponsors)	Proportion with 0–10 Cosponsors	Proportion with >100 Cosponsors
93	16,602	0.30	0	6	0.62	0.00
94	14,882	0.39	0	6	0.64	0.00
95	13,469	0.43	0	7	0.61	0.00
96	7,635	0.41	0	6	0.59	0.02
97	6,778	0.47	0	6	0.61	0.03
98	6,009	0.53	1	7	0.58	0.04
99	5,402	0.60	1	9	0.53	0.04
100	5,293	0.64	2	11	0.49	0.05
101	5,755	0.65	2	10	0.50	0.05
102	6,044	0.62	2	10	0.51	0.05
103	5,121	0.64	2	9	0.53	0.04
104	4,200	0.65	3	9	0.53	0.05
105	4,751	0.68	4	11	0.49	0.05
106	5,523	0.69	4	11	0.50	0.06
107	5,662	0.70	4	11	0.50	0.05
108	5,337	0.73	4	10	0.51	0.06

a dichotomous measure of bipartisanship. Bills are defined as bipartisan if they have cross-party support at or above this threshold, and as partisan if they have less cross-party support. This approach captures whether the cosponsorship coalition is predominantly made up of members from outside the sponsor's party (bipartisan) or inside the sponsor's party (partisan). Since cosponsorship is similar to only yea votes and only a subset of members cosponsor any given bill, it is impossible to use the same threshold – at least 50 percent of Democrats *and* 50 percent of Republicans in support – used in the CQ measure of roll call votes. Instead, the primary measure used throughout the book classifies bills as bipartisan if at least 20 percent of the cosponsors are from the party opposite the original sponsor. All substantively important patterns are nevertheless robust to higher thresholds.[15]

When all House bills are considered, the percentage of bills with bipartisan cosponsorship increases over time (see dashed lines in Figure 2.2). This pattern

---

[15] Additional definitions of bipartisanship, including different percentages of cosponsors from the opposing party (30, 40, and 50 percent) have been used for comparison. In all cases the pattern over time is similar to the 20 percent measure, with the primary difference being a shift in the intercept (see Figure A2.1). The 20 percent threshold is used as the primary measure throughout the book since it captures coalitions that are reasonably balanced between the two parties and, as I will show later in this chapter, it sufficiently differentiates bipartisan and partisan coalitions in subsequent coalitions, including voting.

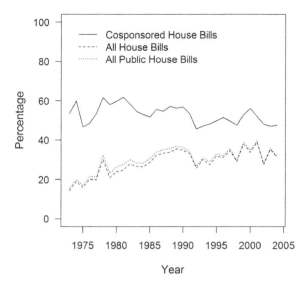

FIGURE 2.2 Bipartisanship in House Cosponsorship Coalitions

holds regardless of whether all House bills are included, or whether private bills are dropped from the analysis. Here, between 20 and 40 percent of *all* House bills introduced between 1973 and 2004 are bipartisan. While this finding suggests that bipartisanship has become increasingly common despite the parallel decline in bipartisan voting, the upward trend is affected by the overall increase in the frequency of cosponsorship. Because the denominator of this measure combines bills of all types – those with bipartisan cosponsors, partisan cosponsors, and no cosponsors – trends in bipartisan agreement are conflated with trends in the frequency of cosponsorship.

Bipartisan agreement declines less than expected based on the conventional wisdom even when the analysis is restricted to cosponsored bills (solid line in Figure 2.2). Although there is variation in the measure over time and a slight downward trend in bipartisanship, the magnitude of the change is surprisingly small. Over the entire period of analysis, the frequency of bipartisan agreement hovers around 53 percent, ranging from 46 percent in 1992 to 61 percent in 1981. In fact, if the analysis is restricted to cosponsored bills sponsored by majority party members, a positive trend in bipartisanship emerges (see Figure A2.2), indicating that bipartisanship is not simply occurring on minority-sponsored legislation that is unlikely to receive further legislative attention. Nor does this trend reflect a substantial decline in the percentage of cosponsors that are not in the sponsor's party. Across the period of analysis, the mean fluctuates around 31 percent, indicating that, on average, nearly one-third of a bill's cosponsors are from the opposing party of the original bill sponsor. What is remarkable here is that there is essentially no decline in the percentage of bipartisan cosponsorship coalitions over time. Common ground between members persists in the form of bipartisan cosponsorship coalitions.

Bipartisan cosponsored legislation includes both major and minor policy changes, and is not merely an artifact of commemorative legislation.[16] For example, legislation with bipartisan coalitions in 2003 included both a major authorization for $15 billion to fight AIDS, tuberculosis, and malaria in both Africa and the Caribbean (H.R. 1298) and a more minor bill to enhance criminal enforcement of copyright laws (H.R. 4077). The former had a bipartisan cosponsorship coalition of two Democrats and two Republicans (as well as a bipartisan final passage vote) while the latter had a bipartisan cosponsorship coalition of four Democrats and three Republicans (and passed the House on a voice vote). The variation in the magnitude of policy changes sought by legislators in these bills provides an important reminder that much of what Congress attempts to do through bill introduction and floor voting reflects routine policy changes and small policy adjustments, not just major efforts at policy reform (Adler and Wilkerson 2013).

Multiple robustness checks confirm that measures of bipartisan cosponsorship are, in fact, revealing patterns of cross-party agreement over time. Bipartisan coalitions occur at similar rates on bills with many cosponsors and on bills with few cosponsors, suggesting that the observed rates are not driven solely by bills with very few cosponsors (see Figure A2.3 for more information). Nor do these patterns appear to be driven by either a shift in policy areas over time or from the actions of only moderate members (see Appendix for more information).

Not only does the bipartisan cosponsorship measure reveal continued agreement over time, it also differentiates bipartisan from partisan coalitions in subsequent roll call votes. Among cosponsored bills that receive a roll call vote, an average of 89 percent of the bills defined as bipartisan (using the 20 percent cosponsorship definition) received at least one bipartisan vote (as measured by the CQ definition). In contrast, an average of 69 percent of the bills defined as partisan received at least one bipartisan roll call vote. The differences are similarly strong for differentiating the likelihood of bipartisan final passage votes. Of the bipartisan cosponsored bills, an average of 81 percent received bipartisan final passage votes. Of the partisan cosponsored bills, the average is 55 percent. The difference between the percentage of bipartisan votes for bipartisan and partisan cosponsored bills is statistically significant in all Congresses

---

[16] Although all House bills are included in the analysis here, omitting commemorative legislation does not change the results. The measures of bipartisanship with and without commemorative legislation for the 93rd to 106th Congresses are correlated at 0.99 (where commemorative legislation is based on the classification in the Congressional Bills Project, but is missing for the 107th and 108th Congresses). Moreover, the percentage of cosponsored bills that are bipartisan only declines by 0.02 percent to 1.8 percent in any given year when commemorative legislation is removed.

except the 96th (1979–80).[17] Certainly, the cosponsorship measure does not perfectly predict the type of voting coalition, and there is some noise in the measures.[18] However, the bills classified as bipartisan are always more likely to receive bipartisan votes than those bills classified as partisan. This suggests that the cosponsorship measure, even with a threshold of 20 percent and based on the actions of relatively few members, captures important variation in the degree of bipartisan agreement. Agreement on legislation at the cosponsorship stage can signal the likely voting patterns of the chamber as a whole, pointing to the validity of the cosponsorship measure.

Although the cosponsorship-based measure of bipartisan agreement is not directly comparable to the roll call vote-based measure of agreement, an exact comparison is impossible given the nature of cosponsorship. That is, individuals who do not cosponsor cannot be assumed to be voting no on the bill in question. However, cosponsorship patterns do tell us about the type of coalition formed around a particular proposal by making inferences from the behavior of a smaller number of members in favor of the bill. Because of these differences, the *level* of bipartisan cooperation may not be comparable across roll call and cosponsorship-based measures. More important for this analysis, however, is the *trend* over time within each measure, which is comparable. As depicted for roll call measures in Table 2.1, Table 2.3 presents a regression of the percentage of cosponsored bills with bipartisan coalitions on time. Two results are particularly notable. First, while the effect of time is negative and significant, the magnitude of the effect is smaller than in any of the roll call based analyses. Whereas the frequency of bipartisanship in voting coalitions declined by 50 percent from the early 1970s to 1995, bipartisanship in bill cosponsorship coalitions declined by less than 20 percent over the same period. This suggests that there remain places of policy agreement between members of the two parties across this period that are captured in cosponsorship coalitions but not in roll call voting. Second, neither time variable is significant in the model of bipartisan agreement with a quadratic term for time. In contrast to the patterns for the regressions using roll call votes, these results indicate that there is not a significant non-linear relationship between bipartisan cosponsorship and time. This suggests that the increase in bipartisan voting in the latter half of the 1990s is not driven simply by an increase in the pool of available bipartisan cosponsored bills.

---

[17] Congresses rather than years are used here to address the fact that legislative attention is not independent between sessions of a Congress. The full results of this analysis are presented in Table A2.1.

[18] Although these analyses include only those bills that received roll call votes, bipartisan cosponsored bills that did and did not receive roll call votes are similar on many observable features related to the extent of bipartisan agreement (e.g., the percentage of cosponsors from the party opposite the sponsor, the difference in party support score, the extremity of the sponsor's DW-NOMINATE score, etc.). These similarities hold among all bipartisan cosponsored bills and among majority-sponsored bipartisan cosponsored bills.

TABLE 2.3 *Regression of Percentage of Bipartisan Cosponsorship Coalitions on Time (1973–2004)*

	Model 1	Model 2
Intercept	57.2***	55***
	(1.49)	(2.3)
Time	−0.248**	0.151
	(0.0788)	(0.322)
Time Squared	–	−0.0121
		(0.00946)
N	32	32
R^2	0.248	0.288
Adjusted R^2	0.223	0.239

Standard errors in parentheses.
^$p < 0.1$, *$p < 0.05$, **$p < 0.01$, ***$p < 0.001$.
Note: The dependent variable is the percentage of cosponsored bills that are bipartisan in each year. If the analysis is restricted to majority-sponsored bills, the effect of time is positive (0.051, $p < 0.001$).

A continuous measure of cross-party agreement using roll call votes and cosponsorship coalitions reiterates the patterns discussed above. Since the dichotomous measures of bipartisanship in voting look at what majorities of the two parties are doing, they may miss the extent of skew within those coalitions. For instance, both a vote that pitted 90 percent of one party against 90 percent of another party and one that pitted only 51 percent of one party against 51 percent of another party are classified as party unity votes. The same is true for the dichotomous measures of bipartisan cosponsorship. A "Difference in Party Support Score" for each vote and cosponsorship coalition parses out variation in the extent of bipartisanship.[19] For each vote, I calculate the percentage of voting Democrats voting yea and subtract the percentage of voting Republicans voting yea. The resulting score ranges from −100 to 100, where −100 indicates a vote on which no Democrats voted yea and all of the Republicans voted yea, and where 100 indicates a vote on which all Democrats voted yea and no Republicans voted yea. The midpoint of 0 indicates bills where the same percentage of Democrats and Republicans voted yea. Thus, the ends of the scale reflect the greatest partisanship, and the middle represents the greatest bipartisanship. Technically, the middle of scale captures instances in when each party has an identical division over the vote. In many cases, these are unanimous or near-unanimous votes.

Density plots (Figure 2.3) reveal the relative frequency of each type of coalition. Plots in Figure 2.3(a) capture the coalitions voting in favor of legislation.

[19] The analysis focuses on yea votes since they are most similar to cosponsorship coalitions in indicating support for a piece of legislation.

The trend over time shows an increase in the frequency of both highly partisan bills and near-unanimous bills, at the expense of moderately bipartisan bills.[20] Both the tails and the center of the distribution grow over time. In the 1970s, bills tend to be highly bipartisan or moderately bipartisan, with few votes pitting all of one party against all of another party. By the mid-1980s, the number of highly partisan bills increases. By the mid-1990s, most votes are either highly bipartisan or highly partisan, with very few coalitions remaining moderately bipartisan (e.g., differences around +/− 50). All of these patterns suggest that by the late 1990s and early 2000s votes either pitted the two parties against one another or garnered nearly unanimous support.

Although the overall pattern of roll call voting in the House does show declining bipartisanship between 1973 and 2004, the frequency of unanimous and near-unanimous votes emphasizes that bipartisanship is not absent in congressional policy making during this period. For example, during the 108th Congress (2003–04), bills passing by unanimous or near-unanimous margins cover a wide range of legislation that include appropriations for military construction (H.R. 2559 passed the House on a vote of 417–5), appropriations for the Department of Homeland Security (H.R. 2555 passed the House on a vote of 425–2), increases for disability compensation for veterans (H.R. 1683 passed House on a vote of 426–0), authorizations for spending on the Trafficking Victims Protection Act (H.R. 2620 passed House on a vote of 422–1), and an extension of unemployment compensation (H.R. 2185 passed House on a vote of 409–19). While these near-unanimous votes do not tend to occur on party-defining legislation, they occur on a variety of types of legislation, including the routine governing matters that confront Congress (Adler and Wilkerson 2013). Importantly, these unanimous votes are typically omitted from ideal point estimates like NOMINATE, thereby downplaying the occurrence of bipartisan agreement in these measures.

A difference in party support score can also be calculated for each cosponsorship coalition. Since cosponsorship occurs only as policy agreement, this score is similar to looking at the roll call vote-based measure of yea votes. For each cosponsored bill, the measure subtracts the percentage of Republican cosponsors from the percentage of Democratic cosponsors. Like the roll call vote-based measure, the resulting scale ranges from −100 to 100, where the endpoints reflect bills with all Republican cosponsors and all Democratic cosponsors, respectively. The midpoint reflects bills with equal numbers of Democratic and Republican cosponsors.

Density plots of the difference in party support score indicate that bipartisanship in cosponsorship coalitions persists over time. Figure 2.3(b) shows that although the distribution of cosponsor coalitions is bimodal, with a relatively large number of both Democratic and Republican partisan bills, the middle (i.e., the most bipartisan bills) has not vanished over time. Regardless of

---

[20] Although Congresses are used to simplify the number of plots necessary to convey the patterns, the results are similar when examining each year separately.

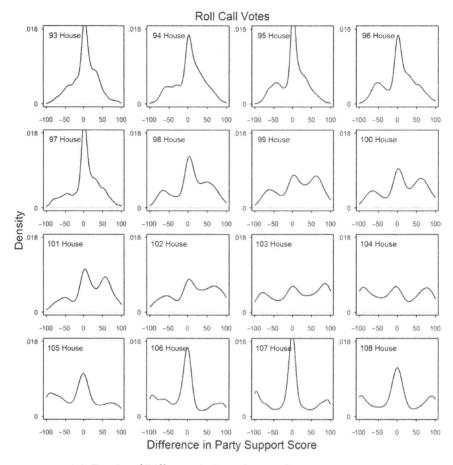

FIGURE 2.3(A) Density of Difference in Party Support Score

the Congress, a similar proportion of bills receive the most bipartisan score (at or around 0). The primary change in the distribution of bills is that it becomes less lopsided toward the Democratic side, particularly once the Republicans gained majority status in the 104th Congress. Whereas partisan bills before this Congress are predominantly Democratic, Democratic and Republican partisan bills are at near parity in more recent Congresses. The finding that the center of the distribution persists across time, including both highly and moderately bipartisan bills, is critical. If there were a substantial decline in bipartisanship, there would be growth in the density of both tails at the expense of the center, creating a greater U-shaped pattern over time. This pattern is not evident.

The relationship between each of these measures and time reiterates that bipartisanship has declined in voting but persisted in cosponsorship. When using the difference in party support scores, the mean of the absolute value of

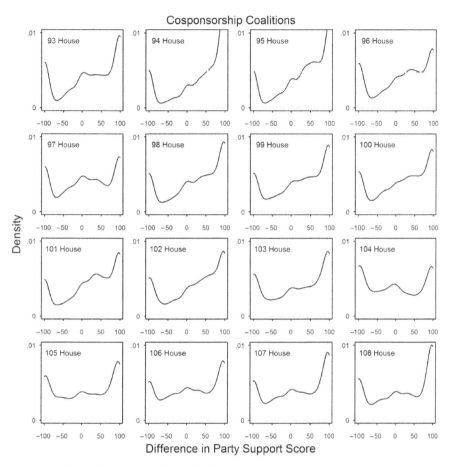

FIGURE 2.3(B) Density of Difference in Party Support Score

the scores in each year captures the average degree of partisanship in the coalition. In this form, the measure is similar to Binder's (2003) measure of the degree of partisan conflict on a bill. In the resulting models, the direction of the coefficient on time is expected to be positive if bipartisanship declines over time, since lower absolute values of the scale reflect greater bipartisanship and higher values reflect greater partisanship. With this dependent variable used in a simple regression on time, the estimated coefficient on time is 0.74 ($p < 0.001$) when looking at roll call votes and –0.02 ($p = 0.72$) when looking at bill cosponsorship coalitions. These relationships further demonstrate that bipartisan cooperation declines more over time in roll call votes than in bill cosponsorship coalitions. Members of the House continue to join cosponsorship coalitions with members from the opposing party even as their votes become more partisan.

All of these patterns suggest that the potential for bipartisan policy agreement in the House declined less between the early 1970s and mid-2000s than the observed roll call voting patterns show. The evidence in this chapter makes it clear that, among cosponsored bills, bipartisan agreement fell relatively little over time. However, the classification of coalitions as bipartisan or partisan ignores non-cosponsored bills since they do not provide any information about the supporting coalition. Using the observed patterns of bipartisanship on cosponsored bills to make broader inferences about the underlying level of policy agreement in the House hinges on an important assumption that cosponsored bills are representative of all bills. Moving from observed patterns of cosponsorship coalitions to inferences about the chamber as a whole assumes that cosponsored and non-cosponsored bills have similar distributions of "potential" bipartisan support (if they had all been cosponsored). Analyses comparing cosponsored and non-cosponsored bills on observable features related to bipartisanship, including bill sponsor ideology and issue area, lend credence to this assumption (see Appendix for details). Importantly, I am able to rule out the possibility that the "potential" bipartisan support on non-cosponsored bills is very high in the early years of analysis but very low in the later years, a pattern that would contrast with and mitigate the observed trend that bipartisan agreement at this early legislative stage declines little over time. As a result, the observed patterns of bipartisan cosponsorship shown in this chapter provide an important insight into the underlying potential for policy agreement between members of the two parties across introduced bills. Rather than falling dramatically over time, bipartisanship has persisted throughout this critical period of American politics.

CONCLUSIONS

This chapter has examined the extent to which bipartisan agreement has fallen in the House of Representatives over time. After assessing the pros and cons of using roll call votes for gauging the extent of common ground across time, and articulating a rationale for why cosponsorship coalitions provide an important avenue for the measurement of substantive agreement, I presented measures of bipartisan cooperation. I found a striking divergence over time in the degree of bipartisan cooperation between the roll call vote and cosponsorship measures. Whereas bipartisanship dropped significantly in roll call vote-based measures between the 1970s and 1990s, it declined little in cosponsorship-based analyses. These two patterns provide a puzzle. The cosponsorship patterns suggest that there continues to be agreement between members of the two parties on the substance of bills, a pattern that is not seen in roll call voting. The divergence over time between these measures suggests that the storyline of declining bipartisanship on the House floor cannot be just about a lack of common ground between members of the two parties. If it were just about policy preferences, bipartisanship in bill cosponsorship coalitions should have declined as well. Something more must be going on.

The remainder of this book seeks to solve this puzzle by looking at the changes that have occurred over time in the content of the congressional agenda and in the issues that receive roll call votes. Having established the existence of divergent patterns of bipartisanship between roll call voting and cosponsorship coalitions, Chapter 3 establishes the theoretical basis for understanding this phenomenon through agenda-setting. What sorts of conditions might lead party leaders and their members to pursue either a bipartisan or partisan agenda in roll call votes?

3

Strategic Partisan Agenda-Setting

A Theoretical Framework

At any given point in time, bipartisan voting patterns in the House can reflect two distinct, but not mutually exclusive, underlying conditions. Bipartisan votes can be the result of members having similar preferences on all bills, or they can result from a selection process that privileges votes for bills with cross-party support. Likewise, the decline of bipartisan cooperation in voting patterns can be caused either by increased polarization of member preferences across issues and bills or a floor agenda that is increasingly skewed toward partisan legislation, or both. The evidence in this book points to agenda-setting as an overlooked component of declining bipartisanship. For example, in the wake of the Enron scandal, the Republican leadership's choice to pursue the partisan version of pension reform legislation despite the presence of a bipartisan alternative suggests the importance of agenda-setting. Similarly, the increase in bipartisan voting between the 104th and 105th Congresses, despite relatively few changes in membership (and therefore preferences), can only be caused by a change in the agenda. Finally, the relative lack of decline in bipartisan cooperation in cosponsorship coalitions over time also cautions against a purely preference-driven story as members from both parties continue to find common ground on legislation at this pre-agenda-setting stage. All of this suggests that agenda-setting is important for explaining the rise of partisan conflict in Congress.

This chapter explicates why the agenda is important for understanding the decline of bipartisanship, and how leadership considerations produce tensions between bipartisan and partisan legislation that vary across contexts. How the leadership resolves this tension determines the type of agenda that is pursued. The primary goal of this chapter and those subsequent to it is not to explain or test every facet of agenda-setting, but rather to explain why the extent of bipartisan agenda-setting has shifted over time. To do so, I draw on key insights about the considerations that confront leaders setting the agenda, developing hypotheses about the conditions under which bipartisan or partisan agenda-setting is pursued. Ultimately, I propose that the agenda has changed over time in a way that precludes bipartisan cooperation and manufactures partisan conflict. I call this process *strategic partisan agenda-setting.*

Strategic partisan agenda-setting emphasizes that the pursuit of partisan or bipartisan legislation on the House floor reflects the complex nature of political parties and institutional governance. In setting the agenda, the majority party leadership must weigh the policy and electoral interests of individual members against the collective interests of maintaining a majority, governing the institution, and building the party brand. As a consequence, the content of the agenda does not reflect the pursuit of one single goal, but rather the strategic balance of multiple goals.[1] Leaders must structure floor choices in ways that keep the peace within the party and ensure the passage of legislation (Sinclair 1983). While partisan legislation can help achieve policy goals and differentiate one party from the other, it can damage the electoral interests of members and hamper the ability of the majority party to produce a record of legislative success. As a result, bipartisan legislation may be advantaged on the agenda in some contexts but may be shunned in favor of partisan legislation in other contexts. Because the content of the agenda affects the choices that members have when voting on the floor, decisions of whether to prioritize bipartisan or partisan legislation will affect whether votes are bipartisan or partisan.

The theoretical framework for understanding strategic partisan agenda-setting rests on four guiding insights. First, the content of the agenda affects the voting behavior of members. Second, members and parties must balance individual and collective goals. Third, parties – and especially the majority party – care about legislative success and a record of effective governance. Fourth, party conflict, particularly on roll call votes, offers opportunities for signaling to external audiences. Combined, these four claims provide the under-pinnings of the theoretical framework I use to explain why the House roll call agenda has, on average, changed over time from prioritizing bipartisan legislation to prioritizing partisan legislation. The first insight emphasizes the importance of the agenda as an intermediate step in policymaking that is consequential for voting outcomes. The remaining insights help explain the leadership's considerations when setting the agenda and point to the conditions when bipartisan or partisan legislation is their best option on the agenda.

From these insights, I develop a number of hypotheses that, when combined, shed light on the decline in bipartisanship in House voting. First, I hypothesize that the selection of bipartisan bills for roll call votes will be related to the degree of bipartisanship in voting coalitions. Second, I hypothesize that bipartisan cosponsored legislation will be advantaged on both the floor and roll call agendas when there are many cross-pressured members in the House. Only

---

[1] The use of the term "strategic" refers to the calculated balancing of various goals and interests. It is used more broadly here than in some portions of the political science literature where strategic actions are those that violate sincere preferences at one stage in order to achieve a more desirable outcome at a subsequent stage.

when congressional districts are well sorted – with district and party interests aligning for most members – can the majority party pursue legislation with only partisan support. Third, I hypothesize that divided government and small majority seat shares will constrain the pursuit of partisan legislation. As a result, leaders may pursue bipartisan legislation more in these political contexts. Finally, I hypothesize that leadership efforts to shift from a bipartisan agenda to a partisan agenda will be most pronounced on the roll call agenda and on party differentiating issues since these instances allow both parties to take public positions and differentiate themselves. In contrast, the broader floor agenda, which also includes voice votes, will continue to prioritize bipartisan legislation. To build up to these hypotheses, each guiding insight is explored below. A final section combines these insights to hypothesize about when party leaders will prioritize bipartisan or partisan legislation on the agenda.

AGENDA CONTENT AFFECTS VOTING

The Clinton impeachment vote (mentioned in the introductory chapter of this book) is one of the more notorious examples of a case where control over the agenda – in this case, the decision to allow a vote on impeachment but not on censure – contributed to the near-perfect party-line vote. The theoretical framework of strategic partisan agenda-setting begins from the insight captured by this and similar examples: the content of the agenda affects the voting behavior of members. This claim garners support from across the literature, but few analyses of roll call voting have considered the impact of agenda-setting as a precursor to voting by explicitly looking at the selection of bills for votes.

Agenda-setting is one of the foundational elements of the legislative institution, affecting nearly everything else that happens, from committees to parties to policy outputs (e.g., Shepsle and Weingast 1987; Tsebelis 2002; Weingast 1996). The development of political parties may even have reflected the need to develop agendas that avoided the perils of cycling over issues, a situation in which a majority cannot agree on a most preferred policy when faced with multiple options over which to choose (Aldrich 1995; Arrow 1951; Black 1958; Riker 1961). Moreover, the floor agenda-setting process itself creates much of the one-dimensional structure of congressional politics (Talbert and Potoski 2002). Whereas the decision to sponsor or cosponsor legislation involves a "complex process involving staff, colleagues, lobbyists, ... issues related to constituency, ideology and personal preference" (Talbert and Potoski 2002, 870–1), floor voting is simplified by the one-dimensional arrangement created by the agenda. Thus, agenda-setting determines the structure of conflict.[2]

---

[2] In general, my framework, and the empirical approach of classifying bills as bipartisan and partisan, is not focused on placing bills and members on a one-dimensional policy space and predicting voting patterns in this way. However, I rely on these insights to build a broader story of how the agenda affects changes in partisan conflict and bipartisan agreement in policymaking over time.

Agenda-setting affects the degree to which various types of coalitions, including bipartisan coalitions, support legislation. Patterns of yea and nay votes, and patterns of which members end up on the winning side of a vote depend on how the majority party uses its power of agenda control (Clinton 2007; Lawrence et al. 2006). For instance, if the majority party blocks legislation that divides its own party, then all roll call votes should, at a minimum, have the support of the majority of majority party members (Cox and McCubbins 2005). More generally, partisan voting coalitions become likely when extreme proposals (Carrubba et al. 2008) or highly salient issues in the media (Carson et al. 2010a) are brought to the House floor. In contrast, bipartisan voting coalitions are likely when less controversial issues are brought to a vote, particularly under suspension of the rules procedures (Crespin et al. 2013). Variation in the content of the agenda affects the likelihood of bipartisan votes, and changes in the content of the agenda over time can affect the degree of partisan conflict and polarization (Clinton 2012).[3]

Gate-keeping by majority party leaders allows them to limit the votes on which members can take positions. "[T]he Rules Committee not only determines whether legislation shall come before the House, but what legislation, and how it is presented – in effect, it sets the terms of debate. It is possible for this power to be used to compel votes – by making it more difficult for opponents to advocate politically acceptable alternatives" (Democratic Study Group 1961, underlines as per original). Gate-keeping limits the inferences that opponents and constituents can make about the policy positions of members. For instance, the Democratic Study Group report quoted above went on to say that "If a member cannot support an alternative education bill, he can be made to look as if he is against having any education bill at all" (Democratic Study Group 1961). Similarly, in his analysis of the connections between descriptive and substantive representation, Minta (2009, 194) notes that, if we only rely on vote-based studies, "we may overstate the degree of partisan unity among legislators and understate black and Latino members' responsiveness on minority interest issues" because "controversial race issues are censored by party leaders before they come to the House floor for a vote." As a result of agenda-setting, members may appear more (or less) partisan than they would be under other agenda scenarios.

In sum, the content of the floor agenda and of the roll call agenda, in particular, will affect whether voting coalitions are bipartisan or partisan. When bipartisan legislation is pursued, bipartisan votes are likely. In contrast, when partisan legislation is pursued, party unity votes are likely. Recall from

---

[3] It is important to note that various measures of partisan conflict and polarization are more or less affected by agenda-setting. Whereas NOMINATE scores are less sensitive to the agenda (McCarty et al. 2006), party voting rates (Roberts and Smith 2003), interest group scores (Snyder 1992), and other scaling techniques (e.g., homals) all reflect greater sensitivity to the agenda. In all cases, however, agenda-setting procedures that aim to align particular groups of members with each other and differentiate them from other members (i.e., majority versus minority members) will be reflected in the resulting measures of polarization.

Chapter 2 that, among bills that received roll call votes, bills with bipartisan cosponsorship coalitions were always more likely to receive a bipartisan roll call vote than bills with partisan cosponsorship coalitions. More generally, I expect that, over time, patterns in the rate at which bipartisan bills are selected to receive roll call votes will mirror the trends in bipartisan roll call voting. If agenda-setting helps explain the divergence between patterns of cosponsorship and roll call voting, the selection of bills for votes must shift over time from prioritizing bipartisan legislation to prioritizing partisan legislation, with a low point for bipartisanship in the mid-1990s.

MEMBERS AND PARTIES BALANCE INDIVIDUAL AND COLLECTIVE GOALS

The second guiding insight of the theoretical framework is that both members and their party must balance individual and collective goals.[4] The pursuit of both sets of goals requires that members concede agenda power to the leadership. The leadership, in turn, must weigh whether bipartisan or partisan legislation better achieves these goals. The choice of which type of legislation is pursued will hinge on whether members' electoral incentives conflict with policy goals and collective interests. Whether these goals push in the same direction (e.g., toward partisan legislation) or opposing directions will depend on the political context.

I start from the premise that both rank-and-file members of Congress and the leadership want to influence policy. While members must have a proximate goal of reelection (Mayhew 1974), their participation in Congress is further driven by their policy interests (Hall 1996, 68). With this in mind, members cannot remain solely focused on electoral interests and they may be willing to take some political risks for the sake of good public policy (Bessette 1994, 136).[5] Like others who have argued that members have multiple goals (Fenno 1978; Kingdon 1973), my framework emphasizes the importance of *both* policy and reelection goals.

Members pursue reelection through many actions, including the cosponsorship of bills, but they also concede some power to their party leadership in an effort to coordinate actions and create opportunities for policy benefits. In effect, "to meet their reelection and policy goals, members need legislation" (Sinclair 1995, 301). Under certain conditions, individual members can further their own policy goals by restricting control over the agenda (e.g., Diermeier and Vlaicu 2011). They may also be willing to make individual sacrifices to achieve collective goals.

[4] This insight has the potential to illuminate many broader aspects of congressional organization, member-party relationships, and policymaking. Its purpose here is more narrow. This insight offers implications for agenda-setting and when a bipartisan or partisan agenda better meets the multiple considerations that leaders face when constructing the agenda.

[5] For instance, scholars have noted that members' legislative behavior, including their support for reforms in the 1970s that vested greater power with party leaders, is inconsistent with a pure reelection, position-taking perspective that does not consider the additional interest of policy outcomes (Martin 2001; Rohde 1991).

Beyond these individual interests, members that make up a political party have a collective interest in being in the majority (Aldrich 1995; Cox and McCubbins 1993; Lee 2009; Smith 2007). Since the party label and its accompanying brand provide a signal to constituents (Kiewiet and McCubbins 1991; Snyder and Ting 2002), members of the party ultimately care about the reputation and record associated with their party. In their collective efforts, members of the majority party seek both positional (i.e., policy) goals and valence (i.e., good governance) goals (Stokes 1963). The combination of individual and collective goals sheds light on the resulting legislative behavior of members and on efforts by the Speaker to set the agenda and influence his party (Green 2010; Roberts and Smith 2003, 316), since leaders must consider possible trade-offs between these goals.

At the cosponsorship stage of legislation, members' individual interests dominate; when it comes to setting the agenda, however, collective interests rise. Cosponsorship, in particular, is at the intersection of members' reelection and policy influence goals. Members of Congress have incentives to engage in a particular mix of bipartisan and partisan behaviors depending on their district preferences, on their own ideology, and on the match between their preferences and those of others in their party. Bill cosponsorship is an arena in which members are relatively free to engage in bipartisan or partisan coalitions to pursue their individual interests (see Chapter 2). The roll call agenda, in contrast, constrains the behavior of individual members of Congress because only a subset of bills are brought to the floor. While cosponsorship is possible on all introduced bills, the agenda-setting process in the House restricts what legislation receives attention beyond introduction and possible cosponsorship.[6] Most bills die in the standing committees. Those bills that are reported from these committees may die in the Rules Committee or when brought to the floor. As a result, members will be forced to take further public positions only on the subset of bills that make the floor and roll call agendas. Since position taking in roll call votes and records of partisanship affect members electorally, they may be wary of agendas that hurt their electoral prospects. However, more partisan agendas may better reflect their policy goals and collective efforts to differentiate the two parties.

When majority party leaders set the floor agenda, they must consider how the selection of particular types of bills will affect individual members and the party as a whole.[7] Voting for partisan legislation holds potential risks for members if it

---

[6] There are, of course, multiple tracks that legislation can take. Particularly when party leaders use task forces or other means of bypassing the regular order, legislation does not merely proceed from introduction/cosponsorship, to committee consideration, then to the floor.

[7] In setting the floor agenda, party leaders select bills from the pool of introduced bills. Of course, leaders can write their own bills as well, but even these can gather cosponsorship coalitions from other members. Since these introduced bills are the same bills that members cosponsored in the pre-agenda step of the legislative process, the cosponsorship coalitions on these bills provide information to the leadership (Koger 2003). Cosponsorship coalitions can be informative about policy content, the type of coalition that would support the bill on the floor, and the resulting likelihood of passage.

makes them appear out-of-step with constituent interests (Canes-Wrone et al. 2002; Carson et al. 2010b). Thus, partisan legislation is most risky for members when they are cross-pressured by their constituents and their party; for members in these "unsorted" districts, bipartisan legislation is less risky. Although a partisan agenda may always be more risky for a subset of individual members, it is important to remember the dichotomous nature of voting. Members just need to be on the "right" side of an issue, as the public is not likely to know the full range of options for the agenda (Arnold 1990, 12; Van Houweling 2012). As a consequence, members may support a partisan floor strategy if it allows them to end up on the "right" side of an issue for their constituents. Moreover, party members may support an agenda that serves multiple goals of policy influence, reelection, and majority party status, even if that agenda does not include the most preferred policy of their constituents. Finding the appropriate balance of these goals is critical for the majority party when setting the agenda.

The floor agenda as a whole, and the roll call agenda in particular, represent the priorities and strategies of the majority party and its collective interest in influencing policy through legislation. Although the role of party leaders in the Senate is debated (see Den Hartog and Monroe 2011), scholars agree that party leaders in the House, particularly the Speaker, have important resources and powers that allow them to influence the construction of the agenda even if they cannot exert direct influence over the votes of members (Cox and McCubbins 1993, 2005; Rohde 1991; Smith 2007). Not only does the Speaker control the Rules Committee, which acts as a "narrow isthmus" through which bills must pass (Brownstein 2007, 66), but the Speaker's power to recognize members allows him to leverage the suspension of the rules procedure (Bach 1990). Setting the agenda allows the leadership to dictate which bills receive floor attention, to put forward bills sponsored by majority party members, and to prioritize bipartisan or partisan bills. While the House leadership plays a central role in this legislative process, parties should nonetheless be viewed as voluntaristic teams (Lee 2009). A partisan floor agenda is only possible when it has the support of the party members.[8]

When members of each party are more homogenous in their preferences, and the alignment of district and party interests is high, party leaders are more likely to exercise power of all kinds. The conditional party government theory emphasizes this historical pattern: when members are not pulled in different directions by their constituents and their party, they cede more power to their party leaders (Aldrich and Rohde 2001; Rohde 1991). This power can be used as direct influence – controlling committee chairs or pressuring members – but also as

---

[8] On any given bill or vote, party leaders may impose a partisan agenda on members (or at least a subset of members who may prefer an alternative bill). However, the voluntaristic nature of congressional parties suggests that, in general, legislators empower leaders to construct these partisan agendas. Members, not just the leadership, benefit from coordinating party activity, developing a party brand, and pointing out differences with the opposing party.

indirect influence – controlling the agenda. Party leaders can then use their heightened power to shape the character of the issues on the agenda and the nature of legislative alternatives (Rohde 1991, 192), including the pursuit more partisan legislative strategies. Consistent with the conditional party government framework, recent findings by Diermeier and Vlaicu (2011) indicate that members of the majority party receive policy benefits by giving disproportionate agenda power to party leaders over the chamber median (i.e., the member whose policy position places him as the median). This is true, however, only when members of the majority party have similar preferences. When parties are heterogeneous and many members face cross-pressures from their constituents and their party, the risks of giving party leaders power increases.

Party cartel theory offers a somewhat different view on agenda-setting and the power of the majority party to balance individual and collective goals (Cox and McCubbins 2005). Since each individual has incentives to pursue actions that hurt (or at least do not help) the party's collective reputation, party leaders are needed to "to internalize the collective electoral fate of the party" (Cox and McCubbins 1993, 132–3). These leaders are then charged with using their negative power to keep party-splitting issues off of the agenda and using their positive power to advance legislation only when it has wide support in the majority party (Cox and McCubbins 2005). As members become better sorted, with Democrats representing Democratic (liberal) leaning districts and Republicans representing Republican (conservative) leaning districts, party leaders are better able to construct floor agendas that pursue partisan policies without substantial electoral risks for members. Members can support this strategy because the pursuit of partisan policies is no longer at odds with constituent preferences.

Figure 3.1, which draws on the cartel agenda model of Cox and McCubbins (2005), presents a stylized picture of Congress. The figure depicts two time periods. In both time periods, the policy positions of the majority party median (M), the minority party median (m), and the floor median (F) are presented on a single policy dimension, which runs from liberal to conservative. These policy positions may be induced by their constituents. Assuming that the status quo and possible bill proposals can also be depicted on this dimension, and that if a bill is brought to the floor, it will be considered under an open rule (meaning that it will

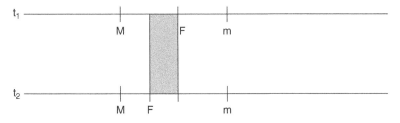

FIGURE 3.1 Illustration of How Member Sorting Contributes to a Partisan Agenda

be amended to the policy position of the floor median), this stylized picture emphasizes how sorting can produce more partisan agendas. Between the first and second time periods, the position of the floor median moves to the left, indicating greater homogeneity or sorting within the Democratic Party. Note, however, that the positions of the majority and minority medians have not moved apart, or become polarized.

As sorting occurs, the status quo policies in the shaded area open up to allow policy change. In t_1, the majority party median prefers to move policy from these status quos toward himself, but he knows that if the issue is placed on the agenda (under an open rule), the floor median's favored position will prevail, ultimately moving policy away from the majority median. As a result, in t_1 the majority median opts not to pursue policy change for those status quos in the shaded area. However, the increase in sorting between t_1 and t_2 allows the majority party median to raise issues with status quos in the shaded area and place them on the agenda. Although the floor median will ultimately prevail, policy movement from the shaded status quos to F yields outcomes closer, and more preferable, to the majority party median (M). As a result, the change between t_1 and t_2 increases the number of proposals that can reach the threshold of support from the majority party for being placed on the agenda. Because a majority of the minority party wants to move policy in the opposite direction, these policy proposals will likely result in party unity votes on the floor. Thus, sorting clearly contributes to a more partisan agenda and, therefore, to more partisan voting patterns.[9]

More generally, working from the assumption that members care about reelection and policy, but also share collective goals with others in the party, the presence of large numbers of cross-pressured members will limit support for the pursuit of partisan policies since individual and collective goals may conflict. As a result, party leaders will be forced to structure the agenda in a way that balances these individual and collective goals, and remain attentive to the costs borne by their party members. When there are many cross-pressured members, partisan legislation is more costly. But when there are few cross-pressured members, the agenda (and particularly, the roll call agenda) can be skewed toward more partisan legislation with fewer costs to individual members.

Although conditional party government and party cartel theories help us understand the relationship between agenda control and intra-party agreement, they do not tell us why bipartisan legislation is common on the agenda. The degree to which bipartisan or partisan legislation is pursued by party leaders via

---

[9] This figure is illustrative of one possible connection between the cartel theory and whether the agenda (and resulting vote) is partisan or bipartisan. The broader argument of this book, which focuses on the notions of bipartisan and partisan as a way to capture coalitions and understand party conflict, does not assume the presence of a one-dimensional policy space for bills, particularly at the cosponsorship stage, or seek to predict precisely what bills will be brought to a vote given preferences, bill content, and the status quo. The view of sorting used throughout the book is also broader than its use in this example.

positive agenda control, in particular, remains ambiguous. In the stylized version of the cartel framework in Figure 3.1, bipartisan votes are common only when legislation changes policies from extreme status quo points, which may be rare since each Congress inherits status quo policies from the previous administration (Krehbiel 1998). Nonetheless, Brady and Han (2006, 131–2) show that party unity has risen in recent decades along with bipartisan unity. Roll call votes are often either highly partisan or highly bipartisan (see Chapter 2). This suggests that a party can pursue *either* partisan or bipartisan legislation by utilizing positive agenda control, prompting the need to consider the additional incentives of party leaders to pursue each type of legislation.

A REPUTATION FOR LEGISLATIVE SUCCESS AND THE NEED FOR BIPARTISAN LEGISLATION

The third insight driving my theoretical framework is that congressional parties – and especially the majority party – have incentives to create a record of legislative success. Because bipartisan legislation is easier to pass and enact into law than partisan legislation, the majority party has reasons to pursue bipartisan legislation that go beyond the potential electoral costs to members from being out-of-step. These incentives may be particularly pronounced in periods with small majority seat shares or divided government.

Party brands can include both a positional component and a valance component (Stokes 1963). Whereas the positional component rests on policy positions and outputs, the valence component refers to the intrinsic attractiveness of a party, including a reputation of legislative accomplishments and efficient governance (Butler and Powell 2014). At a minimum, this requires that the House pass the bills that the majority party puts forward on the floor, but it may also require that the party advance legislation into law. As a result, the valence component of the party brand may require bipartisan legislation even if the positional component requires partisan legislation. The two components of the party brand present a tension that manifests in the pursuit of bipartisan and partisan legislation.

The need to establish a record of legislative success, including the passage of legislation into law, constrains partisan agenda-setting if there are consequences for the party as a collective and for individual members if they fail to govern. Pundits who assert that the electorate is enraged by inaction and will electorally punish members for gridlock (e.g., Capehart 2010; Koszczuk 1995) seem to suggest that these consequences are real. The perspective from scholars is more mixed, but a growing body of research finds that members of Congress should be, and are, concerned with institutional performance and governance. While earlier work by Mayhew (1974) and Fenno (1978) suggested that members care relatively little about institutional performance, running away from Congress and focusing on their own accomplishments instead, recent evidence suggests that members should, and do, consider the need to pass legislation. For instance,

Arnold (1990) proposes that voters hold Congress accountable, either by judging incumbents on their individual policy actions or by judging them on their performance as a party. Lipinski (2004) finds evidence suggestive of the latter, with members referencing legislative accomplishments and institutional performance in their constituent newsletters, ultimately running *with* Congress rather than *against* Congress.

A growing body of evidence emphasizes the importance of legislative success, suggesting that the fates of individual members in the majority are tied both to the performance of their party and to the performance of the institution (e.g., Wawro 2000, 19). This record of performance includes passage of bills in the chamber and enactment of bills into law. While some voters hold both the majority and minority parties responsible for institutional actions, public opinion surveys indicate that few voters fail to hold the majority party responsible.[10] Partisan conflict damages approval of Congress (Ramirez 2009), and congressional approval affects the vote shares of majority members, challenger emergence, and strategic retirement (Jones and McDermott 2010). Jones (2010) finds that congressmen, and particularly those in the majority party, are held electorally accountable for the accomplishments of Congress (or the lack thereof). Most extensively, Adler and Wilkerson (2013) provide a wide range of evidence that voters hold congressmen accountable for institutional performance, adding a third avenue of institutional retrospective accountability to Arnold's individual and partisan approaches. Perhaps most importantly, Adler and Wilkerson's work indicates that members of Congress believe that voters will judge them on institutional performance, including their ability to enact laws that deal with the policy problems confronting Congress.[11] These results suggest that members should be wary of partisan conflict if it damages productivity.

Because voters hold Congress accountable on the basis of party and institutional accomplishments, this drives the majority party to prioritize a record of legislative success. Although a partisan agenda helps the party pursue collective policy goals it can also hurt members if it damages productivity. With this in mind, party leaders will consider the electoral and policy interests of members, in

[10] For instance, public opinion surveys by Stanford University as part of the 2008 Cooperative Congressional Election Study point to perceptions of accountability for both the majority and the minority party. Following up on a congressional approval question, respondents were asked who they thought was responsible for congressional performance. The timing of the survey meant that this question was asked when Democrats held the majority in the both the House and Senate. Of the respondents, 24.6 percent answered that the Democrats in Congress were responsible, and an additional 33.7 percent answered that both Democrats and Republicans in Congress were responsible. Only 3.4 percent of respondents thought that the minority Republicans alone were responsible. Another 24.7 percent of respondents said that congressional Democrats, Republicans, and President Bush were responsible for congressional performance (Fiorina and Brady 2008).

[11] Many studies that point to electoral consequences for failing to govern, including Adler and Wilkerson's (2013) work, draw on evidence from years included in the analyses in this book: the period from 1973 to 2004. This suggests that even as polarization and partisan conflict in voting has risen, governance has been important.

conjunction with the need to produce a record of legislative success, when determining when to pursue a partisan agenda and when to opt for a more bipartisan one.

The need for party leaders to balance the pursuit of policy goals with a record of effective governance provides two expectations within my framework of strategic partisan agenda-setting. First, when partisan legislation is not a viable option for the majority party due to the constraint of cross-pressured members, the majority party can pursue bipartisan legislation.[12] As a result, bipartisan legislation should be relatively common on the agenda, and should increase when partisan legislation cannot pass. Second, the pursuit of a partisan agenda may be constrained by the size of the majority seat share and divided government. The incentive to pursue bipartisan legislation is heightened when political conditions hamper the passage of partisan legislation. Whereas the presence of cross-pressured members and small majority seat shares affect passage within the House, divided government affects movement of legislation from the House and into law. Partisan legislation may be unable to garner support from a majority of the House when members cannot support it without electoral risk, or when slim majorities leave little room for members to deviate from the party line. Even when partisan legislation passes in the House, however, it may die in the Senate or be vetoed by the president during divided government.

Although party cohesiveness has attracted more attention from scholars than seat share (Smith 2007), the size of the majority constrains legislative behavior. A large majority can pass bills without the support of all of its members, while the support of nearly all members may be necessary with a small majority. Partisan legislation may fail to pass when there are small seat shares, particularly in instances when some majority members cannot support a bill because of constituent opposition. As a result, small majorities may need to focus more on pieces of legislation with bipartisan support. For instance, Speaker Carl Albert expressed this sentiment in the early 1970s: "The more Democrats we have in Congress, the better able we are to fend off opposing coalitions and to enact progressive legislation for the nation's well-being" (Albert 1973, 12–13). Discussions of the Republican's rise to majority status in the 104th Congress also suggest that their small seat share should have been a constraint on partisanship. "The narrowness of Republican control appeared to dictate a cautious approach to governing" (Dodd and Oppenheimer 2004, 29).

Similarly, the presence of divided or unified government affects whether leaders can pursue bipartisan or partisan legislation.[13] Although divided

---

[12] Both the theoretical framework and the empirical approach of this book focus on the agenda that *is* pursued in the House, not on the overall size of the agenda relative to a baseline need for legislation. Given changes in the role of government over time, external events, and reauthorizations of legislation for set periods of time (among many other factors), assessing whether House majorities pursue the "right" size of agenda is beyond the scope of this book.

[13] Whether the Senate or the president is the dominant constraint on partisan agenda-setting during divided government will depend on the form of division. For instance, in cases where the same

government does not affect the ability of the majority party to pass legislation in the House, it is likely to affect the policy proposals that can gain simultaneous support in the House, the Senate, and by the president. Assuming that partisan bills are more likely to be opposed by the Senate or President when party control differs from the House, divided government may force a more bipartisan agenda (Trubowitz and Mellow 2005). A memo from John Barriere to Speaker Carl Albert regarding the accomplishments of the House and its leadership in the 94th Congress highlights this institutional constraint:

> The first term Members must recognize that there is some usefulness in building a record. On the jobs bill, for example, the leadership and the Appropriations Committee put together the best possible bill they could devise to accomplish the Party's goals ... In a divided government, with a conservative President and a moderately liberal Congress, this is probably the best one can really hope for. (Barriere 1975)

Thus, a majority party that cares about producing a record of legislative success may see advantages to pursuing bipartisan legislation. Not only does bipartisan legislation benefit the electoral interests of members who are cross-pressured, but it may be easier to pass in the House when there are small majority seat shares. Regardless of the internal make-up of the House, bipartisan legislation is likely to fare better than partisan legislation in the Senate or with the president during divided government.

PARTISAN CONFLICT IN ROLL CALL VOTING PROVIDES EXTERNAL SIGNALING

House leaders use their control over the floor agenda to send messages to external audiences. Although the majority party controls which bills receive floor attention, both parties use roll call votes to signal how they differ from the opposing party. This is important because the ability to point out partisan differences may produce rewards for party branding that bipartisan agreement cannot.

Although bipartisan legislation sends external signals related to governance, partisan legislation offers an important means of signaling to voters, primary constituencies, interest groups, and others who may want to know how members of the two parties differ. "Floor agenda control provides majorities with strategic options for getting out their message" (Sinclair 2006, 278). For instance, Republican members want their leaders to publicize Republican

party controls both the House and the Senate, the president and his veto will be the limiting factor. In cases where the same party controls both the House and the presidency, the Senate will be the limiting factor. While the president must sign or veto legislation (with the latter giving the legislature a chance for an override), the Senate can opt to simply not act on legislation, thus killing it. These differences are potentially important for theorizing about whether House majorities view governance in different ways depending on the configuration of parties in the Senate and Presidency. However, limited variation across the arrangements of divided government over this time period yields empirical results that show similar patterns across types of divided government.

positions while keeping the Democrats' agenda off the floor, particularly on issues where the Democrats and the public agree (Sinclair 2006, 227). Interviews with former House members and staffers similarly highlight floor partisanship as a purposeful choice of the leadership and a means of partisan differentiation. Mike Castle (former at-large representative of Delaware) noted that when the majority party sets the agenda, votes are designed to point out differences, and bipartisan efforts by members are not embraced on the House floor because of partisan priorities (Castle 2011). The Chief of Staff to a current member reiterated this view, saying that bipartisan legislation is difficult to get on the agenda because it does not highlight differences between the two sides (Lausten 2011). These comments suggest that the party leadership not only is wary of putting up issues for votes that create divisions within their own party, but also has incentives to place divisive issues (between the parties) up for votes, with the expectation that their party will come out on the winning side. Agenda-setting makes this possible. "The rules of the game are easy enough to manipulate by a majority party to foreclose opportunities to vote on alternatives that would attract bipartisanship" (Sarah Binder, quoted in Poole 2004, 2907).

Thus, parties can consciously choose partisan conflict as part of their legislative strategy. A growing number of scholars focused on member-party relationships have explored partisan differentiation as a possible goal of agenda-setting (e.g., Lebo et al. 2007; Lee 2009; Patty 2008). These theories speak to partisanship as a strategic choice, and not merely as a byproduct of people's preferences. If partisan conflict reduces the uncertainty about the political positions of individual candidates, the resulting electoral benefits suggest that the pursuit of the positional component of the party brand may favor bills that differentiate the parties over those that do not (Cox and McCubbins 1993, 2005; Grynaviski 2010; Snyder and Ting 2002). "Whatever the virtues of bipartisanship, they muddle party images and make it more difficult for citizens to distinguish Democratic and Republican positions on the issues" (Groeling and Kernell 2000, 83). As a result, legislators may prefer disagreement to compromise (Gilmour 1995).

Since the roll call agenda is the subset of the floor agenda where individual positions are recorded, efforts to point out differences through partisan legislation will be concentrated on the roll call agenda. If the broader floor agenda (which includes voice votes) consists of both partisan and bipartisan legislation, roll call votes are both necessary and politically useful on partisan bills. Roll call votes may be necessary if the winning coalition is not obvious on a voice vote, but they may also be politically useful because they point out differences between the two sides. The public audience for roll call votes can incentivize each side to try to make the other look extreme (Groseclose and McCarty 2001).

Both the majority and minority parties can make efforts to differentiate their positions. Although the minority party lacks the agenda-setting power of the majority, its members can also request roll call votes to mitigate or exacerbate partisan conflict on the floor. In the most adversarial form, the minority may seek to block even bipartisan bills at the expense of governance and against their own policy positions. This has not, however, generally been the case in the House. Voters hold members of both parties accountable for legislative problem solving, especially during divided government (Adler and Wilkerson 2013, 15). However, even when it does not hinder governance, minority opposition enables minority members to point out differences between the parties and to insulate themselves from primary competition. Thus, both the majority and minority parties may face incentives to emphasize partisan differences.

Since the early 1970s, numerous factors have further heightened the benefits that parties and their members receive from pursuing a partisan legislative strategy. These factors include interest groups and their effect on fundraising, primary election concerns, changes in the media environment, and competition for the majority. Not only do these factors point to the reasons why parties want to focus on places of partisan disagreement, but they also explain why congressional partisanship is not necessarily dependent on mass polarization.

The expansion of interest groups during this period focused attention on new issues, forced politicians to take sides, and institutionalized conflict (Brownstein 2007, 117–18). Campaign fundraising became dependent on interest groups that hold positions at the extreme of an issue, and on political action committees (PACs) that often give to only one party (FEC 2009; McCarty et al. 2006). In recent years, although some types of PACs contribute to members across the ideological spectrum, many PACs concentrate money on members at the ideological extremes, and few concentrate money on those in the middle (McCarty et al. 2006, 149). Former House member Dan Glickman, who later became Secretary of Agriculture, summed it up well: "There are no 'Reach Across the Aisle' PACs" (Glickman 2011). Although the relationship between campaign fundraising and legislative strategies is likely a circular relationship, donations from interest groups encourage party leaders to craft agendas that put their party on the favorable side of an issue and the opposing party on the unfavorable side.

Members' primary election interests also make them more likely to benefit from a partisan legislative strategy. Brady, Han, and Pope (2007) argue that primary challengers (particularly since the 1970s) come from the far left and far right, that primary electorates punish moderation (even if it is line with the general electorate's preferences), and that, over time, candidates learn to cater to the base. Thus, primaries have a centrifugal force, pulling candidates toward the ideological poles (Burden 2004, 2001). The rise of the Tea Party movement in the Republican Party in 2010 highlights this pattern. In previous eras, the expectation was that even if candidates were pulled toward the base of the party by primary elections, they would move back to the center for general elections. However, the expansion of 24–7 media (which now tracks the positions a candidate takes and calls him out for "flip-flopping") has made this movement back to the center more difficult and less desirable (Fiorina and Abrams 2009, 166). While concerns about the ability to win a general election can lead members (particularly cross-pressured members) to support bipartisan agendas, primary election concerns can lead members to support partisan agendas.

Changes in the media environment have similarly forced members to pay more attention to the interests of their primary electorate. Prior (2007) suggests that the expansion of media options creates an environment where people who once watched network news no longer watch any news programs because of other entertainment options available on cable television. Without the inadvertent political knowledge that comes from watching the nightly news, these people turn out to vote at lower rates than in previous eras. As a result, the electorate is increasingly comprised of strong partisans with high political interest as the less interested and less committed partisans stay home. Combined with the rise of partisan media (Levendusky 2013), the high-choice media environment incentivizes members of Congress to respond to their primary election constituencies rather than to their geographic or general election constituencies. Partisan legislative strategies allow members to better appeal to their primary electorate.

Competition for majority status further heightens incentives for both parties to pursue partisanship over bipartisanship. When a party seeks to keep or gain majority status, it does not want to provide political cover to even the most moderate members of the opposite party, since both parties are competing for those seats in the next election. Crafting bipartisan solutions limits the ways in which one party can attack the voting records of members of the other party. Reaching a place of bipartisan agreement can insulate the more moderate members in the opposing party from electoral criticism and defeat. A Democratic House staffer made the following assessment, noting a change from times when Republicans were the permanent minority and were willing to cozy up with Democrats:

Blue Dogs [and] the Boll Weevils before that, ... desperately want to have Republican friends. They would prefer that their Republican friends would go down into their districts and tell them what a friendly guy they are to Republicans, because almost all of the Blue Dogs and Boll Weevils represented districts that were conservative and had a lot of Republican supporters ... But the idea in the back of their minds was, "you guys aren't going to attack us, ok and you're going to let us survive." But to Newt, to the political people who came in the '90s, those are the districts that they had the best chance to take, so why in God's name would they be giving all these guys passes – trying to work with them and make them well? You don't want to make them well! You want to make them look like they are with Clinton or Obama or whoever, and you want to exterminate them! (Democratic Staffer 2011)

In environments where there is greater competition for majority status, legislators delegate more power to the party leadership to constrain individualistic behavior (Carroll and Eichorst 2013). As a result, competition for the majority may provide incentives to pursue partisan legislation.

Ultimately, both the party leadership and individual members can benefit from the pursuit of a partisan legislative strategy. Because a partisan strategy appeals to the base, it helps with fundraising efforts and primary elections. When parties use a base strategy rather than a swing strategy, candidates are criticized for *not* having proposals that are appreciably different than their opponent (Fiorina and Abrams 2009, 158). Thus, both parties may favor pursuing opportunities for partisan differentiation. A partisan roll call agenda is one way to accomplish this.

While House parties always see potential benefits in pointing out partisan differences, these benefits may be greatest during divided government (Gilmour 1995). When different parties control the branches of government, voters may not know what each party stands for unless the two sides come into conflict. As a result, the leadership may pursue partisan legislation to point out these differences during divided government. This expectation is at odds with the arguments in the previous section, which suggested that the need to govern would drive more bipartisan agenda-setting during divided government. In subsequent analyses, I consider both possibilities, and also explore whether governing constraints play out on the broader floor agenda but not on the roll call agenda. That is, party leaders may pursue bipartisan legislation during divided government, but these bills may receive voice votes rather than roll call votes, since the majority party does not to want to give credit to the opposing party or show external audiences where the two sides agree.

BRINGING IT TOGETHER: LEADERSHIP CONSIDERATIONS IN SETTING THE AGENDA

While the first guiding insight of my theoretical framework pointed to the importance of looking at agenda-setting as a critical determinant of voting patterns, the next three insights pointed to various considerations that influence the leadership as they set the agenda. The discussion highlighted the ways that the bipartisan and partisan bills would affect the leadership's ability to balance individual and collective goals, achieve a record of legislative success, and point out partisan differences. In some circumstances, these goals push in the same direction, either toward bipartisan or partisan legislation. In other circumstances, however, these goals push against each other, with some favoring the pursuit of bipartisan legislation and others favoring the pursuit of partisan legislation. Drawing on the expectations from these broad insights, this concluding section summarizes the trade-offs between a bipartisan and partisan agenda and offers predictions of when each type of agenda will best achieve the goals of the majority party.

The decision of whether to pursue bipartisan or partisan bills hinges on how well each type of bill meets the objectives of the party leadership. The leadership must consider (at least) three key factors: the costs to members of the party, the probability of legislative success, and the contributions to building a party brand that differentiates the two parties. If leaders factor all three considerations into their decisions, their agenda will contain a mixture of bipartisan and partisan bills. The relative proportion of these two bill types will vary depending on how well each type of bill fulfills the goals of the leaders. The strategic partisan agenda-setting framework, in conjunction with the empirical tests that follow, helps us better understand how parties balance these considerations.

First, party leaders want to minimize the costs of the agenda to their membership. The second guiding insight of this chapter suggested that although the policy interests of the party may best be obtained through partisan bills, members' electoral interests may be put at risk if they support these bills when they are cross-pressured between their party and constituency. In contrast, bipartisan legislation allows cross-pressured members to meet constituent needs while not breaking away from the party. Thus, I hypothesize that periods with many unsorted districts will be associated with bipartisan agenda-setting, and periods with more sorted districts will be associated with partisan agenda-setting. Applied to changes in the historical period covered by this book, this hypothesis suggests that an abundance of cross-pressured members in the 1970s would encourage the leadership to shape the congressional roll call agenda to prioritize bipartisan legislation, but the emergence of more sorted districts, particularly after the later 1980s and early 1990s, would encourage the leadership to prioritize partisan legislation. The concomitant decline in bipartisan cooperation in voting would thus stem from sorting in the electoral coalitions of the parties and the resulting ability of the leadership to build a partisan floor agenda.

Second, party leaders want to increase their chances of legislative success. This means that they must pass bills through the House, and move at least a portion of these bills into law. The third guiding insight emphasized that the size of the majority would affect House passage, with bipartisan legislation being easier to pass in environments with small majorities. Likewise, divided government would differentially affect bipartisan and partisan bills in terms of enactment into law, since partisan bills face a tougher road with a Senate or President of the opposing party. Since passing legislation is a difficult process in general, bipartisan bills provide one route to reduce the time and effort involved, and the risk of legislative failure. Whether bills are bipartisan or partisan can affect the amount of resources and floor time needed, or the transaction cost, for leaders. The transaction cost to move legislation forward is substantially lower for bipartisan bills (Koger 2003). From the insights on the importance of governance and legislative success, I hypothesize that institutional contexts will affect the pursuit of bipartisan legislation. In particular, if leaders prioritize governance, *all else being equal*, bipartisan legislation will be advantaged over partisan legislation to a greater extent during periods with small majority seat shares or divided government than during periods with large seat shares or unified government.

Implicit in the argument above is the assumption that bipartisan cosponsored bills are the less risky option for passage. Empirically, this assumption means that the passage rate of bipartisan bills (among those bills that receive a vote) should be greater than that for partisan bills. Moreover, if majority seat shares and divided government are constraints on the passage of partisan legislation, there should be differences in the success rates of bipartisan and partisan legislation under these contexts. House passage rates should be higher for bipartisan bills than for partisan bills during periods with small majority seat shares, and the rate of enactment into public law should be significantly affected by divided government for partisan bills but not for bipartisan bills.

Third, party leaders want to pursue legislation that helps build the party brand by pointing out differences between their own party and their opponents. The fourth guiding insight suggested that partisan bills provide more opportunities for differentiation and that roll call votes, rather than voice votes, are necessary for achieving this goal. "To give voters a choice, parties need to be cohesive *and* distinctive" (Coleman 1996, 79). As a result, benefits to the party brand increase when the parties take largely different stances on a bill. This suggests that the degree of district-party sorting within both parties, not just within the majority party, will drive partisan agenda-setting. The need for cohesion and distinction also suggests that shifts to partisan agenda-setting will be larger on issues with higher degrees of partisan differentiation – that is, on those issues that each party owns. Moreover, goals of party branding provide an alternative to the governance hypothesis. If party leaders prioritize partisan differentiation rather than governance, the pursuit of partisan legislation will not decline in periods of divided government or small seat shares.[14] Finally, since the benefits of differentiation are only realized through roll call votes, I hypothesize that shifts toward partisan agenda-setting will be concentrated in this form of voting.

In sum, when party leaders weigh the effects of partisan versus bipartisan legislation on the costs to members, the probability of successful legislative outcomes, and emphasizing party differences, they will pursue bipartisan legislation more or less depending on the political environment. Whereas partisan legislation helps meet policy objectives and creates a party brand, it can be costly to individual members (particularly in cross-pressured districts) and may reduce the ability to enact legislation into law. In contrast, bipartisan legislation offers fewer benefits for policy goals and partisan differentiation but imposes fewer costs on cross-pressured members. Bipartisan legislation also has a greater likelihood of becoming law, particularly during periods with small seat shares or during divided government. As a result, there may be tensions between the pursuit of partisan and bipartisan legislation. How the leadership resolves these tensions will affect which bills are brought forward on the floor and roll call agendas. Whether the agenda is predominantly bipartisan or partisan will subsequently affect whether voting patterns are bipartisan or partisan.

---

[14] Leadership considerations of governance and party differentiation may come into conflict. However, if the party loses the majority for failing to govern, benefits from party differentiation are wiped out, suggesting that governance may trump partisan differentiation. I allow the data in subsequent chapters to show which effect dominates or whether they differ among the broader floor agenda and the roll call agenda.

The theoretical framework of *strategic partisan agenda-setting* established here seeks to explain the divergence of bipartisanship between cosponsorship and roll call voting, and sheds light on the role of agenda-setting in manufacturing partisan conflict on the floor. It emphasizes the importance of agenda-setting in explaining the decline of bipartisan agreement on the House floor and, in particular, in roll call voting. This approach helps explain not only how agenda-setting affects voting patterns, but also why party leaders might want to pursue bipartisan or partisan legislation. The remainder of this book explores the hypotheses suggested by this framework. Chapter 4 focuses on the expectations from the first guiding insight, using agenda-setting as a way to resolve the puzzle of declining bipartisanship. Chapters 5 and 6 analyze the expectations from the remaining three guiding insights, examining when bipartisan or partisan legislation is pursued on the agenda. A focus on the degree of district-party sorting, divided government, and majority seat shares sheds light on how party leaders weigh the electoral interests of members, governance, and party differentiation. Chapter 6 also considers whether shifts from bipartisan to partisan agenda-setting are concentrated among issue areas that tend to differentiate the two parties – a pattern that would be expected if the benefits of partisanship occur most when the parties are cohesive and distinctive.

4

Agenda-Setting and the Decline of Bipartisan Cooperation

In 1974, just over 70 percent of all roll call votes had bipartisan voting coalitions. By 1995, only 27 percent of roll call votes were bipartisan. By this metric, bipartisan cooperation fell by more than three-fifths over a 20-year period. Over the same time period, however, bipartisan agreement in cosponsorship coalitions declined by less than one-fifth. The comparison of these two years highlights the broader pattern, and the empirical puzzle, at the heart of this book – bipartisan agreement in roll call voting has declined substantially, but bipartisan agreement in cosponsorship coalitions has declined much less. Agenda-setting provides one avenue to reconcile this puzzle.

This chapter focuses on the first guiding insight of my theoretical framework, which argues that the content of the agenda affects voting patterns. The primary goal of the chapter is to describe the extent to which party leaders pursue bipartisan legislation on the House agenda over time. These patterns of agenda-setting, at least for the roll call agenda, must track with observed patterns of roll call voting in Chapter 2. The secondary goal of this chapter is to consider the connection between increasing partisanship in the roll call agenda and the overall degree of bipartisanship in the legislative process and in policy outputs. I examine patterns of bipartisanship in public laws, differences between roll call and voice votes, and opportunities to craft legislative compromises. All of these patterns speak to how often party leaders pursue bipartisanship in the House and the policy consequences for doing so.

AGENDA CONTROL AND THE DECLINE OF BIPARTISANSHIP

Assessing Agenda-Setting

If agenda-setting is important for explaining the observed patterns of bipartisanship in roll call voting, then patterns of legislative attention for cosponsored bills should show that bipartisan bills received less attention between the 1970s and 1990s and that partisan bills received more attention. Given the observed resurgence of bipartisanship in roll call voting after the 104th Congress, changes in agenda-setting should also show a similar increase in the attention given to bipartisan bills. That is, if the expectation of strategic partisan agenda-setting is correct, then variation in bipartisanship in roll call voting should mirror variation in the relative prioritization of bipartisan versus partisan bills on the roll call agenda. This is the first and necessary step for understanding how strategic partisan agenda-setting contributes to vote-based partisanship.

The House roll call agenda provides an important point in the legislative process to assess the extent of bipartisan agenda-setting. It is not, however, the only place to consider shifts in the agenda. Party leaders repeatedly narrow the legislative agenda between the introduction of bills and roll call voting – first by standing committees, and then by the Rules Committee. As a result, the patterns of bills reported from committee and those receiving any type of floor attention (not just the subset receiving roll call votes) provide information about the party's agenda. Committee chairs can act as agents of the majority party (e.g., Aldrich 1995; Cox and McCubbins 1993), suggesting that the first step of the party's agenda may be seen in whether committees report bipartisan or partisan bills. The House Speaker controls the floor agenda through the Rules Committee and his power to recognize members. The full floor agenda includes every bill considered on the House floor, including those receiving roll call votes, but also those receiving voice votes. Thus, it includes all of the legislative priorities of the majority party. The roll call agenda, by contrast, includes just the subset of floor bills that receive roll call votes.

The legislative agenda at each of these stages is defined empirically by the subset of cosponsored House bills that reach a particular step of the legislative process.[1] The extent to which these bills are bipartisan or partisan captures whether the agenda is characterized as bipartisan or partisan. The committee agenda includes all cosponsored bills that are reported from committee. The floor agenda includes all bills that either received a roll call vote or passed the House without receiving a roll call vote. Although this measure misses any bills that received a voice vote but did not pass, these more controversial bills are likely picked up by the roll call measure. Finally, the roll call agenda includes all bills identified as the underlying bill at stake in any roll call vote. Although this definition includes both amendment and final passage votes, subsequent analyses show that the patterns of agenda-setting are quite similar if restricted to

---

[1] Throughout the analyses, measures of subsequent legislative attention for bills come from combining the bill cosponsorship data with the Policy Agendas Project roll call data (Baumgartner and Jones 2000), and also by using Rohde's (2004) roll call data. If a bill is listed as the root bill of a roll call vote, it is classified as having a roll call vote. Data on whether the bill was reported from committee comes from the Congressional Bills Project (Adler and Wilkerson 2008) and data on whether the bill passed the House comes from Fowler's (2006a) cosponsorship data.

bills receiving final passage roll call votes. For each measure of agenda-setting, I aggregate the attention given to bipartisan and partisan bills by Congress instead of by year, since a bill may be introduced in the first session but not receive attention until the second.

I include multiple categories of legislative attention for two reasons. First, the assessment of the degree of bipartisanship at the broader floor stage helps shed light on Congress' efforts at governing. If partisan legislation has replaced bipartisan legislation in roll call votes but not on the broader floor agenda, then concerns about partisan policymaking and party conflict in roll call voting may mask efforts at bipartisanship that occur elsewhere. Second, patterns of agenda-setting at three stages of the legislative process – committee, floor, and roll call votes – provide information about where the bipartisanship that continues to be observed in cosponsorship coalitions is replaced by partisanship. Whether party leaders choose to advance bipartisan legislation or partisan legislation in committees or after committees does not affect the ultimate conclusions of whether the roll call agenda has changed. However, it sheds light on the routes by which partisan agenda-setting occurs.

These measures of agenda-setting capture each of the underlying bills that are recorded as being reported from committee or at issue in a vote. While this approach misses bills that receive attention through non-standard channels like omnibus legislation, this omission is unlikely to systematically bias the results. In particular, when a partisan bill is the primary vehicle for an omnibus bill, it is likely that other bills incorporated in the omnibus legislation are also partisan (and vice versa for bipartisan bills). For example, the primary bill underlying the Energy Act of 2003 was a partisan bill (H.R. 6), sponsored by Republican Billy Tauzin and cosponsored by four other Republicans. The omnibus bill consolidated H.R. 6 with an energy tax bill (H.R. 1531), an energy research and development bill (H.R. 238), and a bill that allowed drilling in the Alaska National Wildlife Refuge (H.R. 39) (Goldreich 2003a, 2003b). Only one of these bills (H.R. 238) had a bipartisan cosponsorship coalition, while all of the other component pieces of legislation were partisan.[2] In contrast, a number of bipartisan provisions were excluded from the House omnibus bill, including the repeal of the 1935 Public Utility Holding Company Act (H.R. 1627) and the Homeland Infrastructure Power Security and Assurance Incentives Act of 2003 (H.R. 1458) ("Senate-House Energy Bills Compared" 2003). Not surprisingly, the final passage vote of this omnibus bill split along party lines, with 207 Republicans in support and 157 Democrats opposed. Although the exclusion of additional bills in omnibus legislation misses one route by which legislation receives attention, it does not detract from the broader evidence of agenda-

---

[2] H.R. 1531 did not have any cosponsors. However, the vote to report the bill from the Ways and Means Committee was 24–12 and all of the report's dissenting views came from Democrats on the committee (*House Report 108-067 Energy Tax Policy Act of 2003* 2003), suggesting that this bill was also partisan in content.

setting presented in this chapter, particularly if the degree of partisanship in various bills within omnibus legislation is correlated.[3]

Tracking Bipartisan Agenda-Setting

Can patterns of agenda-setting bridge the gap between the patterns of bipartisanship in cosponsorship coalitions and roll call votes? Variation over time in the likelihood that legislation with bipartisan cosponsors receives roll call votes that tracks with patterns of bipartisanship in roll call voting would support this claim. More generally, variation in the likelihood that legislation with bipartisan cosponsors receives any subsequent legislative attention – including committee, floor, and, ultimately, roll call voting – offers a first step toward understanding how agenda-setting magnifies the degree of partisanship in Congress.

Figure 4.1 plots the percentage of cosponsored bills that are bipartisan among all House bills, among bills that are reported from committee, among bills that receive any floor attention, and among bills that receive a roll call vote.[4] In order to simplify the discussion, I refer to these patterns as the extent of bipartisanship that occurs in four areas: in cosponsorship, in the committee agenda, in the floor agenda, and in the roll call agenda. Since these measures capture the percentage of cosponsored bills on the agenda that are bipartisan, higher percentages reflect greater bipartisan agenda-setting. For example, a value of 67 on the y-axis for the category of roll call votes in the 100th Congress indicates that, of all of the cosponsored bills to receive roll call votes in that Congress, 67 percent had bipartisan cosponsorship coalitions. Only 33 percent were bills with partisan cosponsorship coalitions.

Party leaders frequently pursue bipartisan legislation on all legislative agendas – committee, floor, and roll call. The solid line in Figure 4.1 presents the percentage of all cosponsored bills with bipartisan coalitions that occur in each Congress (similar to those presented by year in Chapter 2). This trend captures the underlying pool of bipartisan legislation that party leaders could pursue. Each of the dashed lines presents the percentage of bipartisan bills on the roll call, floor, and committee agendas. These agendas frequently include bipartisan legislation. Compared to cosponsorship coalitions where roughly half of all bills have bipartisan agreement, more than half of the bills at each subsequent legislative stage have bipartisan cosponsorship coalitions. The fact that

---

[3] If the presence of omnibus legislation combines partisan and bipartisan measures such that the nature of the legislation is no longer like that of the original bill, cosponsorship coalitions should not be related to subsequent voting patterns on the bill. The evidence in Chapter 2 that the bipartisan and partisan cosponsorship measures do translate into different likelihoods of bipartisan voting coalitions suggests that omnibus bills are not substantially obscuring the underlying degree of bipartisan agreement on the legislation.

[4] Unless otherwise specified, all measures of bipartisan and partisan bills are based on the 20 percent definition presented in Chapter 2. Bills are bipartisan if at least 20 percent of the cosponsors are from the party opposite the party of the bill sponsor and are partisan otherwise.

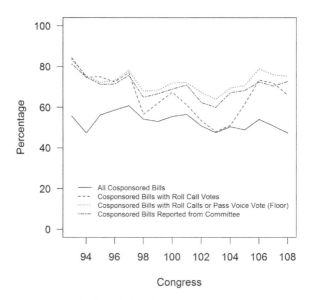

FIGURE 4.1 Bipartisanship by Legislative Stage

bipartisan bills remain on all of these agendas highlights the potential need for leaders to pursue these bills in order to garner a record of legislative success.

Despite high average levels of bipartisanship, the extent of bipartisan agenda-setting varies over time. For each of the legislative agendas, the pursuit of bipartisan legislation falls from the 93rd Congress (1973–74) to the 103rd or 104th Congress (1993–96), and then increases again until the 107th Congress (2001–02). These patterns mimic those seen in roll call voting coalitions. Although all three measures of agenda-setting show similar trends over time, the decline in bipartisanship is largest on the roll call agenda. On the committee and floor agendas, the decline is smaller. Bipartisanship on the committee agenda declined from roughly 80 percent in the 93rd Congress (1973–74) to 60 percent in the 103rd Congress (1993–94). Agenda-setting on the floor follows a similar pattern, although the percentage of bills that were bipartisan is higher than among bills reported from committee. In contrast, the roll call agenda exhibits greater variation over time and a larger decline in bipartisanship during the mid-1990s.[5] Between the 93rd and 103rd Congresses, the percentage of bills with bipartisan cosponsors declined by more than 30 percentage points.[6]

---

[5] When using the Policy Agendas Project data to align roll call votes with the underlying bill, I am including all types of roll call votes (final passage, amendments, etc.). The pattern of bipartisan agenda-setting on the roll call agenda is nearly identical when the analysis is restricted to bills receiving final passage roll call votes. Figure A4.1 plots the percentage of cosponsored bills that were bipartisan for all cosponsored bills, bills receiving any roll call vote, and bills receiving a final passage roll call vote.

[6] Similar shifts in bipartisan roll call agenda-setting are seen with thresholds of 30 percent, 40 percent, and 50 percent to define bipartisan bills, but are most apparent for the 20 percent and 30 percent definitions (as seen in Figure A4.2).

These patterns reveal that changes in agenda-setting, reflecting a shift toward party leaders pursuing less bipartisan legislation, are most evident on the roll call agenda. Throughout the early Congresses considered in this analysis, the prevalence of bipartisan legislation at each legislative stage – committee, floor, and roll call voting – is similar. However, by the 1980s, the percentage of bipartisan bills on the roll call agenda diverges from the patterns of bipartisanship on the other two legislative agendas. Between the mid-1980s and mid-1990s, bipartisan legislation is more prevalent in committees and on the floor than on the roll call agenda. These patterns suggest that leadership decisions further drive the shift from a bipartisan agenda to a partisan agenda after committees report bills. As suggested by former Appropriations staffer Mike Stephens, the decline of bipartisanship on the floor exaggerates the extent of conflict between members and in committees and subcommittees (Stephens 2011).

Paired with the discussion in Chapter 2 of bipartisanship in roll call voting for bipartisan and partisan cosponsored bills, the patterns in Figure 4.1 point to a very strong relationship between the leadership pursuing bipartisan legislation on the roll call agenda and bipartisan voting coalitions in the House. The correlation between the percentage of bipartisan bills on the roll call agenda (i.e., agenda-setting) and the percentage of roll call votes that are bipartisan (i.e., voting outcome) is 0.93 (p<0.001). For final passage votes rather than all roll call votes, this correlation is 0.94 (p<0.001). These correlations between agenda-setting and voting patterns point to how agenda-setting connects bipartisan agreement in cosponsorship to partisan disagreement in roll call voting.

Legislative attention to high-salience bills also shows a shift over time from bipartisan to partisan priorities. I include two measures of salience (i.e., important legislation). The first measure focuses on the discussion of bills in the Congressional Quarterly Almanac (CQ);[7] the second focuses on important legislative accomplishments and failures.[8] For each category of high-salience bills, I calculate the percentage of cosponsored bills that are bipartisan among bills that receive a roll call vote *and* are classified as high-salience. Figure 4.2 plots both the raw data and the trend of bipartisan agenda-setting for each measure. The percentage of bipartisan bills receiving roll call votes in each of these categories declines across the period of analysis, with low points around the 103rd and 104th Congresses. Clearly party leaders in the 1990s and 2000s did not pursue bipartisan legislation at the same rate as leaders in the 1970s.

Analyses that compare bipartisanship in agenda-setting to bipartisanship in cosponsorship coalitions rely on *all* cosponsored bills as the measure of

---

[7] The Policy Agendas Project data on high-salience legislation, as gauged by CQ, includes all bills mentioned in the annual editions of CQ Almanac.

[8] An updated list of Mayhew's important legislative enactments and George Edward's major legislative failures was graciously provided to the author by Sean Theriault. The bill numbers of the specific piece of legislation, as well as duplicate bills, related bills, and other similar proposals, were coded using CQ Almanac, the Library of Congress, and relevant newspaper articles on the legislation if necessary.

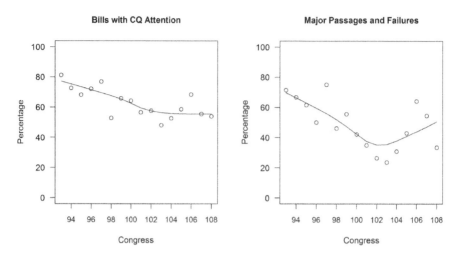

FIGURE 4.2 Bipartisan Cosponsorship of Significant Bills Receiving Roll Call Votes

underlying policy agreement. While it may be tempting to examine just the subset of *high-salience* cosponsored bills, this approach becomes problematic because measures of legislative importance are correlated with legislative attention and with party conflict. Given these correlations, measures of legislative importance likely capture the argument that I am trying to test – that bills with bipartisan cosponsors make it onto the agenda more frequently at some times than others. That is, if the bills identified as important are the ones on the roll call agenda, it is no surprise that the degree of bipartisanship on these bills would change over time (as fewer bipartisan bills received attention on the roll call agenda). For the 93rd–108th Congresses, an average of nearly 50 percent of bills receiving CQ coverage received roll call votes, and nearly all of them received substantial legislative attention, which is, in part, why they receive attention by CQ. Measures of bill salience are also associated with partisan conflict. Carson et al. (2010a) found that conflict is more likely to arise on legislation receiving CQ coverage than on other types of bills. While the number of legislative actions and the amount of partisan conflict may indicate that bills that receive CQ coverage are important, it does not distinguish ex ante importance from ex post importance on the legislative agenda. As a result, measures that are useful for differentiating the magnitude of legislative change in roll call votes are problematic when applied to all introduced bills. This suggests that the appropriate baseline measure of bipartisan agreement should draw from all cosponsored bills, and not just from high-salience cosponsored bills.

While the percentage of bills on an agenda that are bipartisan (i.e., the patterns displayed in Figure 4.1) conveys an intuitive measure of bipartisanship in each step of the legislative process, these measures may miss other bill features (e.g., the party of the sponsor) that would affect whether bills receive legislative attention. They may also miss the extent to which changes in agenda-setting reflect small declines in bipartisan cosponsorship itself. A second approach to measuring changes in bipartisan agenda-setting, presented in Tables 4.1 and 4.2, addresses these concerns by calculating the conditional probability of a bill reaching a specific stage in the policymaking process (committee, floor, or roll call vote), *given* that it is either bipartisan or partisan in its cosponsorship coalition.[9] I also calculate the difference in the conditional probability between bipartisan and partisan bills. Since the House majority controls the selection of committee chairs, the Rules Committee, and the floor agenda, party leaders typically choose to pursue bills that have been sponsored by and supported by their own members. These bills can be either bipartisan or partisan. In contrast, bills sponsored by minority party members receive little attention, particularly if they are partisan.[10] Therefore, the analysis of conditional probabilities for bipartisan and partisan bills looks separately at bills sponsored by majority and minority party members. Table 4.1 presents the conditional probability of legislative attention for majority-sponsored bills; Table 4.2 replicates the analysis for minority-sponsored bills.

As shown by the positive values in the "Difference" columns of Table 4.1, bipartisan bills with majority sponsors generally have a greater probability of garnering legislative attention at each stage – committee reporting, floor attention, and roll call voting – than partisan bills. For each legislative stage, however, variation in these columns mirrors the patterns of declining bipartisanship in roll call voting. Generally, the largest (positive) difference between attention for bipartisan and partisan bills occurs in the earliest Congresses of the analysis. For instance, in the first three Congresses considered, bipartisan bills were roughly 3 to 5 times more likely to receive a roll call vote than partisan bills. The advantage for bipartisan legislation declines in subsequent Congresses. By the 102nd Congress (1991–92) bipartisan bills were only marginally more likely to receive a roll call vote, and by the 104th Congress (1995–96) partisan bills were actually more likely to receive roll call attention. The rise in bipartisan voting observed after the 104th Congress (1995–96) is most evident in the conditional probability of a roll call vote. The advantage for bipartisan bills on the roll call agenda increases between the 104th and 107th Congress (2001–02) before dropping again. The pattern is similar for the broader floor agenda. The committee agenda, by contrast, does not show any heightened attention to bipartisan legislation after the 104th Congress. Rather, the committee agenda shows the advantage for bipartisan bills declining across the entire period, with a low point in the 107th Congress.

---

[9] The conditional probability of a roll call vote for bipartisan bills is calculated as the probability of receiving a roll call vote and having bipartisan cosponsors divided by the probability of having bipartisan cosponsors. The same calculation can be made for partisan bills.

[10] Majority or minority sponsorship of a bill refers to the party of the primary sponsor of the legislation. The definition of whether the cosponsorship coalition is bipartisan or partisan captures the party make-up of the coalition relative to the party of the sponsor.

TABLE 4.1 *Conditional Probability of Legislative Attention Given Cosponsorship Coalition (Majority Party Sponsor)*

Congress	Conditional Probability Reported from Committee			Conditional Probability Floor Attention			Conditional Probability Roll Call Vote		
	Bipartisan	Partisan	Difference	Bipartisan	Partisan	Difference	Bipartisan	Partisan	Difference
93	0.145	0.033	0.112	0.126	0.025	0.101	0.087	0.016	0.072
94	0.171	0.036	0.135	0.165	0.034	0.131	0.102	0.022	0.079
95	0.145	0.058	0.087	0.132	0.050	0.082	0.090	0.030	0.060
96	0.222	0.121	0.101	0.209	0.102	0.107	0.091	0.049	0.042
97	0.188	0.080	0.108	0.165	0.060	0.105	0.068	0.026	0.042
98	0.224	0.124	0.100	0.215	0.104	0.111	0.079	0.064	0.015
99	0.216	0.102	0.113	0.207	0.089	0.118	0.061	0.033	0.028
100	0.224	0.118	0.106	0.231	0.108	0.123	0.078	0.045	0.034
101	0.195	0.101	0.094	0.203	0.096	0.107	0.047	0.037	0.010
102	0.176	0.108	0.068	0.187	0.094	0.093	0.045	0.037	0.008
103	0.176	0.108	0.068	0.196	0.099	0.098	0.048	0.046	0.001
104	0.194	0.133	0.061	0.200	0.124	0.076	0.064	0.090	−0.025
105	0.179	0.130	0.049	0.198	0.134	0.064	0.080	0.079	0.001
106	0.177	0.130	0.048	0.229	0.124	0.105	0.094	0.076	0.018
107	0.143	0.108	0.034	0.154	0.110	0.085	0.082	0.067	0.016
108	0.169	0.110	0.058	0.205	0.133	0.073	0.084	0.087	−0.003

TABLE 4.2 *Conditional Probability of Legislative Attention Given Cosponsorship Coalition (Minority Party Sponsor)*

Congress	Conditional Probability Reported from Committee			Conditional Probability Floor Attention			Conditional Probability Roll Call Vote		
	Bipartisan	Partisan	Difference	Bipartisan	Partisan	Difference	Bipartisan	Partisan	Difference
93	0.021	0.024	-0.003	0.015	0.018	-0.003	0.005	0.010	-0.005
94	0.016	0.025	-0.009	0.015	0.027	-0.012	0.009	0.002	0.006
95	0.022	0.024	-0.001	0.018	0.022	-0.003	0.005	0.004	0.001
96	0.045	0.028	0.017	0.045	0.036	0.009	0.014	0.005	0.009
97	0.037	0.036	0.001	0.037	0.030	0.007	0.012	0.012	0.000
98	0.048	0.052	-0.004	0.051	0.049	0.002	0.010	0.005	0.005
99	0.052	0.050	0.002	0.058	0.052	0.006	0.003	0.013	-0.009
100	0.071	0.022	0.049	0.075	0.016	0.060	0.017	0.002	0.015
101	0.074	0.021	0.053	0.071	0.027	0.044	0.012	0.006	0.006
102	0.050	0.019	0.032	0.057	0.012	0.045	0.003	0.000	0.003
103	0.034	0.019	0.014	0.035	0.036	0.000	0.005	0.003	0.002
104	0.051	0.016	0.035	0.060	0.014	0.046	0.009	0.000	0.009
105	0.062	0.015	0.047	0.104	0.016	0.088	0.015	0.003	0.012
106	0.105	0.031	0.073	0.155	0.029	0.126	0.043	0.006	0.037
107	0.080	0.026	0.054	0.108	0.029	0.079	0.030	0.005	0.025
108	0.069	0.016	0.053	0.177	0.021	0.156	0.045	0.003	0.042

The extent to which bipartisan legislation is favored over partisan legislation across each agenda is also important. For both the floor and committee agendas, the leadership always advantages bipartisan bills over partisan bills. Consistent with the argument laid out in Chapter 3, the leadership only disadvantages bipartisan bills relative to partisan bills on the roll call agenda. This shift toward disadvantaging bipartisan legislation becomes even more obvious when the roll call agenda is measured relative to the subset of bills that are reported from committee.[11]

Differences in the conditional probability of a roll call vote point to substantively large differences in the treatment of bipartisan and partisan bills. Over time, these patterns mirror those of bipartisanship in roll call voting. The correlation between the difference in conditional probability of a roll call vote (i.e., agenda-setting) and the percentage of bipartisan roll call votes on the House floor (i.e., voting outcome) is 0.76 ($p < 0.001$). Likewise, the correlation between this agenda-setting measure and the percentage of bipartisan *final passage* roll call votes on the House floor is 0.67 ($p < 0.01$). Both correlations speak to the close connection between bipartisan agenda-setting and bipartisan voting.

Legislative attention for minority-sponsored bills follows a very different pattern. Table 4.2 shows the same sorts of conditional probabilities and differences as in Table 4.1, but for minority-sponsored bills. For majority-sponsored bills, the difference between attention for bipartisan and partisan bills declined over time. In contrast, for minority-sponsored bills, the difference between attention for bipartisan and partisan bills increases over time. Partisan bills have a slight advantage in the earliest Congresses that gives way to a growing benefit to bipartisan bills over time. This pattern suggests that, in the 1970s, minority Republican members were able to get some legislative attention for their priorities, but that the only way minority Democrats got attention for their bills in the 1990s was through bipartisan legislation. Not surprisingly, minority party members are less successful than majority party members at getting attention for their bills, no matter at what legislative stage they are considered (Volden and Wiseman 2014). This observation holds for bills with either bipartisan or partisan coalitions. As a result, the dominant effect in congressional agenda-setting is that observed for majority party sponsors – where bipartisan legislation changes from being advantaged on the agenda to being similar to or disadvantaged relative to partisan legislation.

While the evidence presented above documents the role of agenda-setting in the decline of bipartisanship in the House, it also points to the continued

---

[11] Even when taking into account the shift in agenda-setting via committee reporting, the roll call agenda has still seen a change toward greater prioritization of partisan legislation. Figure A4.3 presents results of the conditional probability of a roll call vote given a bill's coalition *and* that it was reported from committee. As with the results in Table 4.1, there is a downward trend over time in the difference in conditional probabilities, with a low point in the 104th Congress. However, in all but four Congresses, partisan legislation was prioritized over bipartisan legislation.

presence of bipartisanship in congressional policymaking. Bipartisan legislation dominates on the broader floor agenda, and in most Congresses more than half of all roll call votes occur on legislation with bipartisan cosponsors. When considering the roll call votes themselves, the percentage of votes that were bipartisan dropped below 40 percent in only three Congresses. These data make clear that bipartisanship remains present in the House even as partisanship has risen in roll call voting over the last several decades. The continued pursuit of bipartisan legislation suggests that bipartisanship continues to be a central component of governance.

ROUTES TO BIPARTISAN FORMS OF GOVERNANCE

If bipartisanship has declined on the roll call agenda, are there other ways for greater bipartisanship to enter the legislative process? This section considers a variety of ways to understand how bipartisanship continues to play out in congressional policymaking. First, I connect agenda-setting with the degree of bipartisanship in policy outputs, focusing on those bills that become public law. Second, I emphasize the differences in bipartisan agenda-setting between roll call votes and voice votes, and point to how a legislative strategy can shift toward greater partisanship in roll call voting but continue to show bipartisanship in voice votes. Third, I consider routes to reaching compromise in the legislative process, and examine whether members' opportunities to pursue bipartisan compromises have changed over time. While no single approach can cover the entire complexity of this process, my aim is to shed light on the implications of agenda-setting for governance, and on where bipartisanship remains in the policymaking process. Ultimately, the degree of bipartisanship in politics and policy outputs depends on where we look.

Bipartisanship in Policy Outputs

Congressional production of public laws is a central component of governance. While House leaders' use of agenda control produces very few legislative failures on the House floor, those bills that pass the House do not necessarily pass in the Senate or ultimately garner the president's signature. Over the period from 1973–2004, just over half of House bills (H.R.) that passed in that chamber became public law. Given limited and variable success in enacting laws, agenda-setting affects governance and policy outputs in at least two ways. First, a partisan agenda will result in more partisan public laws than a more bipartisan agenda. Second, a partisan agenda can lead to legislative failures, as bills that pass the House fail to become public law.

Whether party leaders pursue a bipartisan or a partisan agenda affects whether public laws consist of bipartisan or partisan bills. Figure 4.3 shows the percentage of bills that originated with bipartisan cosponsorship coalitions among all cosponsored House bills (H.R.) that became public law. On average,

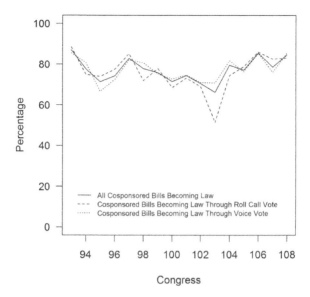

FIGURE 4.3 Bipartisanship in Policy Outputs

77 percent of cosponsored bills passed into law originated from bipartisan coalitions. The dashed and dotted lines separate those public laws that passed the House by roll call and voice votes. While the patterns for both lines move together, the decline in bipartisanship from the 1970s to the early 1990s is more obvious among those bills becoming law by roll call vote than among those becoming law by voice vote. In particular, the 103rd Congress (1993–94) had the most partisan policy outputs via roll call votes.

While a full assessment of the relationship between agenda-setting, policy outputs, and legislative gridlock is beyond the scope of this project,[12] two simple correlations speak to the relationship between agenda-setting and governance. The first considers the relationship between bipartisanship in the roll call agenda and bipartisanship in the bills that become public laws. The correlation between the percentage of cosponsored House bills with roll call votes that were bipartisan (i.e., the roll call agenda) and the percentage of cosponsored House bills that became public law that were bipartisan (i.e., policy outputs) is 0.55 (p = 0.028). When the roll call agenda is more bipartisan, policy outputs are more bipartisan as well. The converse is also true: when the roll call agenda is more partisan, policy outputs are more partisan.

---

[12] In particular, this project does not assess the many ways in which gridlock (i.e., legislative inaction) can occur, both internally in the House and between chambers or branches. A wide body of literature explores many of the patterns of Congressional gridlock, both in terms of the number of major policy initiatives (Mayhew 1991) and in terms of enactment relative to attention (Binder 2003).

The second correlation examines the relationship between bipartisanship in the roll call agenda and overall success in enacting House bills into public law, regardless of whether they are bipartisan or partisan. The correlation between the percentage of cosponsored House bills with roll call votes that were bipartisan (i.e., the roll call agenda) and the percentage of bills that passed the House that were signed into law (i.e., legislative success) is 0.65 (p = 0.0061), indicating that bipartisan roll call agendas result in greater rates of legislative success than partisan agendas. Not surprisingly, the highly partisan agenda of the 104th Congress (1995–96) resulted in the fewest number of public laws enacted across the period of analysis. Only 337 bills were signed into law during that Congress, compared to 473 in the previous Congress and 404 in the following Congress. Both correlations speak to the ways in which the roll call agenda affects governance: bipartisan agendas produce more bipartisan laws and more legislative success than do partisan agendas.

Voice Votes vs. Roll Call Votes

Bipartisan legislation can remain part of the majority party's strategy for governance even when the roll call agenda becomes more partisan. Voice votes offer one means by which the House leadership advances bipartisan legislation. The distinction between roll call votes and voice votes raises two important observations. First, bipartisan legislation can dominate voice votes even as the roll call agenda becomes more partisan. Second, voice votes and roll call votes can serve different purposes for the party. While voice votes allow for the passage of non-controversial legislation, members of both parties use roll call votes to signal positions to external audiences, including partisan differences. As a result, an overall agenda that includes both bipartisan and partisan legislation is likely to concentrate partisan legislation on the roll call agenda. It is the *combination* of voice votes and roll call votes that allow majority party leaders to balance governing, partisan policy goals, and partisan differentiation.

Tracking which bills receive legislative attention through voice votes is difficult to assess systematically using existing data sources. To capture where voice votes are used, I look at bills that passed the House or became law that did not have a roll call vote. Figure 4.3 shows that an average of 77 percent of bills becoming law without a roll call vote had bipartisan rather than partisan cosponsorship coalitions. This suggests, unsurprisingly, that party leaders utilize voice votes for the passage of non-controversial bipartisan legislation. Despite a slight decline in bipartisanship through the 1980s, the percentage of public laws with bipartisan cosponsorship coalitions never fell below 67 percent. The role of bipartisan legislation on the voice vote agenda is also seen among bills passing the House. Figure 4.4 captures the extent to which cosponsored bills passing the House without roll call votes (i.e., with voice votes) had bipartisan cosponsorship coalitions. Across Congresses, an average of 76 percent of the bills that

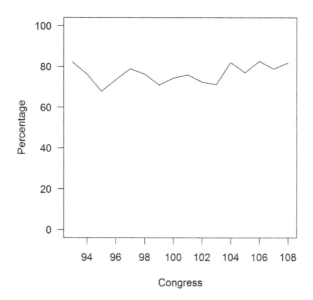

FIGURE 4.4 Bipartisanship in Voice Votes

passed the House through voice votes had bipartisan support. Moreover, there is not a significant downward trend over time.

While the legislative significance of bills passing through voice votes varies substantially, many pieces of routine and governance-related legislation pass by voice vote. For example, bills passing by voice vote in the 108th Congress included legislation to improve microenterprise development assistance programs abroad (H.R. 3818, Public Law 108–484), legislation to alter the District of Columbia Mental Health Civil Commitment Act of 2002 (H.R. 4302, Public Law 108–450), legislation to enhance the competitiveness of U.S.-grown specialty crops (H.R. 3242, Public Law 108–465), and legislation to support research and development to advance high-end computing (H.R. 4516, Public Law 108–423). Not only did these bills pass the House by voice vote, but each bill met my definition of bipartisanship based on its cosponsorship coalition.

The relative frequency of voice and roll call votes also speaks to the extent of bipartisanship in the House. Lynch and Madonna (2008) estimate that from 1807 to 1990, between a tenth and a quarter of landmark bills with votes received voice (or other unrecorded) votes. In the modern House (measured as 1973–90 in their analysis), roughly a tenth of landmark bills received voice rather than roll call votes. However, the frequency of voice and roll call votes varied across types of issues, with highly salient, party-defining issues being less likely to receive a voice vote. My analyses of the frequency of roll call and voice votes on all House bills that passed the chamber between 1973 and 2004 also show that voice votes are common. Of all House bills (H.R.) that passed the House in each Congress, roughly 30 percent to 40 percent received roll call votes, while the remainder received voice votes. In the first three Congresses of this analysis (93rd–95th, covering the years 1973–78) this number was higher, suggesting a change over time in the use of roll call versus voice votes that may also reflect a changing agenda strategy that focuses roll call votes on partisan legislation.

Voice votes allow party leaders to dispose of bipartisan legislation quickly, but roll call votes allow members from both parties to signal their positions and point out differences between the parties. As a result, members of both parties may want to move pieces of legislation from the broader floor agenda onto the roll call agenda. The House rules indicate that a recorded vote can be demanded by one-fifth of those present, by one-fifth of quorum, by a point of order regarding quorum, or automatically for bills dealing with general appropriations, raising taxes, or the annual budget resolution (Library of Congress 2000). In practice, a single member typically asks for a recorded vote after the completion of a voice vote.

Both majority and minority members make these requests. Although the majority party leadership exercises control over which bills receive floor attention, members of both parties can push bills from the broader floor agenda onto the roll call agenda. Moreover, prior research has suggested that minority party members may be more likely to demand roll call votes as a way to express displeasure with committee and leadership decisions (Cox and McCubbins 1993, 273). My own analysis finds that most requests for recorded votes were split fairly evenly between majority and minority members, a finding that is consistent with the idea that roll call votes provide potential benefits to both the majority and minority parties.

From the pool of cosponsored bills that received a roll call vote, I took a random sample of 30 bills with bipartisan cosponsors and 30 bills with partisan cosponsors for each of three Congresses. These Congresses include the 93rd, the 103rd, and the 106th. While not necessarily representative of all congressional terms, these three were selected to provide a range of party control and polarization. The first two Congresses reflect Democratic majority control, with one from a less polarized period and one from a more polarized period. The 106th Congress reflects another relatively polarized period with Republican control.[13] With the exception of votes to recommit bills to committee, which were nearly always requested by minority members, most requests for recorded votes split

---

[13] The sample of votes was selected by identifying all cosponsored House bills with a roll call vote and then taking a random sample of 30 votes on bipartisan cosponsored bills and 30 votes on partisan cosponsored bills (using the 20 percent definition) within each selected Congress. For each bill, I read the Congressional Record to see which member asked for a roll call vote. I also separated the votes according to whether they were amending, passage, recommitting to committee, instructing conferees, and other types of votes.

TABLE 4.3 *Who Requests a Recorded Vote?*

	Amend	Pass	Recommit	Instruct Conferees	Other	Total
93rd Congress						
Majority Ask	7 (10)	1 (2)	1 (0)	0 (0)	0 (0)	*9 (12)*
Minority Ask	7 (8)	13 (7)	1 (2)	0 (0)	0 (0)	*21 (17)*
Don't Know	0 (0)	0 (0)	0 (0)	0 (0)	0 (1 override)	*0 (1)*
103rd Congress						
Majority Ask	5 (4)	8 (1)	0 (0)	0 (0)	0 (0)	*13 (5)*
Minority Ask	7 (10)	8 (7)	0 (3)	2 (3)	0 (2)	*17 (25)*
Don't Know	0 (0)	0 (0)	0 (0)	0 (0)	0 (0)	*0 (0)*
106th Congress						
Majority Ask	7 (3)	7 (11)	0 (0)	0 (1)	0 (0)	*14 (15)*
Minority Ask	5 (6)	6 (2)	1 (4)	2 (1)	0 (1)	*14 (14)*
Don't Know	1 (0)	0 (1)	0 (0)	1 (0)	0 (0)	*2 (1)*

Note: In each cell, the number of requests for a roll call vote on the sample of bipartisan bills is listed first, followed, in parentheses, by the number of requests for roll call votes on the sample of partisan bills. There were 4 instances in which no one was identified as requesting a vote.

fairly evenly between majority and minority members (see Table 4.3). This was particularly true when bipartisan bills were brought forward for amendment votes. The table shows a slight bias toward minority members requesting recorded votes on partisan legislation in both the Democratic 103rd and the Republican 106th Congresses.

Among votes on passage, the results vary by Congress. In the 93rd Congress, the minority was more likely to ask for a recorded vote on both bipartisan and partisan cosponsored bills. This pattern is consistent with statistics compiled by David Rohde (reported in Cox and McCubbins 1993, 263) that show that minority Republicans called for 60 percent of all roll call votes in 1969, 68 percent of all roll call votes in 1979, and 74 percent of all roll call votes in 1987. The patterns of requests for roll call votes in Table 4.3 are more mixed in the 103rd and 106th Congresses. In the 103rd Congress, the requests split evenly between the parties on bipartisan bills, but were dominated by the minority party on partisan bills. This pattern reverses in the 106th Congress. Again, both parties requested recorded votes on bipartisan bills, but the majority requested votes more frequently on partisan bills. The differences seen between the 103rd and the 106th Congresses may reflect which party thought it had the public on "their" side. The small sample size precludes making any definitive claims about how each party uses bipartisan versus partisan legislation in external signaling, but these results do suggest that members of both parties see benefits in requesting roll call votes.

Special Rules, Bipartisanship, and Opportunities for Compromise

The primary focus of the analyses so far has centered on bipartisanship resulting from substantive agreement between members. While House leaders effectively use the floor and roll call agendas to prioritize bipartisan or partisan legislation, House members can also find routes to legislative compromise by amending legislation on the House floor and through conference committee (or other means of reconciling differences with Senate legislation). Although a systematic analysis of legislative compromise and whether that compromise creates legislation with more bipartisan support is beyond the scope of this book, this section briefly explores these routes to crafting bipartisan agreement in the House. For floor amendments, I also consider how closed rules limit the opportunities for compromise.

Examples of floor amendments and reconciliation with Senate legislation emphasize the potential for these routes to produce more bipartisan legislation. For instance, in 1973 members offered (and adopted) a compromise measure as a substitute to strongly partisan legislation giving limited home rule to the District of Columbia. Members also passed other weakening amendments as a legislative compromise. The substitute to H.R. 9682 offered six major concessions to home rule opponents, including retention of congressional control over the city's budget and a prohibition on the city council from making any changes to the criminal code ("Congress Grants Nation's Capital Limited Home Rule" 1973). As a result, the bill passed with bipartisan support: Democrats voted 204 yea to 27 nay and Republicans voted 139 yea to 47 nay. Later, in the 108th Congress, members from both chambers made concessions on the omnibus Energy Policy Act of 2003 (H.R. 6) discussed earlier in this chapter through compromises in conference committee. In particular, the revised bill included some of the more bipartisan Senate provisions and dropped the highly partisan provision allowing drilling in the Alaska National Wildlife Refuge (Anselmo 2003). Although these compromises did not prevent failure of the bill in the Senate via filibuster, they nevertheless illustrate that legislation can become more bipartisan through policy compromise.

However, the majority party's increasing use of closed rules across all types of legislation, but particularly on partisan bills, limits the opportunities members have to use amendments to forge compromise. Since the 1970s, the House Rules Committee's membership ratio has been weighted toward the majority party – 9 majority party members and 4 minority members. However, it was not until the late 1970s that the dominance of Southern Democrats on the Committee receded, and the Rules Committee fell under the firm hand of the Speaker (Rohde 1991), who used the Committee to pursue partisan priorities. In addition to determining which bills receive subsequent legislative attention, the Rules

Committee is responsible for crafting special rules that set the terms of debate and amendment opportunities for each bill on the floor. The majority party utilizes these rules, which range from open to closed (among other more complicated rules), to control whether amendments can be offered on the floor. Whereas open rules allow members to offer unlimited amendments to bills, closed rules restrict members' ability to make changes. As a result, when bills receive open rules, members of Congress have greater opportunities to forge compromise on legislation. The increasing use of closed rules – a trend that has emerged in parallel with party polarization (Brady et al. 2008; Galston and Nivola 2006; Mann and Ornstein 2006) – can stifle compromise. Moreover, Sinclair (1994) finds that restrictive rules are more likely when bills are expected to divide Democrats against Republicans. Within my framework of strategic partisan agenda-setting, this phenomenon suggests that closed rules may be increasingly concentrated among partisan bills, thereby limiting the opportunities for members to craft further compromises.

To examine how often special rules can foster compromise through amendments and whether these rules differ across bipartisan and partisan bills and over time, I collected data on all special rules from the 98th to 108th Congresses and combined them with data on cosponsored bills.[14] Merging the bill cosponsorship data with the rules data captures not only the overall increase in the frequency of closed rules, but also the variation of closed versus more open rules for bills with bipartisan and partisan cosponsors. For the purposes of these analyses, I divided special rules into four categories – open rules, modified open rules, modified closed or structured rules, and closed rules. These categories range from rules that allow members the most flexibility to offer amendments to those that offer the least opportunity for amendments.

Although over time the frequency of open rules declines, and the frequency of closed rules increases, in any given Congress there are notable differences between the rules assigned to bills with bipartisan and partisan cosponsors. Figure 4.5 (left-hand panel) presents a bar plot with the distribution of rules on bills with bipartisan cosponsors for each Congress. Over time, the Rules Committee assigned fewer open rules and more closed or modified closed rules to bipartisan bills. However, even in the 108th Congress, over 20 percent of the bipartisan bills received open or modified open rules. Compared to the distribution of rules for bills with partisan cosponsors (Figure 4.5, right-hand panel), the fact that bipartisan bills continued to receive open rules is noteworthy. In the 108th Congress, no partisan cosponsored bills received an open rule and just under 5 percent received modified open rules.

---

[14] Data from the 105th to 108th Congresses were provided by Don Wolfensberger and data from the 98th to 104th Congress were collected from the Survey of Activities of the House Committee on Rules, found in the U.S. Congressional Series Set House Documents for each Congress. Data for the 93rd–97th Congresses could not be found in a similar form.

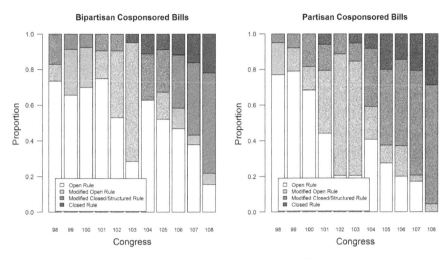

FIGURE 4.5   Distribution of Special Rules for Cosponsored Bills (98th–108th Congresses)

These patterns suggest two important insights. First, the increasing use of closed rules has limited members' opportunities to craft bipartisan coalitions through the amendment process. For both bipartisan and partisan bills, the proportion of open rules has declined, and the proportion of closed rules has increased. Second, the differences between bipartisan and partisan bills, even in recent Congresses with relatively few open rules, suggest that the selection of special rules may further accentuate the bipartisan or partisan nature of these bills. Consider the following cases. When open rules are given to bipartisan bills on the floor, the amendment process allows for policy compromise that can produce even more bipartisan coalitions.[15] When closed rules are given to partisan bills on the floor, there is no amending process to allow any compromise on the legislation. Put another way, the House Rules Committee's recent efforts to grant closed rules to partisan bills has increased the potential for rules to magnify the partisan consequences of strategic partisan agenda-setting by limiting opportunities for compromise.

The Republican Party strategy on the Electronic Surveillance Modernization Act (H.R. 5825) in the 109th Congress illustrates the argument that closed rules limit opportunities for compromise. The original bill, sponsored by Republican Heather Wilson (R-NM) was cosponsored by 13 other members, all of whom were Republicans. When the bill was brought up on the House floor, the special rule (H. Res. 1052) allowed for 1 hour and 30 minutes of debate and no amendments by members. During debate over the bill, Representative Schiff

---

[15] Of course, amendments can also be added that break apart bipartisan coalitions and make legislation more partisan. Here, the interest is in the possibility that amendments open the door for making legislation more bipartisan.

(D-CA) complained about the refusal of the House to take a vote on a bipartisan alternative proposed by Representative Flake (R-AZ) and him, highlighting how the majority strategy of pursuing bills with primarily partisan support precludes consideration of bipartisan legislation and that closed rules accentuate this phenomenon ("Congressional Record" 2006, H7775–H7784).

Despite the general trend that bipartisan bills received more open rules, it is noteworthy that in the 98th and 99th Congresses (1983–84, 1985–86), the opposite pattern held. Bills with partisan cosponsors received a slightly greater proportion of open rules than their bipartisan counterparts. Although data were not available in a similar format to compare rules on legislation in the early-1970s, the pattern from the 98th and 99th Congresses is consistent with arguments made by the Democratic Study Group (DSG). The DSG found that when Southern Democrats still chaired committees, closed rules protected moderate legislation while open rules allowed Democratic Study Group members to make legislation more partisan and ideological on the floor (Conlon 1961; Oppenheimer 1977). Ronald Peters' interview with former Speaker Carl Albert also made the same distinction between these legislative approaches. Speaker Albert said that when conservative southerners were at the head of major committees, the Rules Committee had to take on a strategy of liberalizing legislation on the floor (via open rules), whereas when more liberal members chaired committees, the leadership's job was to try to keep it intact on the floor (via closed rules) and not let the conservatives break it apart (Albert 1979, Tape 3, Side 2, p. 33).

CONCLUSIONS

The agenda for roll call votes has changed over time and, with it, the degree of bipartisanship in voting. This pattern provides the first piece of evidence in support of the framework of strategic partisan agenda-setting. Patterns of roll call voting are strongly associated with patterns of agenda-setting. My evidence further shows that while committee reporting and the broader floor agenda saw some decline in bipartisan agenda-setting, only the roll call agenda showed a strong shift from prioritizing bipartisan legislation to prioritizing partisan legislation. These shifts in agenda-setting have real consequences for the coalitions that produce public laws and for policy action versus gridlock. Less bipartisan agendas result in less bipartisan policy outputs and a lower rate of converting bills that pass the House into public law.

However, bipartisan policy outputs remain the norm, and even in the most partisan periods of House agenda-setting and voting, bipartisanship is present. Voice votes in particular are dominated by bipartisan bills across the period of analysis. There also remain additional routes for bipartisanship to enter the legislative process. These routes include members' use of floor amendments and conference committees to develop compromise. However, the distribution of special rules in the Houses has increasingly limited members' ability to amend partisan legislation. Combined, the insights from this chapter point to the simultaneous ways in which agenda-setting has become more partisan, while bipartisanship persists outside of roll call votes.

Having tracked patterns of agenda-setting over time, and documented the connection between bipartisan agenda-setting and bipartisan roll call voting in the House, I now move on to the factors that drive attention for bipartisan versus partisan legislation. The next analyses look at how the sorting of constituent interests within a party and institutional arrangements within the House affect when leaders pursue bipartisan or partisan legislation on the roll call and broader floor agendas. In doing so, these analyses point to how majority party leaders balance the electoral concerns of members, the passage of legislation, and establishing a record that emphasizes policy differences between the majority and minority parties.

5

Variation in Strategic Partisan Agenda-Setting

In 1983, majority Democrats pursued bipartisan legislation to reform Social Security. H.R. 1900, which was sponsored by Dan Rostenkowski (D-IL) and cosponsored by one Democrat and one Republican, was based on recommendations from President Reagan's bipartisan National Commission on Social Security Reform. This bill combined increases in the retirement age with delayed cost-of-living adjustments and increased payroll taxes. Not only was the cosponsorship of the bill bipartisan, but the vote to report the bill from the Ways and Means Committee had bipartisan support (32–2 vote), and the House final passage vote also had the support of a majority of both parties (282–148 vote, with Democrats splitting 185–79 and Republicans splitting 97–69).

Ten years later, this bipartisan atmosphere seemed to have been replaced. The majority Democrats not only passed major initiatives like education reform by partisan votes ("House Advances Education Reform Bill" 1993),[1] but this partisan approach extended across many policies, including reform to a 121-year-old law that governed mining operations on federal lands. H.R. 322, which was sponsored by Nick Rahall II (D-WV) and cosponsored by 40 Democrats, 6 Republicans, and 1 Independent, instituted a royalty on extracted minerals, increased fees paid by miners for the land claims, and set up a regulatory regime aimed at protecting the environment from mining related-damage (Benenson 1993).[2] Importantly, the mostly partisan Hardrock Mining Reform Act of 1993 (H.R. 322) was pursued in the House despite the presence of a more bipartisan bill addressing the same policy (H.R. 1708, sponsored by Bill Orton (D-UT) and cosponsored by 2 Republicans). Orton argued that the Rahall bill was supported

---

[1] H.R. 6, the Elementary and Secondary Education Reauthorization, passed the House on a vote of 289–128 (yea–nay). Democrats voted 243–4 while Republicans voted 45–124.

[2] Although this bill had both Democratic and Republican cosponsors, the number of Republican cosponsors does not meet the 20 percent threshold for bipartisan cosponsorship used throughout my analyses.

84

by extreme environmental groups and would cripple the mining industry (Orton 1993). Despite the option of Orton's more bipartisan bill, the Democratic majority pursued Rahall's partisan bill, passing it in a party unity vote of 316–108 (with Democrats voting 245–6 and Republicans voting 70–102).

The theoretical framework of strategic partisan agenda-setting offers a possible explanation of why leaders pursued bipartisan bills in 1983 but partisan bills in 1993. The framework emphasizes the importance of district-party sorting (aligning members' constituent and party interests) for allowing leaders to pursue partisan legislation without substantial electoral costs to members. It also notes the possible tensions between governance and partisan differentiation, suggesting that leaders may need to pursue bipartisan legislation during periods of divided government or small majority seat shares, even though partisan legislation better emphasizes party differences. The two examples discussed above fit these situations exactly. In the case of the 1983 reforms to Social Security, each party had its own preferred version of reform. However, more than a third of all House members, and nearly 45 percent of Democrats, represented districts where the normal presidential vote was less than 50 percent for the party of the member (i.e., there were many unsorted districts). Moreover, the 98th Congress operated within a divided government, with a Republican president and a Republican Senate. The combination of many unsorted districts and divided government meant that the House leadership needed a bipartisan approach if Congress was going to prevent the Old-Age and Survivors Insurance from running out of funds. Members of Congress were able to find places of cross-party agreement when the prospects that Social Security would go bankrupt became increasingly real and action was required ("Social Security Rescue Plan Swiftly Approved" 1983). By 1993, however, district sorting had increased somewhat, particularly among Democrats, and divided government had been replaced by unified Democratic control. As a result, partisan legislation could be pursued with fewer risks of legislative defeat.

More generally, the framework of strategic partisan agenda-setting seeks to reconcile the divergent patterns of bipartisanship over time between roll call voting and bill cosponsorship coalitions, and to explain how the selection of bills for votes affects the degree of partisan conflict in the House. Chapter 4 provided the first pieces of evidence for this argument, demonstrating that the puzzle of diverging bipartisanship trends between cosponsorship and roll call voting can be explained by the selection of bills that receive votes. Continuing with the premise that cosponsorship coalitions reflect pre-agenda-setting behavior, this chapter examines the factors that drive strategic partisan agenda-setting.[3] In

---

[3] As noted in Chapter 3, the focus of this chapter is on the relationship between the three variables of interest – district sorting, divided government, and majority seat shares – and legislative attention for bipartisan versus partisan bills. These tests are not designed to offer a comprehensive test of when certain policies or particular bills get attention (which may include factors like expiring authorizations (Adler and Wilkerson 2013) or shifts in coalitions since legislation was first enacted (Berry et al. 2010)).

particular, it looks at the conditions under which a bipartisan or partisan strategy is pursued in roll call voting and more generally on the floor.[4]

The primary goal of this chapter is to systematically assess whether party leaders pursue bipartisan over partisan legislation under various political contexts. These political contexts include the degree of district-party sorting, divided versus unified government, and the size of the majority seat share. Prior to testing whether party leaders pursue bipartisan or partisan legislation under these contexts, I provide evidence for a key observable implication of the framework that bipartisan bills are more likely to pass than partisan bills, both in general and particularly during times with small majority seat shares or divided government. These passage rates provide the basis for the assumption in the theoretical framework that bipartisan bills offer an easier route to legislative success than partisan bills. The primary empirical tests that follow and make up the bulk of this chapter speak to how leaders focus on members' electoral interests and balance partisan differentiation and governance goals. A discussion of changes in agenda-setting between the 104th and 105th Congresses (1995–98) further emphasizes how leaders balance the competing goals of minimizing the electoral costs to members, governing, and emphasizing partisan differences. These two Congresses point to how the GOP got ahead of district sorting and pursued partisanship at the expense of governance. The party then backtracked in its strategy, pursuing more bipartisan legislation.

A NOTE ON LEGISLATIVE SUCCESS FOR BIPARTISAN AND PARTISAN LEGISLATION

Throughout the theoretical framework of strategic partisan agenda-setting, I suggested that bipartisan legislation is the less risky choice for a majority party interested in passing legislation and creating a record of legislative success. Passing legislation and showing an ability to govern is one part of party branding (i.e., valence component), and one goal of party leaders. Given the majority party's negative agenda control, it is not surprising that the bills brought up for votes on the House floor typically pass, regardless of their cosponsorship coalition. Nonetheless, there are significant differences in the success rates for bipartisan and partisan cosponsored bills among the subset of bills that receive roll call votes. Overall, among bills receiving any roll call vote during the 93rd to 108th Congresses, 92 percent of bipartisan cosponsored bills and 89 percent of partisan cosponsored bills passed the House (difference is significant at $p = 0.053$).[5] The difference in success rates between bipartisan and partisan bills is even

---

[4] Although parties may influence the work of committees, as noted in the previous chapter, the primary focus of the theoretical framework is on how parties structure the content of the agenda on the floor, primarily through roll call votes but also through voice votes. Thus, this chapter focuses on only these outcomes.

[5] These measures capture the passage rates of bills that received any roll call votes (not only final passage votes). The 93rd Congress (1973–1974) is an outlier among other Congresses with lower passage rates for both bipartisan and partisan legislation. The Congressional Bills Project notes

TABLE 5.1 *Floor Passage Rates for Bills with Roll Call Votes*

	Majority Seat Share			
	1st Quartile (0.51–0.55)	2nd Quartile (0.55–0.59)	3rd Quartile (0.59–0.64)	4th Quartile (0.64–0.67)
Bipartisan Cosponsors	97.8%	76.4%	93.0%	93.7%
Partisan Cosponsors	91.5%	74.3%	90.0%	95.2%
Difference	6.3%	2.1%	3.0%	−1.5%
	($p < 0.001$)	($p = 0.66$)	($p = 0.15$)	($p = 0.53$)

Note: Calculations based on House passage of cosponsored bills receiving a roll call vote. The low values for the 2nd Quartile are affected by the 93rd Congress, which has errors in the Library of Congress database on bill passage. These values are presented here to show the differences between types of bills (bipartisan versus partisan) but the overall rate of passage is likely higher than that presented here.

more striking for the enactment of bills into public law. Among bills that passed the House, 52 percent of bipartisan bills became public law compared to only 42 percent of partisan bills (the difference is significant: $p < 0.001$).[6]

If governance concerns are to force House leaders to prioritize bipartisan bills over partisan bills during periods with small seat shares or divided government, then bipartisan legislation should be particularly successful relative to partisan legislation during these periods.[7] For a range of majority seat shares, Table 5.1 shows the percentage of bills with roll call votes that pass on the House floor for both bipartisan and partisan cosponsored bills. Bipartisan legislation fares better than partisan legislation in all but the largest seat shares. As expected, the difference is significant for only the lowest quartile. When party leaders face small

that the Library of Congress (THOMAS) acknowledges errors in the House and Senate passage data for this Congress, suggesting that rates are likely higher. If this Congress is excluded, the passage rate for bipartisan bills receiving a roll call vote is 95 percent and 91 percent for partisan bills (difference is significant, $p < 0.001$).

[6] If the analysis is restricted to just those bills passing the House *and* receiving roll call votes, the difference is even larger: 50 percent of bipartisan bills become law compared to just 33 percent of partisan bills ($p < 0.001$).

[7] Because leaders tend to pursue bills that can pass the House, most bills pass on the floor. However, the combination of some uncertainty in whether bills will pass the House (much less become law), along with leaders balancing governance and other goals, means that not all bills will pass. The resulting variation in passage rates should capture which bills are more likely to pass, and are thus the easier option for leaders to pursue. My theoretical framework emphasizes that both electoral interests and governance interests could provide incentives for party leaders to pursue bipartisan legislation. Whereas the extent of district sorting affects the agenda through its effect on members' electoral interests, the institutional dynamics of majority seat shares and divided government are more likely to affect the agenda through their effect on governance interests. As a result, the assumption that bipartisan bills are easier to pass is of theoretic interest in terms of general passage rates and under different institutional arrangements that would make partisan legislation more difficult to pass.

majority seat shares, bipartisan legislation is a significantly less risky option to procure House passage.

Divided government is a stumbling block for the passage of partisan legislation but not for the passage of bipartisan legislation. Among bills with roll call votes that pass on the floor, the percentage of bipartisan bills that become law varies little between unified and divided governments. Under unified government 52 percent of bipartisan bills become law; under divided government 49 percent of bipartisan bills become law (and the difference is not significant: $p = 0.27$). In contrast, partisan bills have a lower success rate in general, and a larger difference between unified and divided government. During unified government 39 percent of partisan bills become law. In contrast, only 30 percent of partisan bills become law during divided government. This is a statistically significant difference ($p = 0.015$). Not only are bipartisan bills more likely than partisan bills to become law, but bipartisan bills are affected little by divided government. In contrast, the success of partisan bills is significantly hampered by divided government. If party leaders care about enacting legislation, divided government becomes a constraint on the pursuit of partisan legislation.

All of these patterns support the theoretical framework's assumption that bipartisan bills are the less risky option when the goal of policymakers is floor passage or enactment into law. The passage of legislation in the House favors bipartisan bills over partisan bills during periods with small majority seat shares. The enactment of bills into law favors bipartisan bills over partisan bills in general and particularly during divided government. Thus, pursuing bipartisan bills rather than partisan bills is more likely to help a party produce a record of legislative success.

POLITICAL CONDITIONS THAT PROMOTE BIPARTISAN AGENDA-SETTING

As House leaders consider the potential costs to members, legislative success, and partisan differentiation resulting from any given agenda-setting strategy, they will construct an agenda that contains a mixture of bipartisan and partisan bills. The extent to which the leadership pursues bipartisan bills over partisan bills will vary as the political context changes. These changes include whether House districts are sorted or unsorted, whether there is divided versus unified government, and whether the majority has a small or large seat share. Testing the role that each of these factors plays in determining the leadership's roll call and floor agendas not only explains variation in the pursuit of bipartisan versus partisan bills over time, but also sheds light on how party leaders balance multiple considerations, particularly those of governance and party differentiation.[8]

---

[8] As discussed in Chapter 3, some of the factors that may contribute to incentives to differentiate the parties – perceived competition for the majority, fundraising strategies, and fear of primary challengers – are difficult to specify and test empirically because they rest on the beliefs of

The framework of strategic partisan agenda-setting provides the following expectations for how political contexts affect the pursuit of bipartisan versus partisan legislation (among majority-sponsored bills). First, bills with bipartisan cosponsorship coalitions should be more likely to receive legislative attention than partisan bills when the parties are poorly sorted and there are large numbers of cross-pressured members. In contrast, partisan bills should be increasingly likely to receive legislative attention relative to bipartisan bills as the parties sort.[9] Second, if leaders prioritize governance over partisan differentiation, bipartisan bills should be more likely to receive legislative attention than partisan bills during divided government relative to unified government and during periods of small majority seat shares relative to large seat shares.

The theoretical framework explicitly suggests that the shift from bipartisan to partisan agenda-setting will be most evident on the roll call agenda. However, it offers fewer predictions about whether the relationship between bipartisan cosponsorship and each political context will be more pronounced on the roll call or broader floor agenda. For instance, if divided government leads to a greater prioritization of bipartisan legislation, it is not obvious whether this pattern will occur on the roll call agenda, the broader floor agenda, or both. There are several possible ways that the roll call and floor agendas can capture how party leaders balance bipartisan and partisan legislation. First, since the roll call agenda sees the most dramatic shift from bipartisan to partisan legislation, and passage by voice vote occurs overwhelmingly on bipartisan legislation across the period of analysis, it is likely that the relationship between bipartisan agenda-setting and district sorting will be most pronounced on the roll call agenda since this is where partisan bills are concentrated. Second, the theoretical framework noted that divided government may provide an incentive to pursue bipartisanship in order to produce a record of legislative success, but could also produce incentives to pursue partisanship in order to differentiate the parties in a fight for majority status. Since the payoff for differentiation requires partisan bills and the knowledge of how members of each party voted, roll call votes are required. Because bipartisan legislation does not offer a way for the parties to differentiate themselves, but can be more easily enacted into law, efforts to pursue bipartisanship during divided government may only be evident on the broader floor agenda where bipartisan legislation can become law through voice votes. Whether the governing constraint of small majority seat shares leads to changes in the roll call agenda, the broader floor agenda, or both is less clear.

politicians. As a result, this chapter takes a first step toward understanding changes in agenda-setting by examining those variables that can be measured more concretely.

[9] Sorting, defined in detail later in the chapter, captures the extent to which members represent districts that align with their partisanship. Since sorting within the majority party reduces the costs on members from pursuing a partisan agenda, but sorting within both parties increases the benefits from partisan differentiation, either an overall measure of House sorting or a measure of majority party sorting will capture this phenomenon. Moreover, these two measures are highly correlated ($r = 0.98$) and robustness checks using only majority party districts yield similar results.

Ultimately, I allow the data to speak to the question of whether the relationship between bipartisan cosponsorship and each of these variables is stronger on the roll call or broader floor agenda.

Measuring Electoral Sorting

Before presenting the empirical tests of strategic partisan agenda-setting, I consider electoral sorting as a concept and also as a measure. Divided government and majority seat share are fairly intuitive institutional features, both as concepts and measures. Sorting is a much less concrete concept. Scholars use the term "sorting" to refer to changes in Congress (Brownstein 2007; Theriault 2008) and in the mass public (Levendusky 2009). My usage of the term draws on facets of both congressional and mass public change as my interest lies in the electoral coalitions of parties in the House. From Roosevelt's New Deal era through the 1960s, each party remained an ideological jumble within Congress and in the party's electoral coalition (Brownstein 2007, 183). Democrats, in particular, drew support from a wide coalition ranging from Northern unionists to Southern segregationists. For members of Congress, this meant that their party label likely meant little for voters; similarly, voters' party identification told members little about what policies their constituents would support. Over the next several decades a process of sorting occurred, with changes in Congress and among ordinary citizens resulting in better separated voting coalitions.[10]

Sorting at the mass level meant that voters took increasingly clearer cues from party elites to better align their ideology and party identification (Hetherington 2001; Levendusky 2009). In terms of voting patterns, this change was seen first in presidential voting in the 1960s, as conservatives in the South increasingly voted Republican. This was followed by an alignment of ideology, party, and voting in congressional races during the 1970s and 1980s (Han and Brady 2007). The ideological re-sorting of the electorate allowed each party to deepen its hold on portions of the country that leaned in its direction. "Each now controls a commanding majority of the House and Senate seats in the states they consistently win in presidential elections. Both have partitioned the country into what amounts to competing spheres of influence that they dominate up and down the ballot in federal elections – from the House, through the Senate, to the presidency" (Brownstein 2007, 209).

Conceptually, a sorted district in my analysis refers to a district where the majority of voters identify as Democrats (Republicans), see themselves as moderate to liberal (conservative), and vote for Democratic (Republican) presidential and congressional candidates. Since survey coverage of congressional districts is too sparse for much of the period of my analysis, I cannot empirically assess all of the components of this concept, and especially those inferences about individual party identification and ideology. Instead, I simplify the concept's measurement

---

[10] Sorting can reflect a combination of changes in the electorate and member replacement.

by focusing on voting behavior. I consider whether or not a majority of each district votes for the Democratic presidential candidate and for the Democratic member (or the Republican presidential candidate and Republican member). Put simply, districts are sorted when the majority of voters support a presidential and congressional candidate of the same party.

Although this simplification introduces potential problems for periods where one-party dominance may have meant that self-identified conservatives routinely voted for Democratic presidential and congressional candidates, the restriction of my analysis to the post-1973 period alleviates the worst of these concerns. Evidence from other scholars indicates that the sorting of party, ideology, and voting at the individual level all moved together over the period of my analysis (Abramowitz 2010; Levendusky 2009). For instance, in the American National Election Studies, the percentage of self-identified Democrats who also described their ideological views as liberal increased from 35 percent in the 1970s to 52 percent in the 2000s. Similarly, the percentage of Republicans identifying as conservative increased from 63 percent in the 1970s to 77 percent in the 2000s (calculated by Alan Abramowitz, cited in Brownstein 2007, 190). A similar sorting occurred among voting patterns. The percentage of self-described liberals voting for the Democratic candidate in House races increased from 75 percent in the 1970s to 83 percent in the 2000s. Likewise, the percentage of conservatives voting for Republican House candidates increased from 59 percent in the 1970s to 78 percent in the 2000s (calculated by Alan Abramowitz, cited in Brownstein 2007, 191). The same patterns held for Senate and presidential races. These trends indicate that individual-level sorting of party identification and ideology align with increased consistency in voting for a particular party.

Thus, while a measure based on the alignment of presidential voting and House members' partisanship necessarily simplifies the concept of sorting in electoral coalitions, it is able to capture key components. As the public votes for the same party in congressional and presidential races, and as their votes reflect greater alignment of individual partisanship and ideology, members of Congress increasingly represent districts where the majority of constituents align with their party. This has at least three possible effects that contribute to partisan agenda-setting. First, sorting can result in members getting greater support from constituents for the policy proposals of their party. Second, sorting can make constituents more forgiving of partisanship since even the most partisan positions by a member can still put them on the "right" side of an issue relative to their constituency. Third, sorting reduces members' fear of defeat in general elections even though they may worry about primary challengers, which typically occur from the left or right flank (Brady et al. 2007; Burden 2004), not from the center of the ideological divide. As a result, sorting opens the door for members to pursue partisanship even if the electorate does not grow substantially more polarized.

I define *sorted districts* as those where the *normal presidential vote* is greater than or equal to 50 percent for the party of the House member. The *normal presidential vote* measures the mean two-party presidential vote in the previous two elections by the party of the Representative.[11] Unsorted districts are those where the normal presidential vote is less than 50 percent for the party of the House member. The threshold of 50 percent for defining sorted versus unsorted districts follows from the logic that, with more than 50 percent of the vote, a majority of the district supports the party of the representative. An alternative specification uses the *normalized presidential vote*, which calculates how well the member's party did in his or her district relative to the national average in that election. Robustness checks using this measure, and with sorted defined as greater than or equal to zero (i.e., better than the national average), show results similar to those presented in this chapter. However, I focus on whether districts are sorted or unsorted based on the normal presidential vote since the concept of sorting is more closely related to the actual level of support for the party, and not to whether the party does better than the national average. I focus on the *percentage of sorted districts* in each Congress as the key independent variable since the pursuit of partisan agenda-setting is constrained by the frequency of unsorted districts in any given Congress.

Redistricting introduces the potential for greater noise in the normal presidential vote measure every ten years and creates similar noise in the sorting measure. Jacobson's (2010) data on House elections provides adjusted measures of the presidential vote in the district for changes in boundaries due to redistricting. This adjustment, however, is only available for the most recent election cycle. For instance, data for members elected in 2002 provides adjustments to the presidential vote for 2000, but not for 1996. As a result, the normal presidential vote based on two election cycles may have greater noise for districts where boundaries changed in ways that shifted a district from heavily Democratic to heavily Republican (or vice versa).

Given the trend that redistricting has increasingly created incumbent-protecting and partisan-leaning seats (Cox and Katz 2002; Theriault 2008), the effect of leaving in the noise from the older election cycle likely biases down the normal presidential vote. As a result, this can slightly bias down the percentage of sorted districts as well. One option for dealing with this issue is to use only one election cycle for seats that have substantial redistricting. The downside to this approach is that with only one election cycle, a landslide for one candidate could lead to a normal presidential vote that is too high or too low for a district relative to the underlying partisanship or ideology of the constituents. A second option for dealing with this issue is to use the most recent election

---

[11] The previous two elections are used to mitigate against the impact of any specific presidential election (Canes-Wrone et al. 2002). For instance, if the member is a Republican I use the mean Republican presidential vote in the last two presidential elections and if the member is a Democrat I use the mean Democratic presidential vote in the last two presidential elections. The presidential vote has been found to be an excellent proxy of district-level partisanship (Levendusky et al. 2008), although some scholars point to some tenuous assumptions when it is used to estimate the ideology of the median voter (see Kernell 2009).

TABLE 5.2 *Summary Statistics for Cosponsored Bills with Majority Sponsors* *(1973–2004)*

	Minimum	Maximum	Mean	Standard Deviation
Roll Call Vote	0	1	0.0614	0.240
Floor Attention	0	1	0.137	0.344
Committee Reported	0	1	0.137	0.344
Bipartisan Cosponsorship	0	1	0.531	0.499
Number of Cosponsors	1	399	19.6	34.8
Second Session	0	1	0.324	0.468
Member of Committee of Referral	0	1	0.462	0.499
Chair of Committee of Referral	0	1	0.0870	0.282
Subcommittee Chair of Committee of Referral	0	1	0.0957	0.294
Percent Sorted Districts	52.1	81.2	64.5	10.1
Divided Government	0	1	0.733	0.442
Majority Seat Share	0.508	0.671	0.591	0.0547

Note: 64.8 percent of cosponsored bills in this period were sponsored by majority party members.

in a given Congress, and the next subsequent election for all districts with substantial redistricting. However, if the trend over time is toward more sorted districts, this may bias the percentage of sorted districts upward. Given the pros and cons of each of these approaches, the analyses in this chapter use the previous two presidential election cycles for all seats, acknowledging that there will be noise in this measure because of redistricting. Summary statistics of the resulting measure of sorting are presented in Table 5.2, along with those for other variables. Robustness checks that consider both of the additional approaches outlined above, which result in 1–3 percent more sorted districts in Congresses following redistricting, yield substantively similar results.

Tests of Bipartisan vs. Partisan Agenda-Setting

The relationship between legislative attention for bipartisan cosponsored bills and the three political contexts of interest – electoral sorting, divided government, and majority seat shares – can be empirically assessed, providing tests of the hypotheses in the framework of strategic partisan agenda-setting. In constructing these tests, the roll call agenda and the broader floor agenda (including roll call votes and House passage by voice votes) are considered as measures of legislative attention. Drawing on the universe of all cosponsored bills, analyses are run at the bill level where the dependent variable (i.e., outcome variable) is an indicator of whether a bill received attention on the roll call or floor agendas. For the roll call agenda dependent variable, bills are coded as 1 if they receive roll call attention, and 0 otherwise. For the floor agenda dependent variable, bills are coded as 1 if they receive either a roll call vote or pass the House on a voice vote, and are coded 0 otherwise. The primary independent variables (i.e., explanatory variables) of interest capture the political context and the interaction of each political context with whether or not a bill has a bipartisan cosponsorship coalition. These contextual variables are the percentage of sorted districts (capturing cross-pressures on members), divided government, and majority seat share (both capturing how governance concerns can constrain partisanship).[12] The expectations from the theoretical framework suggest that the effect of bipartisan cosponsorship (relative to partisan cosponsorship) will vary across each of these political contexts in the resulting models.

The primary independent variables are defined as follows. *Bipartisan cosponsorship* is defined as 1 for bills where at least 20 percent of the cosponsors are from the party opposite the party of the sponsor (the omitted category of 0 captures partisan cosponsored bills). The *percentage of sorted districts* measures the percentage of districts in each Congress where the normal presidential vote is greater than or equal to 50 percent. *Divided government* is defined as 1 for Congresses when both Democrats and Republicans held any combination of the House, Senate, and President and as 0 for Congresses when one party held control over all three institutions. The *size of the majority seat share* measures the fraction of House seats held by the majority party.

For each measure of the political context, I include an interaction term between that variable and bipartisan cosponsorship. The interaction term is critical in assessing whether the effect of bipartisan cosponsorship (as opposed to partisan cosponsorship) differs in periods of high and low district-party sorting, in periods with unified or divided government, and in periods with small or large seat shares. That is, my predictions are not simply that these political contexts affect the amount of legislation on the agenda, but that these contexts affect *whether* bipartisan legislation is prioritized over partisan legislation. The interaction terms and resulting predictions from these models allow the effect of bipartisan cosponsorship on agenda attention to vary across each of these variables.

As we have seen in Chapter 4, the party of a bill's sponsor can affect the likelihood of legislative attention. Majority party members are much more likely to receive attention for their bills than minority party members. In order to simplify the interpretation of the models, the analyses presented here use the subset of only majority-sponsored bills. Robustness checks using three-way

---

[12] The framework of strategic partisan agenda-setting suggests that party leaders would often like to pursue partisan legislation, both for policy goals and to point out differences between the parties. As such, unsorted districts, divided government, and small majority seat shares can all constrain the pursuit of partisan legislation. As an empirical endeavor, however, the patterns speak to how the composition of the agenda changes over time and cannot separate constraint from the preferred legislative agenda of the leadership. The empirical patterns are, nonetheless, consistent with the argument that these conditions constrain the leadership.

interactions with majority bill sponsor as an additional variable yield similar results. Moreover, a member is more likely to be able to move his bill through committee and onto the floor if he sits on or chairs the committee to which his bill is referred. As a result, I include control variables for whether the bill's sponsor is *a member of the committee* of referral, is the *chair of the committee* of referral, or is a *subcommittee chair* of the committee of referral. Other control variables include the *number of cosponsors* and an indicator for bills introduced in the *second session* of Congress.[13] In some model specifications, *committee reporting* of the bill is included as an additional control variable. Table 5.2 presents the summary statistics of each of these dependent and independent variables.

Since predictions from the theoretical framework focus on how the effect of bipartisan cosponsorship is likely to change across each political context – district sorting, divided government, and majority seat shares – multi-level models offer a useful route for analysis. These models acknowledge the nested structure of the data, with bills being introduced within Congresses, but the political contexts varying across Congresses. Logistic models including random effects by Congress for both the intercept and bipartisan cosponsorship are used for each dependent variable of whether or not a bill received attention on the agenda (either roll call or floor). This approach allows the average proportion of bills receiving agenda attention and the effect of bipartisan cosponsorship to vary across Congresses (see Gelman and Hill 2007).[14] Table 5.3 presents the results, first for roll call votes and then for the broader floor agenda. However, since the table masks the random effects in the models and makes the interaction terms difficult to assess, I have additionally run bootstrapping simulations of the models to estimate average treatment effects of bipartisan cosponsorship (Figures 5.1 and 5.2). These simulations sample from the observed data and predict the agenda attention for bipartisan and partisan cosponsored bills across the range of values in each contextual variable. The difference between the predicted attention to bipartisan and partisan cosponsored bills captures the effect of bipartisan cosponsorship on legislative attention.

The hypotheses from the framework of strategic partisan agenda-setting suggest the following relationships. First, bipartisan legislation should be advantaged over partisan legislation on the roll call agenda when there are few sorted districts, but should be replaced by partisan legislation when there are many sorted districts. Empirically, this pattern would be captured by a negative coefficient on the interaction between bipartisan cosponsorship and the percentage of sorted districts, and a positive coefficient on the baseline term of the

---

[13] Models using the natural log of the number of cosponsors on a bill yield substantively similar results to those presented here.

[14] Including interactions between the bill-level variable (bipartisan cosponsorship) and Congress-level variables allows these Congress-level variables to be predictors in the regression of the slope on bipartisan cosponsorship (see Gelman and Hill 2007, chapter 13). The random effects, net of the observed variables in the cross-level interactions, are assumed to be independent of all variables.

TABLE 5.3 *Legislative Attention for Cosponsored Bills with Majority Sponsors*

	Model 1 (Roll Call Vote)	Model 2 (Roll Call Vote)	Model 3 (Roll Call Vote)	Model 4 (Floor)	Model 5 (Floor)	Model 6 (Floor)
Intercept	-7.42*	-7.40**	-9.61**	-3.23	-3.37	-3.95*
	(2.88)	(2.86)	(3.01)	(3.24)	(3.22)	(1.60)
Bipartisan Cosponsorship	5.20	5.40	6.03^	0.763	0.984	-0.716
	(4.11)	(4.14)	(3.50)	(2.44)	(2.45)	(3.20)
Number of Cosponsors	0.00725***	0.00742***	0.00704***	0.00371***	0.00423***	0.00274***
	(0.000442)	(0.000444)	(0.000587)	(0.000369)	(0.000374)	(0.000570)
Member of Committee	0.949***	0.977***	0.310***	0.768***	0.872***	0.0684
	(0.0550)	(0.0554)	(0.0660)	(0.0373)	(0.0383)	(0.0555)
Chair of Committee	1.01***	0.981***	0.347***	1.02***	0.973***	0.551***
	(0.0558)	(0.0568)	(0.0670)	(0.0431)	(0.0445)	(0.0720)
Subcommittee Chair of Committee	0.595***	0.569***	0.0543	0.737***	0.733***	0.301***
	(0.0702)	(0.0706)	(0.0852)	(0.0485)	(0.0494)	(0.0750)
Second Session	0.0576	0.0467	-0.0592	0.289***	0.263***	0.416***
	(0.0461)	(0.0462)	(0.0543)	(0.0322)	(0.0327)	(0.0494)
Percent Sorted Districts	0.0383*	0.0377*	0.0431**	0.0150	0.0142	0.0153^
	(0.0160)	(0.0155)	(0.0164)	(0.0175)	(0.0174)	(0.00883)
Divided Government	-0.0832	-0.0934	-0.0831	-0.137	-0.148	-0.188^
	(0.184)	(0.182)	(0.193)	(0.208)	(0.207)	(0.105)
Majority Seat Share	1.70	1.76	3.22	-1.39	-1.28	-1.92
	(3.16)	(3.13)	(3.29)	(3.56)	(3.54)	(1.75)
Bipartisan x Percent Sorted	-0.0515*	-0.0523*	-0.0516**	-0.0142	-0.0149	0.00703
	(0.0223)	(0.0225)	(0.0191)	(0.0132)	(0.0132)	(0.0174)

Bipartisan x Divided Government	-0.0281	-0.0256	-0.109	0.172	0.181	0.151
	(0.263)	(0.265)	(0.224)	(0.156)	(0.156)	(0.206)
Bipartisan x Majority Seat Share	-2.56	-2.84	-4.54	1.39	1.06	1.46
	(4.50)	(4.55)	(3.83)	(2.68)	(2.69)	(3.51)
Committee Reported	—	—	4.02***	—	—	4.77***
			(0.0648)			(0.0505)
$\sigma^2_{Congress}$	0.0540	0.0524	0.0537	0.0832	0.0816	0.0511
$\sigma^2_{Bipartisan\ Cospon\ (by\ Congress)}$	0.120	0.123	0.0670	0.0363	0.0360	0.0556
σ^2_{Policy}	—	0.0527	—	—	0.159	—
N	39554	39554	39554	39554	39554	39554
Log Likelihood	-8245	-8213	-5343	-14019	-13633	-7069

Standard errors in parentheses. $^p < 0.1$, $^* p < 0.05$, $^{**} p < 0.01$, $^{***} p < 0.001$.

Note: Fixed effect estimates and standard errors from multi-level logistic regressions examining the effects of bipartisan cosponsorship and contextual variables on legislative attention. Random effects by Congress are included on the intercept and on the slope of bipartisan cosponsorship.

percentage of sorted districts (since this baseline term shows the effect on partisan bills). In the resulting figure, the effect of bipartisan cosponsorship (relative to partisan cosponsorship) should decrease as the percentage of sorted districts increases. Second, if divided government is a constraint on partisan agenda-setting, there should be a positive interaction between bipartisan cosponsorship and divided government, and a negative main effect of divided government. That is, the effect of bipartisan cosponsorship should be larger in divided than in unified government. Based on the discussion above, this effect may be most apparent for the broader floor agenda since efforts at governance may be offset by partisan differentiation on roll call votes. Finally, if the size of the majority seat share is a constraint on partisan agenda-setting (all else equal), there should be a negative interaction between bipartisan cosponsorship and majority seat share, and a positive coefficient on the size of the majority seat share. In the resulting figure, the effect of bipartisan cosponsorship should decrease as the size of the majority increases.

For each dependent variable of agenda attention, the first model provides the initial test of the expectations from the framework, the second model adds random effects by policy area (drawing on the 19 major topic codes in the Congressional Bills Project), and the third model includes committee reporting of the bill as a control variable.[15] These additional models allow me to examine the robustness of the findings and to explore whether the shift toward partisan agenda-setting occurs after committee reporting. Table 5.3, Models 1–3 present results where the dependent variable is attention on the roll call agenda. Table 5.3, Models 4–6 present results where the dependent variable is attention on the broader floor agenda. While the estimates in Table 5.3 offer preliminary evidence about the variables that are associated with agenda attention, the average effect of bipartisan cosponsorship in each of the figures that follow offers the clearest evidence of the conditions under which bipartisan legislation is significantly prioritized over partisan legislation.

Legislative attention on both the roll call and floor agendas is positively associated with a number of characteristics of a bill. Although these models are based on the subset of majority-sponsored bills, the party of the sponsor is a central determinant of whether bills receive attention. Whereas 6.1 percent of majority-sponsored bills across the 93rd to 108th Congress received a roll call vote, less than 1 percent of minority-sponsored bills received a roll call vote.

---

[15] Since party control over the agenda can extend to control over what bills committees report, this variable captures a portion of changes in agenda-setting that we are trying to understand with the contextual variables in the model. Moreover, committee reporting is excluded from the initial model because it is highly correlated with floor attention ($p = 0.77$) and, to a lesser extent, with bills receiving a roll call vote ($p = 0.53$). When included as a predictor of floor attention, there is little variation to be explained by other variables in the model. However, the robustness of the relationship between bipartisan cosponsorship and sorted districts to the inclusion of committee reporting in the roll call model emphasizes the finding in Chapter 4 that changes in agenda-setting for roll call votes goes beyond changes in committee attention to bipartisan bills.

Among majority-sponsored bills, those with a higher number of cosponsors are more likely to receive legislative attention, as are those introduced in the second session (at least for floor attention). Bills sponsored by members who serve on the committee of referral or chair the committee or subcommittee are also more likely to garner subsequent agenda attention. Committee reporting also has a large and significant effect (seen in models 3 and 6) on legislative attention. Among bills that are reported from committee, 38 percent receive roll call votes.

Preliminary evidence for whether or not the effect of bipartisan cosponsorship varies across the percentage of sorted districts, divided government, and the size of the majority is seen in the interaction terms between these contextual variables and bipartisan cosponsorship. These interaction terms speak to whether each political context alters the relationship between bipartisan cosponsorship and legislative attention. The first dependent variable of interest is attention to bills on the roll call agenda (Table 5.3, Models 1–3). As expected, the sign on the interaction of bipartisan cosponsorship and the percentage of sorted districts is negative, and the sign on the percentage of sorted districts is positive. Whereas the probability of receiving a roll call vote decreases for bipartisan legislation as the percentage of sorted districts increases, the probability increases for partisan legislation. The next two interactions in the model examine whether divided government and the majority seat share affect the pursuit of bipartisan legislation. Although the coefficient estimates for both interaction terms are insignificant, those for the size of the majority seat share generally point in the expected direction (i.e., negative). For majority-sponsored bills, larger majority seat shares decrease the likelihood that bipartisan bills receive roll call votes. These results offer preliminary support for some of the hypotheses. However, the patterns only provide suggestive evidence about the significance of these relationships since the combination of interaction terms and the multi-level model make interpretation of the estimated coefficients and their standard errors more complex.

Estimated effects of bipartisan cosponsorship on agenda attention from bootstrapping simulations make the logit coefficients easier to interpret, account for the random effects in the model, and provide confidence intervals that are not dependent on modeling assumptions about the covariance between the terms. This simulation approach uses the models in Table 5.3 to predict the likelihood of attention on the roll call agenda for bipartisan bills and for partisan bills across each observed level of the three political contexts. The difference between the predicted attention for bipartisan and partisan bills measures the effect of bipartisan cosponsorship (relative to partisan cosponsorship) on agenda attention. The resulting figures show the average treatment effect of bipartisan cosponsorship (relative to partisan cosponsorship) across observed values of the percentage of sorted districts, then across unified versus divided government, and then across majority seat shares. The average treatment effect speaks to how the effect of x on y changes as z changes (Franzese and Kam 2007, 92), where x is bipartisan cosponsorship, z is the percentage of sorted districts (or divided government or majority seat share), and y is a roll call vote. The vertical lines above and below each average treatment effect represent the 90 percent confidence intervals on the estimate. These confidence intervals are formed from the 5th and 95th percentiles of the bootstrapped simulations (based on 1000 samples). If bipartisan legislation is prioritized over partisan legislation in any given political context, the confidence intervals around the average treatment effect will not cross zero. If the effect of bipartisan cosponsorship varies significantly across the political context, however, the confidence intervals around the average effects at one level of the sorting (or divided government or majority seat share) will not overlap with the effect at other levels. For instance, the argument that party leaders are constrained by the electoral interests of members predicts that the effect of bipartisan cosponsorship will be positive and significant when there are few sorted districts, and that the effect will vary significantly across the percentage of sorted districts.

Party leaders pursue bipartisan legislation when few districts are sorted but can pursue partisan legislation when many districts are sorted. Figure 5.1 presents the effects of bipartisan cosponsorship on receiving a roll call vote when Model 1 from Table 5.3 is used to predict attention. As the percentage of sorted districts increases across its observed values, the average treatment effect of bipartisan cosponsorship decreases significantly. At the lowest levels of sorted districts (e.g., the 94th and 95th Congresses in the data studied) the average effect of bipartisan cosponsorship is positive and significant. As hypothesized, party leaders pursue bipartisan legislation more often than partisan legislation on the roll call agenda when there are few sorted districts and many members are at risk of being cross-pressured between their constituents and their party. At the highest levels of sorted districts (e.g., the 107th and 108th Congresses in the data studied) the average effect of bipartisan cosponsorship is negative and significant. When constituent and party interests align for most members, the majority

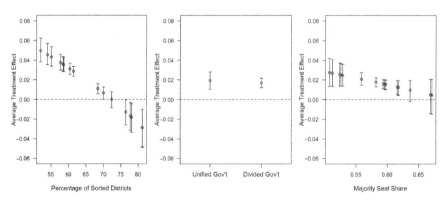

FIGURE 5.1 Effect of Bipartisan Cosponsorship on Receiving a Roll Call Vote

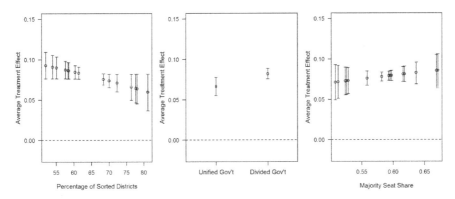

FIGURE 5.2 Effect of Bipartisan Cosponsorship on Receiving Floor Attention

leadership is free to prioritize partisan legislation over bipartisan legislation (yielding a negative effect on bipartisan cosponsorship). Although the estimated effect sizes may appear small, ranging from roughly −0.03 to 0.05, when these effects are aggregated across bills, the consequences on the resulting agenda can be substantively important. In particular, when party leaders allow bipartisan bills on the agenda, more legislation becomes public law and these bills are more likely to have the support from both sides of the aisle.

Party leaders do not advantage bipartisan bills on the roll call agenda any more during periods of divided government than they do during periods of unified government. The second panel of Figure 5.1 captures this phenomenon, showing the effect of bipartisan cosponsorship as the political context varies between unified and divided government. Although the results show that bipartisan legislation is pursued at similar (and statistically indistinguishable) rates in these two contexts, the effect of bipartisan cosponsorship is positive and significant in both unified and divided government. This pattern points to how bipartisan legislation is actually favored in both contexts.

Party leaders are more likely to pursue bipartisan than partisan bills when faced with small majorities. The third panel of Figure 5.1 shows the effect of bipartisan cosponsorship as the size of the majority seat share varies. Here, the results are consistent with the expectations from my hypotheses. Bipartisan legislation is significantly advantaged on the roll call agenda under small seat shares, but is not significantly advantaged under large seat shares. This finding is shown by the positive and significant effect of bipartisan cosponsorship in periods with small seat shares and by the confidence intervals that overlap zero in periods with large seat shares. However, since the confidence intervals on the effect of bipartisan cosponsorship at values of low and high seat shares overlap slightly, I cannot say with a great deal of certainty that the effects of bipartisanship at low and high majority seat shares are significantly different from one another. Nonetheless, these patterns suggest that during periods with small seat shares, governance concerns push party leaders to prioritize bipartisan legislation over partisan legislation.

The same basic patterns found in Figure 5.1 occur when either Model 2 (adding random effects by policy area) or Model 3 (controlling for committee reporting) are used to estimate the effects of bipartisan cosponsorship. Bipartisan legislation is advantaged when there are few sorted districts and disadvantaged when there are many sorted districts. With two important exceptions, similar patterns to those discussed above hold across the contexts of divided government and size of majority seat share. First, when the model controls for committee reporting, bipartisan legislation is no longer significantly prioritized over partisan legislation in either unified or divided government. That is, the effect of bipartisan cosponsorship is smaller in this model than in Figure 5.1 and has confidence intervals that overlap with zero. This suggests that, among the bills reported from committee, party leaders do not disproportionately favor bipartisan bills on the roll call agenda. Second, when the model controls for committee reporting, the effect of bipartisan cosponsorship is not only positive and significant in periods with small seat shares, but the effect is negative and significant in periods with large seat shares. This pattern points to a significant difference in the effect of bipartisan cosponsorship between periods with small and large seat shares. These results are presented in detail in Figure A5.1. Combined, the analyses of attention to bills on the roll call agenda show that district sorting is strongly associated with a change in whether bipartisan or partisan bills are favored in roll call votes, and that small majority seat shares may also lead to the prioritization of bipartisan legislation. There is little support for divided government as a limiting factor in the pursuit of partisan legislation on the roll call agenda.

The second dependent variable of interest is whether or not bills receive attention on the broader floor agenda of *either* roll call votes or passage via voice votes. On the floor agenda, party leaders always advantage bipartisan legislation over partisan legislation and there are fewer changes in agenda-setting across political contexts. As shown in Table 5.3 (Model 4) and Figure 5.2, the effect of bipartisan cosponsorship is not significantly different across levels of district sorting or majority seat share.[16] The confidence intervals on the effect of bipartisan cosponsorship overlap within both sections of Figure 5.2. In all cases, however, the effect of bipartisan cosponsorship is significantly different from zero. That is, party leaders always advantage bipartisan legislation over partisan legislation on the floor agenda. These results speak to the dominance of bipartisan legislation in voice votes. Although Table 5.3 does not capture a significant effect of divided government, Figure 5.2 shows that the estimated effect of bipartisan cosponsorship (relative to partisan cosponsorship) is larger in divided government

---

[16] In model specifications that omit the size of the majority seat share, there is a significant relationship between bipartisan cosponsorship and the percentage of sorted districts (see Figure A5.4 for more details).

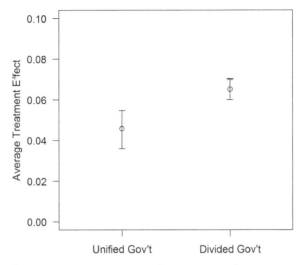

FIGURE 5.3 Effect of Bipartisan Cosponsorship on Passage by Voice Vote

relative to unified government, and that these differences approach statistical significance.[17] Analyses breaking divided government into each possible configuration of House, Senate, and presidential control yield similar patterns (see Figure A5.3 for details). All of these results are similar when the model is estimated with additional random effects by policy area or with a control for committee reporting. The details of these specifications and accompanying figures are presented in Figure A5.2. Across the models, leaders always favor bipartisan legislation over partisan legislation on the broader floor agenda, and this benefit tends to increase during divided government.

Analyses that separate roll call votes from voice votes provide more concrete evidence that divided government does significantly affect whether party leaders pursue bipartisan legislation. Although party leaders advantage bipartisan legislation among all bills passing through voice votes, they advantage bipartisan bills even more during periods of divided government compared to periods of unified government. Figure 5.3 shows the effect of bipartisan cosponsorship across unified and divided government for a model where the dependent variable is House passage by voice vote. During unified government, the average treatment effect of bipartisan cosponsorship is 0.046. During divided government, the average treatment effect of bipartisan cosponsorship increases to 0.065. These estimates reflect a statistically significant difference in the extent to which bipartisan legislation is prioritized over partisan legislation. In contrast, Figure 5.1 showed that there was

[17] With 90 percent confidence intervals, the average treatment effects overlap but only slightly. In unified government, the 95th percentile of the average treatment effect is 0.078. During divided government, the 5th percentile of the average treatment effect is 0.076.

not a significant increase in attention to bipartisan legislation during divided government for roll call votes. Moreover, among cosponsored bills that receive floor attention, significantly more bills pass by voice vote during divided government than during unified government. These patterns suggest that divided government does affect agenda-setting; it leads to an increase in the percentage of bills passing by voice vote as opposed to receiving roll call votes, and it leads to more attention in voice votes (and the floor agenda more broadly) for bipartisan cosponsored bills relative to partisan cosponsored bills. Consistent with expectations in the framework, divided government is a constraint on the pursuit of partisan legislation. Heightened efforts by party leaders to pursue bipartisan legislation, however, only appear in voice votes and not in the roll call votes.

Robustness checks of both the roll call and floor agenda dependent variables yield similar patterns to those discussed above. These robustness checks, discussed in greater detail in the Appendix, include alternate specifications for a number of variables.[18] These variables include the percentage of sorted districts in the majority party (rather than the full chamber); adjustments to the normal vote in congressional districts with substantial redistricting; the percentage of sorted districts based on the normalized presidential vote; 30 percent and 40 percent thresholds for bipartisan cosponsorship; and a continuous measure of bipartisan cosponsorship based on the absolute value of the difference in party support score (from Chapter 2). I also consider specifications where the majority seat share variable is dropped from the model since it is correlated with the percentage of sorted districts (see Figure A5.4). In this specification, attention to bipartisan bills on both the roll call and floor agendas shifts significantly across the percentage of sorted districts. In general, the results are similar across these model specifications, emphasizing that district sorting is strongly related to whether bipartisan or partisan agenda-setting is pursued (particularly on the roll call agenda). Small majority seat shares promote bipartisan legislation on the roll call agenda, and divided government promotes greater bipartisanship on the broader floor agenda (but through voice votes).

The results of these analyses lend support for many of the expectations of the strategic partisan agenda-setting framework. First, electoral sorting has a significant and substantively meaningful effect on whether bipartisan or partisan legislation receives attention. Not surprisingly, this effect is most pronounced for bills receiving roll call votes since this is where the greatest shifts in the agenda occur (and where partisan legislation is concentrated). On the roll call agenda, party leaders significantly advantage bipartisan legislation over partisan legislation in periods with few sorted districts. They significantly disadvantage bipartisan legislation relative to partisan legislation in periods with many sorted

---

[18] All models were also replicated using standard logistic models, estimating the effects of all interacted terms by bootstrapping the results with sampling proportional to the number of the bills in each Congress to yield results similar to clustered standard errors by Congress.

districts. Second, divided government does correspond to greater attention for bipartisan bills, but only through voice votes. This pattern suggests that governance concerns may influence party leaders to put bipartisan bills on the floor agenda (and pass them through voice votes) but that efforts to point out party differences during divided government leave leaders few incentives to take roll call votes on these bipartisan measures. Third, small majority seat shares are associated with a significant advantage for bipartisan bills over partisan bills. For roll call votes, this effect declines (sometimes significantly) as seat share increases. Although party leaders significantly advantage bipartisan bills over partisan bills when there are small seat shares, they do not advantage bipartisan bills when there are large seat shares and may even disadvantage bipartisan bills in these periods. Bipartisan bills remain advantaged on the broader floor agenda.

These results corroborate anecdotal cases where party leaders stressed that the heterogeneity of member and constituents positions limited their agenda options and that partisan bills could not always pass on the floor. Comments from Speaker Carl Albert during an interview with Ronald Peters captured his concerns about members' electoral interests. Peters noted that even when the general positions of the Democrats favored busing or energy reform, a lack of agreement around a specific alternative made it difficult to pursue. Speaker Albert responded that even if they knew the major thrust of the Democratic Party on an issue, they could not pursue it as a partisan bill because individual members would say "Well, gosh, I can't do that. I'd get slaughtered if I did that" (Albert 1979, Tape 2, Side 2, 54–65).

Similarly, a memo from the early 1970s between Speaker Carl Albert and John Barriere, the executive director of the Democratic Steering and Policy Committee, highlights the joint concerns about inter-party agreement and the need to pass legislation. The memo detailed how the committee chair lost the votes of Southern Democratic committee members on the Wage-Price Control Bill (H.R. 6168) and angered Republicans who thought the bill was too extreme (Barriere 1973). "On the basis of past experience, a bill that emerges from the Banking and Currency Committee, opposed by Stephens [a southerner], representing the moderate Southerners, and by Widnall representing the moderate Republicans, is in for rough sledding on the House floor" (Barriere 1973). Predicting that pursuit of this extreme, partisan version of the bill would lead to defeat on the floor, Barriere suggested that Albert not pursue the bill on the floor. While not explicitly framing the discussion as one of partisan versus bipartisan alternatives, these examples suggest that partisan bills were not viable because individuals' electoral interests were at odds with the party position and partisan legislation would result in legislative defeat. As such, party leaders were constrained to pursue more bipartisan legislation. Comparing the perspective of leaders in this era to those in the mid-1990s and onward when many more districts were electorally sorted, it is easy to see how partisan legislation could replace bipartisan legislation on the agenda.

Although I hypothesized that governance concerns would lead party leaders to prioritize bipartisan bills during periods of divided government and small majority seat shares, the empirical evidence for these variables as constraints on partisanship is somewhat weak, particularly for divided government, where the effect is only seen among bills receiving voice votes. There are at least two possible explanations for these more mixed results on the constraining effects of divided government and majority seat shares. First, efforts at partisan differentiation conflict with efforts to build a record of legislative success. This is particularly the case during divided government, a period when the need for differentiation may be greater but when bipartisan legislation may also be needed to enact laws. As suggested by Smith, "Avoiding losses on the floor is not a necessary or a sufficient strategy for enhancing party reputation" (Smith 2007, 137). As a result, balancing goals of governance and partisan differentiation during divided government may result in both bipartisan and partisan legislation being forced onto the agenda, but with bipartisan legislation being concentrated among voice votes and partisan legislation among roll call votes. Second, majority parties may underestimate the extent to which pursuing partisan legislation will hamper a record of legislative success, particularly if they are a new majority. The next section considers this possibility in the context of the Republican Revolution in the 104th and 105th Congresses.

OVER-STEPPING AND BACK-TRACKING IN PARTISAN AGENDA-SETTING

Observers of congressional politics may be surprised to learn that bipartisan voting rose after the Republican Revolution in the mid-1990s, a time when many accounts focused on the dramatic rise of polarization in Congress. Importantly, this rise in bipartisanship is at odds with explanations for partisan conflict that focus on ideological differences, since the membership did not become markedly more moderate during this time. Why, then, did the Republicans choose to pursue a legislative strategy in the 105th Congress that included many more bipartisan bills when they had pursued a strategy focused on partisan legislation in the previous Congress? To explore this question, I briefly examine this period in greater detail, exploring how the agenda changed and whether the changes were consistent with greater efforts at building a record of legislative success during divided government and small majority seat shares. The resulting patterns speak to how much bipartisanship may be necessary for governance and how parties balance governance and partisan differentiation.

A few points are worth noting before delving into the shifting strategies of party leaders during this period. First, the rise in the percentage of roll call votes that were bipartisan tracks with my measures of bill selection. Bipartisanship in voting increased at the same time as the selection of bills with bipartisan cosponsors increased; both co-vary together, rather than just trend together. This pattern lends support to my argument that the level of bipartisanship in voting hinges on which bills are brought up for votes. Second, recent research has noted this increase in bipartisan votes (or decline in party unity votes) and

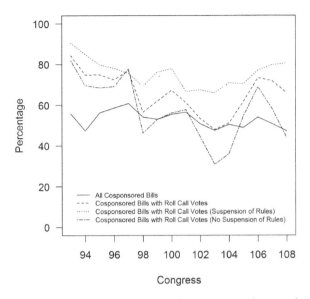

FIGURE 5.4 Bipartisan Cosponsorship by Legislative Stage and Type of Vote

found a partial explanation in the composition of vote types. Crespin et al. (2013) find that the percentage of votes under suspension of the rules – which requires the support of a super-majority – increased during this time.

Although there was an increase in voting under suspension of the rules between the 104th and 105th Congresses, there was also a broader shift in the agenda toward more bipartisan legislation. Figure 5.4 repeats the analysis from Figure 4.1, but in addition to examining the percentage of cosponsored bills that were bipartisan and the percentage of cosponsored bills reaching roll call votes that were bipartisan, I also subset roll call votes into suspension of the rules votes and non-suspension votes. Breaking votes into these two categories shows that changes in the extent of bipartisan agenda-setting occurred on both types of votes.[19] Figure 5.4 shows two important patterns. First, the vast majority of bills receiving votes under suspension of the rules came from bills with bipartisan cosponsors. As noted by Bach (1990, 60), the suspension of the rules procedure is "subject to effective partisan control but which, in practice, usually is suitable only for bipartisan purposes" because it requires super-majority support for passage. Therefore, it is not surprising that bills receiving votes under suspension of the rules are typically bipartisan. Second, bipartisan agenda-setting increased

---

[19] Although these measures do not capture the overall frequency of each type of vote, recent work by Crespin et al. (2013) speaks to this component. The percentage of suspension votes increased from 6.5 percent in the 104th Congress to 10.8 percent in the 105th Congress (followed by 15.4 percent and 17.8 percent in the 106th and 107th, respectively).

dramatically between the 104th and 105th Congresses even on non-suspension votes. In the 104th Congress, 36 percent of bills receiving a non-suspension roll call vote had bipartisan cosponsors, compared to 55 percent in the 105th. Thus, the rise in bipartisan voting, via an agenda that contained more bills with bipartisan cosponsors, was not merely a result of non-controversial items on the suspension calendar. Rather, it appears that the GOP changed its strategy more generally between the 104th and 105th Congresses to include more bipartisan bills on the roll call agenda.

In the 104th Congress, it seems that the Republican strategy got ahead of sorting at the expense of governance. The breakdown in governance was real, as witnessed not only in the shutdown of the government, but also in the enactment of a record low number of public laws. Only 337 bills were signed into law during that Congress, compared to 473 in the previous Congress, and 404 in the following Congress.[20] Party leaders may have been driven to pursue a more bipartisan agenda in the 105th Congress after experiencing legislative failure and the resulting electoral risks to their members. The overly partisan strategy of the 104th Congress put both their collective interest in maintaining a majority in the House and members' own electoral interests at risk.

Arguments by both congressional scholars and journalists suggest that the Republicans did not realize that the confrontational, partisan agenda they pursued in the 104th Congress would not bode well for the realities of governing. For instance, Fenno (1997) argued that 40 years in the minority left the Republicans unprepared to interpret electoral victory or to govern. This institutional deficit created the opening for political firebrands like Newt Gingrich to seize what they may have seen as a one-shot chance to implement Republican policies. As result, the Republican majority in the 104th may have underestimated the constraints imposed by a divided government with small majority seat shares and taken a chance with an unabashedly partisan agenda (Killian 1998).

The first evidence that the Republican majority over-reached in its pursuit of partisan policies in the 104th Congress comes from its members' interpretation of the election victory in 1994. Although the Republicans took their electoral results as a mandate for change, evidence suggests that the election did not reflect major shifts in public mood or a broad endorsement of GOP policy priorities. Even ten days before the election, polls showed that 71 percent of respondents had never heard of the "Contract with America" (the Republican platform in the election). Of the 29 percent of respondents who had heard of the "Contract," one in six said it did not matter to them (Ostrowidski 1995). The Republican majority, however, sought to make the Contract and other partisan items legislative priorities.

[20] Outside of the Congresses analyzed here, this number is beaten by the 112th Congress (2011–12), pointing to the possibility of a similar case of partisanship at the expense of governance. This more recent case is discussed in detail in Chapter 8.

Whether or not the 1994 election offered a mandate for Republican policies, the new GOP majority pursued a partisan agenda. Gingrich's leadership, combined with a cohesive freshman class, drove this pursuit. The newcomers made comments like "We're going to stand for principle. The consequences be damned" (Gugliotta 1996). Majority Whip Tom DeLay adopted a strategy of starting "every policy initiative from as far to the political right as we could" (DeLay and Mansfield 2007, 103–4), clearly pointing to the partisan aims of the GOP in setting policy. Moreover, the Republican goal of self-sufficiency – not having to rely on Democratic support – meant that partisanship was sought despite relatively small seat shares (Brownstein 2007, 271–2). As a result of this legislative approach, party leaders focused on holding the party together, rather than reaching out for consensus (Eilperin 2006, 18–19).

Although 65 of the 73 members of the freshman class in the 104th Congress came from districts that had been represented by Democrats in the 103rd Congress, the percentage of sorted districts increased between the two Congresses. Many members won seats in conservative districts that had already been voting for Republican presidential candidates. By the measure used previously in this chapter, the percentage of sorted districts increased between the 103rd and 104th Congresses from 72 percent to 78 percent, suggesting that the electoral interests of members alone would not have prevented partisanship.

The Republicans' legislative approach, however, contributed to failures in governance as the presence of small seat shares and divided government proved a problem for pursuing their partisan agenda. According to journalist Linda Killian, the Republicans made a number of tactical mistakes: "They tried to ignore for too long the president and his veto power, even when they did not have enough votes to override that veto" (Killian 1998, 416). The passage rates for partisan legislation in the first session of the 104th Congress emphasize the difficulties the Republicans had in pursuing a partisan agenda. Although a well-sorted Republican majority in 1995 was able to pass 93 percent of the partisan bills that received votes on the floor, only 10 percent of these bills became public law. In contrast, 41 percent of the bipartisan bills that passed on the floor became law. As a result of these difficulties passing partisan legislation, only 67 bills were enacted into law in 1995. This was the lowest number of bills passed in a first session of Congress since the end of World War II (Killian 1998, 258).

The combination of partisan agenda-setting and lack of legislative success created by that agenda led many observers to expect widespread Republican losses in the 1996 election as punishment for failing to govern (Cogan et al. 1997). Although losses were not as large as expected, 18 members (including 11 freshmen) lost their bid for reelection; those reelected did not see the typical boosts associated with the incumbency advantage; and the GOP lost the national vote. A number of the electoral losses were by members in competitive and unsorted districts. Of the 18 GOP electoral losses, the normal presidential vote for Republican candidates was less than 55 percent in 14 districts and less than

50 percent in 7 districts. Moreover, roughly half of the GOP freshman saw the Democratic challenger in their race win 45 percent or more of the vote in 1996. These patterns suggest that even though the percentage of sorted districts increased from the previous Congress, individual members should have worried more about the consequences of supporting a partisan agenda, especially those who represented more competitive districts. In their pursuit of a thoroughly partisan agenda that often failed to become law, the Republican majority may have gotten ahead of sorting and found itself needing to backtrack.

The electoral losses in 1996 and the unpopularity of the government shutdowns forced the Republican leadership to consider the costs of a partisan legislative strategy, particularly under divided government (Killian 1998). As a result, the majority leadership shifted its strategy. By the end of the 104th Congress, Republicans acknowledged that bipartisanship was necessary for governing. They were "unnerved by their experience on the budget, and faced with an impending election" (Fenno 1997, 50). Comments by members of the 104th–105th Congresses allude to how they learned that partisan differentiation must be balanced by legislative success. For instance, Sam Brownback (R-KS) was quoted as saying that in 1995 "we showed more guts than brains at times. We did Pickett's Charge. Now we have to say, 'Ok, let's be smarter this time around.' We need to show people we can govern" (quoted in Killian 1998, 273). Likewise, George Nethercutt (R-WA) was quoted as saying that the freshmen had learned the importance of reaching agreements between both sides: "Compromise sounds as if you're sacrificing your principles. We should just say 'reach agreement.' You don't ever get 100 percent of what you want," he said. "This is a change in strategy, not goals or commitments" (quoted in Killian 1998, 273). According to White House domestic policy advisor Bruce Reed, by the 1996 elections the tension between partisanship and governance had become clear: "They [the Republicans] had been humbled by the experience of the last two years ... and they had to decide whether they were going to govern or not" (quoted in Brownstein 2007, 167).

As I showed earlier in the empirical evidence of agenda selection, after losing seats but maintaining their majority in the 1996 elections, the GOP lessened their purely partisan approach, allowing more opportunities for bipartisan cooperation. Aldrich and Rohde (2000, 29) note a similar change in the degree of partisanship, finding that the Republican majority changed its strategy on the Appropriations Committee between the 104th and 105th Congresses, backing off from its previous approach of using appropriations levels to make Democratic priorities take larger cuts. These shifts reflect a greater acknowledgment that governance constrains partisanship. They also reflect members' electoral interests, as sorting decreased slightly following Clinton's reelection in 1996.

Documents from the archives of Richard Armey (R-TX), House Republican Majority Leader from 1995 to 2002, yield additional insights into how the Republicans may have over-reached given the institutional constraints in the 104th Congress, and how they changed strategy in the 105th Congress to better balance goals of governance and partisan differentiation. For instance, in a 1997 memo between Armey staffers David and Kerry[21] regarding the "Criteria for Considering Legislation on the Floor," staffers made it clear that the Republican Party was changing its strategy between the 104th and 105th Congresses, moving from a partisan strategy to one that included some areas for bipartisanship:

Unlike the 104th Congress – where the Leadership played a more active role in setting the legislative agenda – hopefully the 105th will see more bottom-up, bipartisan, committee-driven initiatives. While this means more autonomy and responsibility for committees, it does not mean carte blanche for committees to set the agenda in an ad hoc manner .... Priority for bringing legislation to the floor will be given to committees who have prepared and followed good communications and operational strategies. Specifically, these steps include ... involving, from the beginning, moderate and conservative Democrats in the process. (David 1997)

Balancing the pursuit of partisan legislation with the electoral interests of individual members and governance goals forced the leadership to take into account the interests and needs of these more vulnerable members when crafting a partisan strategy. In a memo titled "The 55 Percent Caucus Project," the Republican leadership detailed a plan to identify and work with members who won reelection in 1998 with 55 percent or less of the vote. The memo indicated that one of the primary purposes of the program was to facilitate communication between these members and the leadership, making sure that members' concerns about how legislative matters would affect their districts would be reflected in the agenda (Ehrlich et al. 1999). Since the Republican majority held only 223 seats, the fact that they had even 27 members on the "55 percent caucus list" left little room for members to deviate if a partisan agenda were pursued.

The simultaneous efforts to pursue a partisan strategy for reasons of policy and partisan differentiation, and a bipartisan strategy to produce a record of legislative success during divided government came across well in a speech by Dick Armey in 1997. The speech outline emphasized that the Republicans needed to find where their agenda overlapped with that of the president and pursue those places of bipartisan agreement, while also picking out battles to highlight differences on flex time, legal reform, and the partial birth abortion ban (Armey 1997). Thus, while the GOP appeared to want to focus on efforts of partisan differentiation, the political environment they faced necessitated that they seek some bipartisanship in order to achieve legislative success with their agenda.

In order to better balance the electoral concerns of members, governance, and party differentiation, the party leaders increased the number of bipartisan issues on the agenda in the 105th Congress. As a result, more bills with bipartisan support were brought up for votes in the following Congresses. However, the

---

[21] Presumably David Hobbs and Kerry Knott, both of whom served as Armey's chief of staff at various times.

degree to which party leaders prioritized bipartisan over partisan legislation was on par with the agendas of the early 1990s, not at the much higher levels of the late 1970s and early 1980s. The minor resurgence in bipartisan agenda-setting came after the nadir of that strategy, as the Republican Party sought to balance the interests of members, the party, and the needs of governing during divided government.

A comparison of legislation with bipartisan cosponsorship that *did not* receive floor attention in the 104th and legislation that *did* receive floor attention in the 105th illustrates this change toward a more bipartisan agenda. This comparison also indicates that in the 104th Congress there were bills with bipartisan cosponsors that could have been considered on the floor that the leadership chose not to pursue. While this comparison does not reflect a random sample of legislation, it highlights the change in agenda.

In the 104th Congress, a number of bills sponsored by Republicans with bipartisan cosponsors died in committee. These included a health care bill to limit disclosures of genetic information (H.R. 2690, cosponsored by 24 Democrats and 10 Republicans), an energy bill to provide tax incentives to encourage the production of oil and gas in the United States (H.R. 987, cosponsored by 7 Democrats and 9 Republicans), and an education bill to evaluate student loan programs (H.R. 530, cosponsored by 20 Democrats and 60 Republicans). In his introduction of the Student Loan Evaluation and Stabilization Act, the bill's sponsor Rep. Goodling (PA-19) noted the common ground on the legislation: "I would also like to thank Bart Gordon and my other Democratic colleagues who have helped to create this bipartisan effort and who share my concerns about integrity and accountability in the student aid programs" ("Congressional Record" 1995, E102). Examples like these are numerous and indicate that there were pieces of legislation with bipartisan agreement that were not legislative priorities in the 104th Congress.[22]

When leaders of the 105th Congress shifted their agenda to include more bipartisan legislation, bills of similar policy importance to those that died in the 104th Congress saw roll call attention.[23] Some of these bipartisan bills passed under suspension of the rules while others passed by large margins under regular roll call procedures. Among the legislation that passed under suspension of the rules were bills with broad, bipartisan coalitions. For instance, legislation to support community efforts to reduce substance abuse among youth passed the

---

[22] Nonetheless, it is important to remember that bipartisan legislation did continue to pass by voice vote in the 104th Congress, so bipartisanship was not entirely absent. Bipartisan cosponsored bills becoming law through voice votes included legislation amending the Public Health Service Act to provide for more studies of traumatic brain injuries (H.R. 248, Public Law 104–166), modifying the farm credit system and mortgage market (H.R. 2029, Public Law 104–105), and authorizing a program to enhance safety, training, research, and development in the propane gas industry (H.R. 1514, Public Law 104–284).

[23] These assessments of policy importance are necessarily rough but are meant to provide examples of the types of legislation that did or did not receive attention.

House with the support of 420 members (H.R. 956, Public Law 105–20). Similarly, legislation to prohibit financial transactions with countries supporting terrorism (H.R. 748) passed the House with a broad bipartisan vote of 377 yea to 33 nay.

Across many issue areas, a number of bills with bipartisan support in their cosponsorship coalitions did receive roll call votes in the 105th Congress, even without suspension of the rules. In education policy, these included a bill to improve employment, training, literacy, and vocational programs (H.R. 1385) and a bill to extend the authorization of programs under the Higher Education Act of 1965 (H.R. 6). In foreign policy and trade, bipartisan legislation included a bill to reauthorize the Export-Import Bank (H.R. 1370). In energy policy, bipartisan legislation included a bill to amend the Nuclear Waste Policy Act of 1982 (H.R. 1270).

These types of changes in the roll call agenda of the Republicans between the 104th and the 105th Congresses were driven in part by the constraints of governing and the realization that they had over-reached when pursuing partisanship during the 104th Congress. When partisan bills failed to become law and both the GOP majority and its members were at electoral risk, the party shifted its strategy. With divided government and a small majority, greater bipartisanship on the roll call agenda was necessary to pass legislation. Leaders pursued more bipartisan legislation, not because they desired bipartisanship above all else, but because they could not produce a record of success with partisan legislation. However, even without increasing the attention to bipartisan bills on the roll call agenda, House majorities can achieve some degree of governance by pursuing bipartisan legislation on broader floor agenda through voice votes. When party leaders seek to balance partisan differentiation and governance, this approach may be beneficial. Whereas roll call votes are unique in allowing for partisan differentiation and putting members on the record, the majority party may still be able to fulfill the governing side of its job, even during divided government or times of small seat shares, by giving bipartisan legislation floor attention and passing that legislation through voice votes. As a result, the majority may have fewer institutional constraints on the construction of a partisan roll call agenda. Thus, the limits on the partisanship of the roll call agenda may be due primarily to the electoral pressures on members and the degree to which members of a party have similar electoral bases of support.

CONCLUSIONS

The extent to which party leaders pursue bipartisan over partisan legislation on the agenda varies across political contexts. As hypothesized, the relative prevalence of partisan and bipartisan legislation on the roll call agenda can be explained, at least in part, by electoral/constituency pressures. Bipartisan legislation is always more likely than partisan legislation to find a place on the roll call agenda when districts are not well sorted. Only when members' electoral bases of support align with the party can congressional parties prioritize partisan legislation. Moreover, bipartisan legislation is significantly advantaged on the roll call agenda when there are small majority seat shares and not when there are large seat shares. Divided government does not always encourage party leaders to pursue bipartisan legislation on the roll call agenda, but it does result in the pursuit and passage of significantly more bipartisan bills through voice votes. However, changes in the GOP agenda strategies between the 104th and 105th Congresses suggest that political leaders ultimately viewed divided government and small majority seat shares as constraints on both the roll call and full floor agendas. The new majority underestimated the importance of bipartisan legislation when governing during divided government and shifted course when the risks to individual members and to the party as a whole became visible. These patterns suggest that even if House parties do not prioritize governance over partisan differentiation, they do seek to balance the two.

Combined, this evidence shows that congressional agenda-setting has changed over time from prioritizing bipartisan legislation to prioritizing partisan legislation. This shift reflects changes in the risk that partisan legislation has had on members' electoral interests. Nonetheless, parties appear cognizant of the institutional constraints and the necessity to govern when holding the majority. Even in the most partisan periods, bipartisan legislation remains present, especially when the broader floor agenda that includes voice votes is considered. The evidence in this chapter and in Chapter 4, combined with the evidence about patterns of cosponsorship coalitions, suggests that some of the partisanship in Congress is manufactured by the content of the agenda. There remain pieces of legislation that can garner bipartisan cosponsorship coalitions, indicating that common ground exists between members of the two parties. However, voting coalitions appear increasingly polarized when bipartisan bills do not make it to the roll call agenda and are replaced by partisan bills.

The next chapter considers how patterns of bipartisan agreement and agenda-setting play out within and across issue areas. It also explores whether the aggregate shift from bipartisan to partisan agenda-setting is driven by particular policy areas that offer greater benefits from partisan differentiation. The framework of strategic partisan agenda-setting suggests that the benefits of pursuing partisan legislation are greatest when the two parties hold distinct positions from one another and issues define the party brand.

6

Strategic Partisan Agenda-Setting Across Policy Areas

In response to a U.S. export subsidy that had triggered international sanctions in 2004, Republican William Thomas (R-CA) introduced a bill to amend the Internal Revenue Code to make manufacturing, service, and high-technology businesses more competitive. The bill (H.R. 4520) provided for a massive corporate tax overhaul, which was enacted into law in October of 2004 (Public Law 108–357). From its inception, the legislation was highly partisan. Not only did a Republican sponsor the bill, but 40 Republicans cosponsored it. The committee markup session ended in a partisan vote, with only 3 Democrats joining all 24 Republicans in support of the bill. The House roll call votes were similarly partisan, with the votes on final passage and on agreement to the conference report falling along party lines. In both cases, an overwhelming majority of Republicans supported the bill (202 on the first vote; 207 on the second) and an overwhelming majority of Democrats opposed the bill (154 on the first vote; 124 on the second vote). In both chambers, partisan conflict ignited from the macroeconomic and labor issues in the legislation (*Corporate Tax Breaks Enacted* 2005).

Contrast this example with legislation that garnered bipartisan support in 2005 on surface transportation. In February 2005, Republican Representative Don Young (R-AK) introduced legislation (H.R. 3) to authorize $244 billion for surface transportation programs in fiscal years 2005 through 2009. The legislation – which became the Safe, Accountable, Flexible and Efficient Transportation Equity Act: a Legacy for Users (SAFETEA-LU) – was bipartisan throughout its development.[1] Of the 79 cosponsors on the original bill, 39 were Democrats and 39 were Republicans (the remaining cosponsor was a delegate

---

[1] The legislation did face battles, both between the White House and Congress, as well as between "donor" states (those that contributed significantly more to the Highway Trust Fund) and "donee" states (recipient states that received more than they contributed), but these conflicts were non-partisan in nature.

from Puerto Rico). All of the roll call votes were also bipartisan. For instance, the House final passage vote had the support of 218 Republicans, 198 Democrats, and 1 Independent. Only 9 members, all fiscally conservative Republicans, voted against the legislation. " 'Every page of this bill has been built on accommodation and compromise,' said Bill Thomas, R-Calif., chairman of the House Ways and Means Committee and a key broker in the conference negotiations" (Compromise Highway Bill Completed After Two-Year Clash 2006).

These examples serve to highlight the range of bipartisan and partisan legislation coming out of Congress, even in recent years. They also suggest that there may be some predictable differences in bipartisan cooperation by issue area, which may affect both the degree of bipartisan cosponsorship on an issue and whether bipartisan or partisan agenda-setting is pursued. At the same time, this is not to say that bipartisan legislation is inherently of a higher quality than partisan legislation: the bipartisan SAFETEA-LU legislation carried billions of dollars in earmarks, including the infamous "Bridge to Nowhere," many of which have become notorious examples of wasteful spending (Cosgrove-Mather 2005). Bipartisan legislation may be an important component of governance in Congress, but bipartisan coalitions on bills need not always signal that the legislation is the best possible policy solution.

Previous chapters have demonstrated that agenda-setting strategies in the House have changed since the early 1970s. As the percentage of sorted districts increased (and the number of cross-pressured members declined), bipartisan legislation was replaced by partisan legislation, particularly on the roll call agenda. Institutional constraints also limited party leaders' pursuit of partisan legislation, with small majority seat shares promoting bipartisanship on the roll call agenda and divided government promoting bipartisanship on the broader floor agenda through voice votes. Importantly, the shift toward greater partisanship on the roll call agenda occurred despite a relatively weak decline in the rate of bipartisan cosponsorship of legislation.

Even so, the examples discussed above serve as a reminder that not all policy areas are created equal (e.g., Clausen 1973; Hurwitz et al. 2001; Jochim and Jones 2013). Whereas some policies divide the parties and may be the basis of the party brand name or the focus of issue ownership (Cox and McCubbins 1993; Lawrence et al. 2006; Petrocik 1996), other policies are largely distributive in nature and either geographically driven (i.e., agriculture) or nonpartisan (i.e., transportation) (Jochim and Jones 2013). These differences are likely to affect the degree of bipartisanship on an issue and may affect the extent of partisan agenda-setting within issues. When the party brand or issue ownership is at stake, the mere desire to pursue partisan policies may be greater, since parties are more likely to be cohesive and distinct on these issues. When the constraints on partisan agenda-setting are low – as the result of well-sorted districts, large seat shares, and unified government – party leaders may pursue partisan legislation more on these issues than on those where the benefits from partisan differentiation are lower.

The opening examples gesture toward how the parties treat these different types of policy. Macroeconomic policies have been associated with party branding and issue ownership, while transportation policies have not.[2] Not only is bipartisan agreement lower on macroeconomic issues than in many other areas, but, as this chapter will show, party leaders have shifted their agenda on this issue over time from one focused on bipartisan policies to one focused on partisan policies. The roll call record reflects this shift. Whereas 49 percent of all roll call votes on macroeconomic issues were bipartisan in the 93rd Congress (1973–74), only 23 percent were bipartisan in the 104th (1995–96) and a mere 14 percent were bipartisan in the 108th Congress (2003–04). Bipartisan voting on transportation policies also declined over time, which is consistent with the broader story of increasing partisanship. However, the record of bipartisan agreement did not decline nearly as much as on macroeconomic policies. Between the 93rd and 108th Congresses, the percentage of bipartisan transportation votes fell from 73 percent to 55 percent, which was still more than three-quarters of the level of bipartisanship in the 93rd Congress. The contrast between the voting patterns on macroeconomic and transportation policies clearly points to disparities in the degree to which party leaders pursued partisan legislation in different policy areas. More generally, on policy areas associated with issue ownership, party leaders may have greater incentive to focus on partisan differentiation (Gilmour 1995). Consequently, the framework of strategic partisan agenda-setting may not only explain aggregate patterns of how leaders select bills for floor and roll call attention, but may also explain differences in how leaders prioritize bipartisan and partisan bills across issues.

The remainder of this chapter has three goals. First, I document the patterns of bipartisanship across policy areas. The observed differences in these patterns across policies are important both because they provide further justification for the cosponsorship measure (since the patterns of bipartisan cosponsorship capture differences that congressional observers would expect between issues), and because they provide the motivation to explore whether agenda-setting plays out differently across issue areas. Second, I empirically test whether strategic partisan agenda-setting plays out within policy areas and whether it is stronger in some issue areas relative to others. I trace which bills receive roll call and floor attention within policy areas, and assess whether party leaders change their strategy over time from pursuing mostly bipartisan bills to mostly partisan bills in all or only some issue areas. As a potential explanation for why shifts in agenda-setting vary across issues, I draw from literature on issue ownership. Finally, I explore the implications of strategic partisan agenda-setting for which issues receive legislative attention over time.

---

[2] After the early 1970s, both House parties showed increasing cohesion on budget votes. These partisan differences on macroeconomic policy increased in the 1980s as a result of the breakdown in the Keynesian model (Coleman 1996).

The findings of this chapter indicate that strategic partisan agenda-setting occurs not only at the aggregate level, as bills are selected for roll call votes (or floor attention), but also within and between policy areas. The evidence shows that the electoral sorting constraint on partisan agenda-setting is strongest for those policy areas that are the most partisan. This result suggests that party leaders pursue partisan legislation when possible on issues that are the basis of the party brand and issue ownership, but that their pursuit of these highly partisan bills is heavily dependent on the degree of district-party sorting. Moreover, as a consequence of the majority party shifting its agenda in general from a largely bipartisan to a more partisan strategy, legislative attention to particular groups of policies has changed over time. I find that when a partisan floor strategy is pursued, those issues that are most likely to achieve bipartisan agreement – foreign trade, agriculture, international affairs, environment, space and technology, transportation, and defense – receive less legislative attention than when a bipartisan strategy is pursued. This result raises a potential concern about governance and legislative action, in that policymakers seeking partisan policies and emphasizing differences between the two parties may ignore some issue areas.

BIPARTISANSHIP BY ISSUE AREA

To explore how strategic partisan agenda-setting plays out within and between policy areas, I begin with some descriptive measures of bipartisanship by issue area, focusing again on bill cosponsorship coalitions. I define the issue area of each bill using data from the Congressional Bills Project (Adler and Wilkerson 2008), which uses the same coding scheme as the Policy Agendas Project (Baumgartner and Jones 2000). The resulting issue codes include 19 major topic areas and over 200 subtopic areas. For subsequent analyses, I focus on the major topic codes listed in Table A6.1. As with the earlier analyses, I define bills as bipartisan in their cosponsorship if at least 20 percent of the cosponsors are from the party opposite the party of the bill's sponsor.

The percentage of cosponsored bills with bipartisan coalitions varies across policies and across time. Like the analysis of all cosponsored bills in Chapter 2, Figure 6.1 plots the percentage of cosponsored bills in each issue area that are bipartisan in each year, along with a trend line through the data. There is significant heterogeneity in both the initial level of bipartisanship and in the trend over time. The policy areas with the highest initial levels of bipartisanship include transportation, space and technology, international affairs, environment, and defense. The policy areas with the lowest initial levels include social welfare, labor, health, and community development. The remaining issues of public lands, macroeconomics, law, government operations, foreign trade, energy, education, civil rights, banking, and agriculture fall somewhere in between.

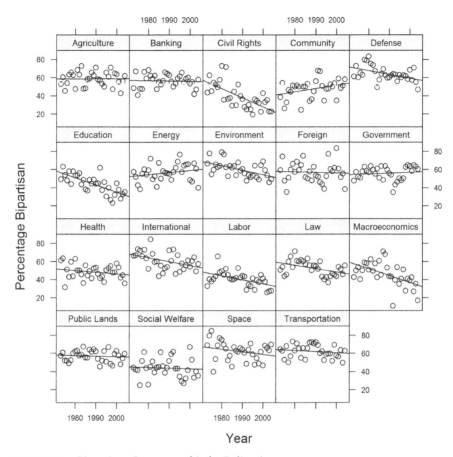

FIGURE 6.1 Bipartisan Cosponsorship by Policy Area

Over time, some policy areas saw significant decline in bipartisan agreement, while others did not.[3] Among the issues with the highest initial levels of bipartisanship, space, international affairs, and environmental issues all had significant negative trends. Among issues with the lowest initial levels of bipartisanship, only labor had a significant negative trend. Among the remaining issues, macroeconomics, law, education, and civil rights had negative time trends. Overall, 8 of the 19 issue areas had negative trends, but 11 did not. Clearly, the degree of bipartisan agreement on legislation varied considerably across issues. Among majority-sponsored bills (not pictured), bipartisan cosponsorship declined even less over time; none of the policy areas yield a significant negative relationship

[3] Significance is based on the 95 percent confidence intervals for the slope and is calculated using the 32 yearly observations within each issue area.

with time, 12 exhibit insignificant trends, and 7 exhibit positive trends. While the average level of bipartisanship varies dramatically across issue areas, if majority leaders focused on bills sponsored by their party's members, they would have encountered bipartisan bills within many policy areas at similar rates in the 1970s and 2000s.

Not surprisingly, many of the policy issues that have either low or declining bipartisanship (among all cosponsored bills) across this time period are the same policies that define the party brand name. This is particularly true for social welfare, civil rights, labor, and macroeconomic (including taxation) policies. Importantly, the different patterns across issue areas provide additional justification for using cosponsorship coalitions to assess bipartisan agreement. The level and trend of bipartisanship across issues aligns with traditional understandings of policies with more or less partisan conflict. Moreover, the number of issues with moderate-to-high levels of bipartisanship, and those with no significant decline over time, reiterate the contention that there remained places of substantive bipartisan agreement between the two parties.

Summary measures of the average level of bipartisan agreement in each issue area further emphasize that there is substantial variation in the degree of bipartisanship across policies. These summary measures, shown in Table 6.1, are based on the average level of bipartisan cooperation, defined as the average of the yearly estimates (below) or as the overall percentage of bills in an issue area that are bipartisan. The first measure considers each year equally, regardless of how many bills were introduced in each issue area, whereas the second gives greater weight to years in which more bills on a given issue were cosponsored. Both yield similar insights.

Both summary measures of bipartisan agreement vary across issues in ways that those familiar with party politics would expect. For instance, the first two columns of Table 6.1 show that defense policy, at 64 percent, has the highest average percentage of bipartisan cosponsorship coalitions, followed by space and transportation policies, and then international and environmental policies. The lowest levels of bipartisan cooperation occur in civil rights, with an average of 39.3 percent bipartisan bills, followed by labor and social welfare. The third and fourth columns, which are based on the overall percentage of bipartisan bills in each issue area, show a similar ordering of policies. Under both measures, it is clear that some issues are much more likely to garner bipartisan support than other issues. As complaints about pork-laden bipartisanship (e.g., Lawler 1997) would suggest, distributive policies (transportation, agriculture, etc.) have a relatively high record of bipartisanship. However, bipartisanship is also relatively frequent in other policy areas, including international and foreign policy, environmental issues, and energy. The more partisan issues include macroeconomics, social welfare, labor, and civil rights – many of which are the same as those that drive the ideological differences between the parties. Whereas policies with greater bipartisan cosponsorship tend to reflect higher issue dimensionality, policies with little bipartisanship fit onto the unidimensional liberal-conservative spectrum (Jochim and Jones 2013).

TABLE 6.1 *Rank Ordering of Most Bipartisan to Least Bipartisan Policy Areas*

Average Yearly Percentage of Bipartisan Cosponsored Bills		Total Percentage of Bipartisan Cosponsored Bills	
Policy Area	Percentage Bipartisan	Policy Area	Percentage Bipartisan
Defense	64.0	Defense	63.8
Space, Science, Tech.	62.0	Space, Science, Tech.	61.5
Transportation	61.9	Transportation	61.4
International Affairs	60.4	Environment	59.4
Environment	59.9	Agriculture	58.9
Agriculture	58.5	International Affairs	58.7
Foreign Trade	56.9	Foreign Trade	57.0
Public Lands	56.9	Public Lands	56.3
Energy	56.4	Banking	55.7
Banking	56.4	Government	55.1
Government	55.9	Energy	54.6
Law, Crime	52.5	Law, Crime	51.7
Health	48.4	Health	48.1
Community Development	47.3	Macroeconomics	47.3
Macroeconomics	45.6	Community Development	45.4
Education	44.1	Social Welfare	44.7
Social Welfare	43.8	Education	43.6
Labor	40.3	Labor	40.3
Civil Rights	39.3	Civil Rights	39.6

With 19 policy areas, the systematic assessment of differences in agenda-setting within and between each area is difficult and may produce results that are dependent on outliers in a given policy (especially since roll call attention may be infrequent for some policies). To simplify some of the subsequent analyses, I therefore rely on three categories of bills that capture the frequency of bipartisan cosponsorship. I separate policy areas based on the level of bipartisan agreement – those with the least (civil rights, labor, education, social welfare, community development, and macroeconomics), medium (health, law, energy, government operations, banking, and public lands), and the most (foreign trade, agriculture, international affairs, environment, space and technology, transportation, and defense) bipartisanship. These categories include roughly equal numbers of issue areas. In all cases, the level of bipartisanship is based on the average percentage of bipartisan cosponsorship coalitions (Table 6.1, Columns 3 and 4). The resulting categories are identical when using the average yearly estimates of bipartisan cosponsorship. These categories allow subsequent analyses to consider two important elements of strategic partisan agenda-setting: first, whether the constraining factors of the framework – district sorting, divided government, and majority seat share – have stronger effects for some categories of issues relative to others, and, second, whether a shift by party leaders toward partisan agenda-setting has implications for issue attention.

STRATEGIC PARTISAN AGENDA-SETTING BY ISSUE AREA

The descriptive data presented above indicate that issues receive varying levels of bipartisan support. Differences in bipartisan support between issues affect the pool of available bipartisan bills that could receive legislative attention. These differences may also affect whether party leaders want to pursue partisan legislation when conditions permit. The framework of strategic partisan agenda-setting suggests that more partisan legislation may be pursued when conditions are favorable – that is, when the majority party faces a Congress with many sorted districts, unified government, and large majority seat shares. In what follows, I attempt to identify the routes by which aggregate patterns of increasingly partisan agenda-setting over time play out across different groups of policies. In order to explore whether party leaders have pursued increasingly partisan agendas within issues and whether patterns of agenda-setting vary across issues, this section focuses on two types of analyses. First, I focus on evidence for strategic partisan agenda-setting *within* issues. Second, I examine differences in the extent of partisan agenda-setting *between* groups of issues, considering issue ownership as one possible explanation for these differences.

The majority party is more likely to pursue a partisan agenda when parties are better sorted and district preferences align with the partisanship of the representative. This strategy involves prioritizing partisan issues on the floor and in roll call voting to pursue policy goals and to build the party brand. The same expectation holds when leaders set the agenda within an issue. As the parties become better sorted on average,[4] I expect that party leaders will increasingly prioritize partisan bills relative to bipartisan bills within each issue area. For instance, among bills on education policy, those with partisan cosponsors will see an increased likelihood of making it to a roll call vote when districts are better sorted, while those with bipartisan cosponsors will see a decreased likelihood of making it to a roll call vote. The conditional probability of legislative attention for majority-sponsored bills, leveraging variation within all 19 policy areas, provides one way to test of the framework of strategic partisan agenda-setting within issues.

---

[4] Both the theoretical concept of district-party sorting and the measure of the normal presidential vote to assess sorting focus on the aggregate or average degree of sorting. Neither is issue-specific. The measure is designed to capture the extent to which members represent majorities that align with their party or whether they are cross-pressured between party and district. This does not exclude the potential for differences in sorting to occur by issue, a possibility that should be explored in future work.

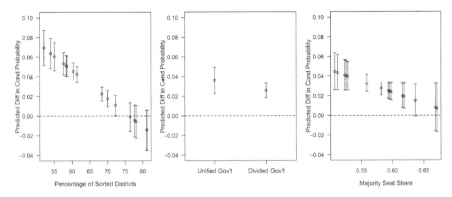

FIGURE 6.2 Predicted Difference in Conditional Probability of a Roll Call Vote (Majority-Sponsored Bills)

For both outcomes of interest – attention on the roll call agenda and the broader floor agenda – I calculate the conditional probability of the outcome given that a bill is bipartisan for each of the 19 issue areas and each of the 16 Congresses (yielding measures for each policy-area Congress). I calculate the same conditional probability of agenda attention for partisan bills. For subsequent analyses, the unit of analysis is the policy area-Congress, and the dependent variable is the difference in conditional probability of legislative attention (first for roll call votes, and then for broader floor attention) between bipartisan and partisan bills. Not only does this measure systematically capture the likelihood of bipartisan and partisan agenda-setting for each issue, but it also accounts for the underlying propensity for bipartisan cosponsorship in each issue area, which can vary over time. Larger values of this outcome measure reflect greater attention to bipartisan bills. I estimate the effect of the percentage of sorted districts, divided government, and the size of the majority seat share on bipartisan agenda-setting using a multi-level linear model with random effects by Congress and by policy. I also control for the proportion of bills receiving roll call votes (or floor attention). These models test whether party leaders pursue bipartisan bills more often than partisan bills as the political context varies.

Figure 6.2 plots the predicted difference in conditional probability of a roll call vote across the observed values of each of the three independent variables of interest. Figure 6.3 plots the predicted outcomes for the broader floor agenda (full model results are in Table A6.2). These predictions are based on bootstrapping simulations of the model, essentially sampling repeatedly from the data and predicting the outcome when each of the independent variables is set to a given observed value.[5] Given the structure of the dependent variable,

---

[5] The bootstrapping process produced model estimates and predicted outcomes for 1,000 samples of the data.

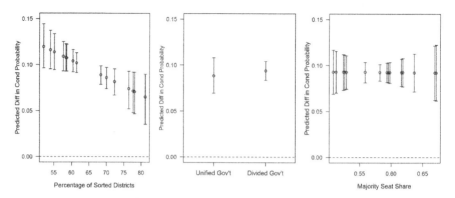

FIGURE 6.3 Predicted Difference in Conditional Probability of Floor Attention (Majority-Sponsored Bills)

positive values for the predicted outcome reflect party leaders prioritizing bipartisan legislation relative to partisan legislation, while negative values reflect party leaders prioritizing partisan legislation relative to bipartisan legislation.

When the outcome of interest is a roll call vote (Figure 6.2), party leaders significantly favor bipartisan legislation when the percentage of sorted districts is low, but do not significantly advantage bipartisan legislation relative to partisan legislation when the percentage of sorted districts is high. Moreover, the difference between predicted outcomes is significantly different across the observed values of the percentage of sorted districts. Here, the effect of moving from one standard deviation below the mean on the percentage of sorted districts to one standard deviation above the mean is −0.058 (90 percent confidence intervals from −0.083 to −0.033). As did the findings in Chapter 5, these results speak to how the content of the agenda differs in periods with few versus many sorted districts (and thus many versus few cross-pressured members), but these results further indicate that this change occurs *within* issues, at least on average. Similar to the bill-level findings of Chapter 5, divided government does not have a significant constraining effect on roll call agenda-setting, while differences between the predicted outcomes approach significance across the range of majority seat shares. Party leaders disproportionately pursue bipartisan legislation when they have a small majority, but pursue bipartisan and partisan bills at similar rates when they have a large majority.

When the outcome of interest is attention on the broader floor agenda (either roll call votes or passage by voice votes), party leaders always favor bipartisan legislation over partisan legislation. This pattern is seen in the positive predictions for the difference in conditional probability in Figure 6.3. Nevertheless, the predicted difference in floor attention for bipartisan and partisan bills is significantly higher in periods with few sorted districts compared to those periods with many sorted districts. That is, the confidence intervals for those predictions at the smallest percentage of sorted districts do not overlap with the confidence intervals at the larger percentage of sorted districts. In this specification of floor attention, party leaders' pursuit of bipartisan legislation is not affected by unified versus divided government or the size of the majority seat share. Though reiterating the weaker effect of divided government, even on the broader floor agenda, these results provide further evidence for variation in agenda-setting within issues as the percentage of sorted districts increased.

Although these results suggest that strategic partisan agenda-setting plays out within issues, these tests do not allow the shifts in agenda-setting to differ between issues. However, anecdotal examples (such as those at the opening of this chapter), the varying patterns across issues in Figure 6.1, and interviews with former members of Congress emphasize the potential for differences in agenda-setting across issues. In an interview with the author, former House member Michael Castle (R-DE) commented that there are many places of bipartisan agreement, but that bipartisanship is lower on hot-button issues. Moreover, he suggested that the hot-button issues receive greater legislative attention (Castle 2011). The raw data from the difference in conditional probability of a roll call vote that were used as the dependent variable in the analysis above further highlights differences in agenda-setting between issues. For each policy area, Figure 6.4 plots the raw data and a smoothed line for the difference in conditional probability of a roll call vote between bipartisan and partisan cosponsored legislation for each Congress, looking again at bills sponsored by majority party members. Values of zero on the y-axis indicate that the conditional probability of a roll call vote is the same for bills with bipartisan and partisan cosponsors. Values greater than zero indicate that party leaders favor bipartisan bills; values less than zero indicate that party leaders favor partisan bills. The trend over time is also important since it speaks to whether party leaders increasingly prioritize partisan bills, even if these partisan bills do not become more likely than bipartisan bills to reach a roll call vote.

A few points are worth noting. First, where there is a discernible trend in agenda-setting over time, it is often downward, suggesting that over time party leaders increasingly prioritize bills with partisan cosponsors relative to bills with bipartisan cosponsors. Second, the magnitude of the downward trend varies across issues. The decline in macroeconomic, labor, and health policies is much greater than that for agriculture, transportation, environment, and many other issue areas. In some of these policies (e.g., macroeconomics, labor, and education), the difference in the conditional probability of receiving a roll call vote crosses zero on the y-axis. This suggests that while bipartisan bills were more likely to have received votes in the early years of the analysis, they were over-taken by partisan bills in the later years of analysis. Importantly, this decline in bipartisan agenda-setting occurs on top of any decline of bipartisan cosponsor-ship in these areas, pointing to the effect of agenda-setting and not just

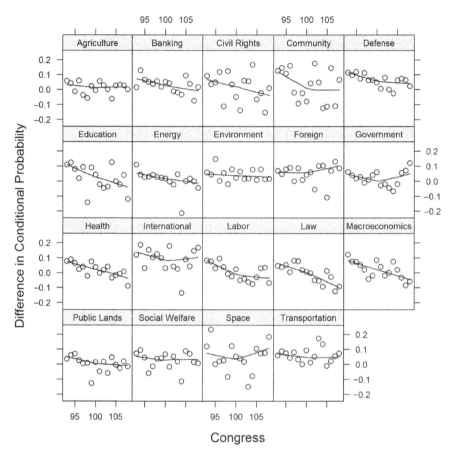

FIGURE 6.4 Difference in Conditional Probability of a Roll Call Vote (Majority-Sponsored Bills)

substantive policy disagreement. For instance, Figure 6.1 provides evidence that bipartisanship on macroeconomic policies declined over time. Figure 6.4 shows that bipartisan agenda-setting declined, even taking the level of bipartisan cosponsorship among majority-sponsored bills into consideration. Finally, some policy areas – for example, space, foreign trade, and government operations – display an upward trend in the latter part of the figure. This trend represents instances where party leaders increased the priority they placed on bipartisan legislation in the mid- to late-1990s. Consistent with the aggregate trends, the low point in bipartisan agenda-setting often occurred in the early to mid-1990s. Combined with the trends in Figure 6.1, the patterns in Figure 6.4 suggest that the degree of bipartisan agreement varies across issues, and that patterns of agenda-setting – and especially the degree to which partisan legislation replaces bipartisan legislation over time – also vary across issues.

Issue Ownership

To summarize these patterns and to identify the routes by which partisan agenda-setting plays out via certain policy areas, I consider issue ownership as one possible explanation for differences in agenda-setting across policies. In particular, I argue that if party leaders' desire to pursue partisan forms of legislation differs across issues, strategic partisan agenda-setting may be more pronounced within some issues relative to others. Gilmour (1995) suggests that strategies of disagreement are likely to be used by parties that own an issue. In contrast, "many [other] issues fail to unite the Democratic members of Congress against Republicans, and thus are not useful for partisan purposes" (Gilmour 1995, 54). While his focus on how members make strategic decisions to avoid reaching a compromise is distinct from my focus on agenda-setting, the same argument about focusing partisan politics around areas of issue ownership may apply.

The concept of issue ownership stems from findings that Americans consistently name one party as better able to handle particular issues (Petrocik 1996). For instance, the public regularly names Democrats as the party better at handling welfare, poverty, elderly issues, unemployment, education, health care, labor/jobs, environment, and Medicare/Social Security, but names Republicans as the party better at handling crime/drug abuse, moral values, foreign policy, defense, inflation, and taxation (Holian 2006; Petrocik 1996; Petrocik et al. 2003; Pope and Woon 2009). Not only does issue ownership exist among the public, but it also shapes the actions of candidates and parties in elections and in governing. In elections, each party emphasizes the issues that are advantageous to them (Petrocik et al. 2003), although there may also be reasons for candidates to trespass on another's territory in order to gain advantage (Hayes 2005). When in office, Democrats and Republicans prioritize their owned issues through lawmaking and spending (Egan 2013).

Given the presence of issue ownership and Gilmour's (1995) assertion that efforts at partisan differentiation will be highest on these issues, I expect that leadership efforts to pursue partisan legislation – when possible – will be greater in policy areas that include many places of issue ownership when compared to policy areas with little or no issue ownership. Moreover, issue ownership coincides with many of the issues that are considered part of the party policy brand, including social welfare, civil rights, labor, and macroeconomic (including tax) issues (Lawrence et al. 2006). In my theoretical framework, I suggested that, as a collective, members of the majority party seek both positional (i.e., policy) and valance (i.e., good governance) goals (Stokes 1963). The incentives to pursue positional goals may be greatest when policies are expected to divide the two parties from one another. Bringing in variation in bipartisanship by policy area and issue ownership, I expect that party leaders' efforts to pursue partisan rather than bipartisan legislation will be most pronounced among policies with a large degree of issue ownership. However, since there is no partisan advantage to be gained if the issue splits the majority party or puts individual members at electoral risk, the constraining effect of unsorted districts should also be largest on these same issues. As a result, the shift from a very bipartisan strategy during periods with few sorted districts to a partisan strategy during periods with many sorted districts may be largest for the subset of policies with a large degree of issue ownership.

Testing for Differences in Agenda-Setting Across Issues

In order to assess how strategic partisan agenda-setting plays out among policies dominated by owned versus non-owned issues, I draw on the three categories of policies discussed earlier – those with the least, medium, and most bipartisan cosponsorship. While these categories do not perfectly match to owned versus non-owned issues, this approach captures key differences across issues both in the degree of cross-party agreement on the policy and the extent of issue own- ership.[6] There are many owned issues among the least bipartisan category of policies.[7] These include the macroeconomic policies related to unemployment, inflation, and taxation (all of which have been identified as places of issue ownership – unemployment by Democrats and inflation and taxation by Republicans); social welfare policies related to welfare, poverty assistance, pro- grams for the elderly, and Social Security (all owned by Democrats); and com- munity development policies related to poverty and elderly assistance via housing programs (again owned by Democrats). Moreover, this category also includes the major topics of labor and education, both of which fall under Democratic issue ownership. In contrast, among the medium bipartisan cate- gory, only health care and law (which encompasses legislation on crime) contain policies with issue ownership, with health care falling under Democratic own- ership and crime under Republican ownership. Among the most bipartisan category, only environmental policies (owned by the Democrats), and foreign policy/defense (owned by the Republicans) fall under issue ownership. Foreign policy and defense, however, are policies that have been historically known for bipartisanship as it is often claimed that partisanship stops at the water's edge (Beinart 2008).

Using these three categories of policies, I explore whether efforts to pursue partisanship (when unconstrained by few sorted districts) are more pronounced

---

[6] The alternative approach – categorizing bills into issue ownership or not – is avoided for two reasons. First, the categories of issue ownership do not perfectly align with the major topic codes, or even sub-topic codes, in the Congressional Bills Project. Given the large number of bills in the analysis, separating bills at a more fine-grained level is prohibitively difficult. Second, differences across policy areas in the level of bipartisanship, even absent issue ownership, may affect agenda- setting strategies since places of agreement are not useful for partisan purposes (Gilmour 1995).

[7] Although ownership of an issue by the majority party will vary over time depending on which party is in the majority, I include all issues here since parties may trespass on issues (Hayes 2005) and the minority party may also call for roll call votes.

within the least bipartisan category (which aligns with the most issue owner-ship). If the insights from the issue ownership literature and Gilmour (1995) are correct, efforts by party leaders to replace bipartisan legislation with partisan legislation, and the resulting differences in the effect of bipartisan cosponsorship on legislative attention across values of the percentage of sorted districts, should be lower among the medium and most bipartisan issues when compared to the least bipartisan issues. In particular, for bills in the most bipartisan category, party leaders may nearly always advantage bipartisan legislation over partisan legislation. Since these issues reflect places of widespread agreement across the parties and relatively little issue ownership, the parties have fewer incentives to seek partisan legislation and may, instead, pursue bipartisan legislation to achieve a record of legislative success. Thus, both the effect of bipartisanship at any given point in time, as well as the degree to which the effects vary across the percentage of sorted districts (or other constraining variables) may differ across categories of issues.

Efforts to assess differences in agenda-setting between issue areas require that analyses consider the impact of sorted districts, divided government, and major-ity seat shares within each category of policies. Given the small-N in the analysis of conditional probabilities, even when focusing on policy-area Congresses, there is relatively little power to detect differences between these categories of issues. Therefore, I return to the bill-level analyses of Chapter 5 and assess the effect of bipartisan cosponsorship on legislative attention for each subset of bills – least bipartisan, medium bipartisan, and most bipartisan. Given that these models already have a number of interaction terms, I opt to model each category of issues as a subset of data, allowing effects of all independent variables to differ between categories, rather than including the categories as additional variables in the interaction. The resulting models focus on either roll call attention or floor attention (either roll call vote or passage by voice vote) as the dependent variable of interest. The primary explanatory variables of interest are the percentage of sorted districts, an indicator for divided government, and the size of the majority seat share. Each of these variables is interacted with bipartisan cosponsorship.[8] The figures below show the effect of bipartisan cosponsorship across each political context. Positive values of this effect indicate that party leaders prioritize bipartisan bills on the agenda. Negative values indicate that party leaders prioritize partisan bills on the agenda.

---

[8] The discussion below relies on the estimated effects from the models, based on bootstrapped simulations. Full model results are available in Table A6.3. Control variables include the number of cosponsors, the second session of each Congress, and whether the sponsor was on the committee of referral, chaired the committee of referral, or chaired a subcommittee of the committee of referral. The treatment effect of bipartisan cosponsorship captures the average effect of bipartisan cosponsorship (relative to partisan cosponsorship) on roll call attention (or floor attention) as the percentage of sorted districts (or divided government or the size of the majority seat share) varies.

Patterns of Agenda-Setting Across Issues

There are clear differences in roll call agenda-setting between the least, medium, and most bipartisan issue areas. Figure 6.5 presents the effect of bipartisan cosponsorship for each category of issues, beginning with the least bipartisan policies on the top row and ending with the most bipartisan policies on the bottom row. Among the least bipartisan category (i.e., those highly partisan

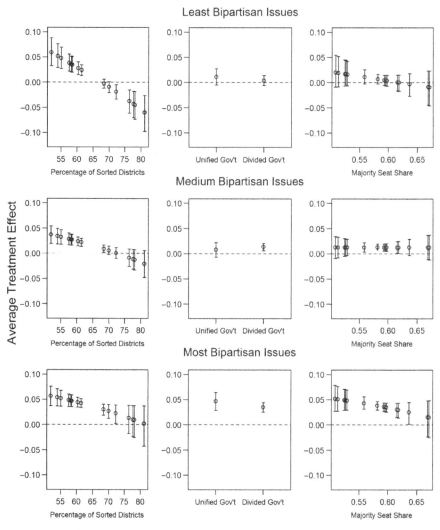

FIGURE 6.5 Effect of Bipartisan Cosponsorship on Receiving a Roll Call Vote by Policy Category

issues that are associated with issue ownership and the party brand), the effect of bipartisan cosponsorship decreases significantly when moving from low to high levels of the percentage of sorted districts. Moreover, at the highest percentage of sorted districts (e.g., the 107th and 108th Congresses in these analyses), bipartisan cosponsorship has a significant negative effect, indicating that party leaders advantage partisan legislation. Among policy areas most associated with issue ownership, party leaders were able to shift from prioritizing bipartisan bills on the agenda when they were constrained by cross-pressured members to prioritizing partisan legislation on the agenda when members' electoral and party interests aligned. While the effects of bipartisan cosponsorship are not different between unified and divided government, they trend in the expected direction across levels of the majority seat share. In neither context, however, is bipartisan legislation significantly prioritized over partisan legislation, as shown by the confidence intervals that overlap with zero.

The second row plots the effects of bipartisan cosponsorship for bills in the medium bipartisan category. Although there are still significant differences in how leaders treat bipartisan cosponsored bills across the range of sorted districts, the magnitude of the effects is smaller than in the least bipartisan category. Because the models are run on separate subsets of data, I cannot make statements about significant differences between the categories, but the results are nonetheless illuminating. The average treatment effect of bipartisan cosponsorship among the medium bipartisan issues is between half and two-thirds of the size of the effect among the least bipartisan issues. Moreover, there is never a significant negative effect of bipartisan cosponsorship among the medium bipartisan issues. This suggests that, among this category of issues, partisan legislation is never significantly prioritized over bipartisan legislation. Although the differences between the effect of bipartisan cosponsorship in unified and divided government are not significantly different, the effects show that party leaders significantly prioritize bipartisan bills over partisan bills on the roll call agenda during divided government but do not do so during unified government. These results speak to the possibility that divided government constrains party leaders.

The bottom row captures the effect of bipartisan cosponsorship among the most bipartisan category. Party leaders significantly advantage bipartisan bills over partisan bills on the agenda in nearly all political contexts. Only when the vast majority of congressional districts are sorted or the majority seat share is very large do party leaders pursue bipartisan and partisan bills at similar rates. Moreover, the effect of bipartisan cosponsorship has overlapping confidence intervals across the range of sorted districts. This is in contrast to the aggregate pattern in Chapter 5 and the pattern in Figure 6.5 for both the least and medium bipartisan categories. For policies that are most likely to garner bipartisan support, party leaders did not shift from pursuing bipartisan bills to pursuing partisan bills as more districts sorted. As in the other categories, the effects of bipartisanship are not different between unified and divided government. Among the most bipartisan policy areas where issue ownership is less frequent, party leaders typically focus their legislative attention on bipartisan bills rather than partisan bills. Even when leaders faced fewer constraints on a partisan agenda, the roll call agenda of bills on the most bipartisan issues tended to remain bipartisan.

In sum, the effects of bipartisan cosponsorship on roll call attention across policy categories suggest that there are differences in how strategic partisan agenda-setting plays out. Across the range of the percentage of sorted districts, the changing prioritization for bipartisan bills is most evident among the least bipartisan issues, consistent with the expectation that issue ownership would drive partisanship when possible. When many districts were sorted, party leaders significantly advantaged partisan legislation on the agenda. When few districts were sorted, party leaders were constrained to advantage bipartisan legislation. In contrast, among the most bipartisan policies, bipartisan legislation was almost always pursued. Even when party leaders did not advantage bipartisan legislation on the agenda in periods with well-sorted districts, they pursued bipartisan and partisan bills at similar rates.

Differences in agenda-setting between these categories of legislation translate onto the broader floor agenda as well (Figure 6.6). Here, it is important to note that the likelihood of bills passing by voice vote differs in each category. This affects whether the dependent variable is driven predominantly by roll call attention, or by both roll call and voice vote attention. Whereas the bills in the most and medium bipartisan categories may often receive voice votes, bills in the least bipartisan category rarely receive voice votes. As a result, the outcome of floor attention for the least bipartisan category will be driven by roll call votes, despite the inclusion of both roll call votes and passage by voice votes in the definition of the dependent variable. Since some legislation in this category does receive voice votes, however, and since those votes tend to be on bipartisan bills, all of the effects shift upward, reflecting greater prioritization of bipartisan legislation on the broader floor agenda.

For bills in the least bipartisan category, agenda-setting on the broader floor agenda is very similar to agenda-setting on the roll call agenda. As in Figure 6.5, the effect of bipartisan cosponsorship differs significantly across the percentage of sorted districts, but insignificantly across unified/divided government and the range of the majority seat share. When party leaders face political conditions in which there are few sorted districts, and many members are cross-pressured, they focus the floor agenda on bipartisan legislation, even in policy areas that tend to have the lowest levels of bipartisanship. In contrast, when the leaders face political conditions with many sorted districts, they focus the floor agenda on both bipartisan and partisan legislation.

Among the medium bipartisan issues, the effect of bipartisan cosponsorship on floor attention is always positive. While there are not significant differences in how leaders prioritize bipartisan legislation across the percentage of sorted districts or majority seat shares, there is a significant difference between unified and divided government. During unified government, the effect of bipartisan cosponsorship on floor attention is 0.051. During divided government, this

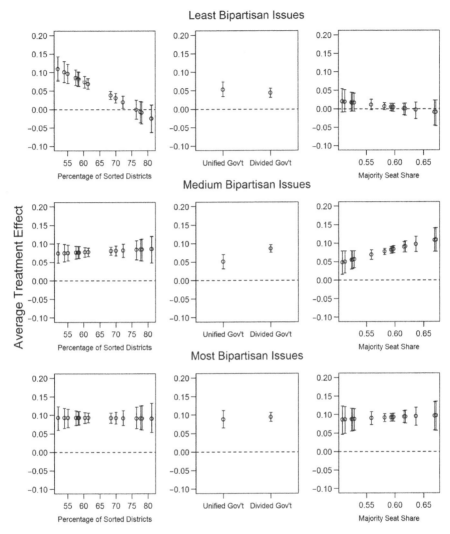

FIGURE 6.6 Effect of Bipartisan Cosponsorship on Receiving Floor Attention by Policy Category

effect increases to 0.086. This pattern suggests that when party leaders face divided government, they significantly increase their pursuit of bipartisan bills in some policy areas (i.e., ones in the medium bipartisan category) but not necessarily in other policy areas.

Among the most bipartisan issues, party leaders always prioritize bipartisan legislation over partisan legislation on the floor agenda. Here, there are no significant differences in the extent to which leaders pursue bipartisan legislation across the three political contexts examined in these analyses. This suggests that for the most bipartisan issues there have been few changes in how party leaders prioritize bipartisan and partisan legislation on the broader floor agenda across political environments.

These patterns are robust to a number of changes in model specification, including controlling for committee reporting and dropping majority seat share from the model.[9] Across specifications, among the least bipartisan issues, bipartisan cosponsorship has a positive effect when there are few sorted districts and a negative effect when there are many sorted districts. This suggests that bipartisan support for a partisan issue can kill a bill in periods when the political conditions favor partisanship. For bills on the medium bipartisan issues, this effect is dampened; for bills on the most bipartisan issues, there is never a significant negative effect of bipartisan cosponsorship. However, when controlling for committee reporting of legislation, the strongest evidence for small majority seat shares promoting bipartisanship is seen among the most bipartisan issues.

Combined, these results speak to how the aggregate patterns of agenda-setting, in which party leaders replaced bipartisan legislation with partisan legislation on the roll call agenda between the 1970s and 1990s, are driven largely by shifts within traditionally partisan areas that align with issue ownership. While party leaders significantly prioritized bipartisan legislation over partisan legislation in every category of issues when there were few sorted districts, party leaders' decision to shift from pursuing bipartisan legislation to partisan legislation when there were many sorted districts is contingent on the type of policy. One possible explanation for these differences is the extent of issue ownership. When parties seek to offer distinctive positions on these policies, they are more likely to pursue partisan legislation. In contrast, when policies reflect little issue ownership, there is not a significant shift in strategy. Returning to the opening examples, the empirical patterns suggest that as district sorting increased over time, the shift from party leaders pursuing bipartisan legislation to partisan legislation significantly changed the agenda in areas like macroeconomics, but had a much more minimal effect on the agenda in areas like surface transportation.

The results of this section indicate that some policy areas contribute more than others to the aggregate patterns of declining bipartisan agenda-setting seen in Chapters 4 and 5. Those issues that contribute the most to a shift toward partisan agenda-setting are civil rights, labor, education, social welfare, community

---

[9] Given the correlation between the percentage of sorted districts and the majority seat share, including both variables in the model yields larger confidence intervals than when majority seat share is omitted. However, the key results and patterns across the models hold even when omitting the majority seat share. For the roll call agenda, the effect of bipartisan cosponsorship shifts from significantly positive to significantly negative among both the least and the medium bipartisan issues. In contrast, bipartisan legislation is always favored among the most bipartisan issues. Moreover, for floor attention, the effects of bipartisan cosponsorship differ significantly across the percentage of sorted districts in the least bipartisan issues but do not yield significant differences among the medium or most bipartisan issues. In both of the later categories, bipartisan legislation is always favored.

development, and macroeconomics. Those issues that contribute the least (and where bipartisan agenda-setting remains) are foreign trade, agriculture, international affairs, environment, space and technology, transportation, and defense.

IMPLICATIONS OF STRATEGIC PARTISAN AGENDA-SETTING FOR ISSUE ATTENTION

The final goal of this chapter is to assess whether changes in agenda-setting result in trade-offs between issue areas that receive legislative attention. If the majority party leadership crafts a legislative strategy that focuses floor attention and roll call votes on issues that highlight partisan divisions rather than on places of bipartisan agreement, some issues may be left off the agenda.

I begin by considering the distribution of issues at two stages in the legislative process – the introduction of bills and roll call votes. The percentage of bills introduced on any given issue captures the extent of early legislative attention for that issue. Likewise, the percentage of roll call votes on an issue captures the extent of roll call voting attention to that issue.[10] Comparing the percentage of bills at each stage points to whether an issue shows up frequently in the introduction of bills but not in roll call votes, or vice versa. Although this comparison does not account for variation in external "need" for legislation on an issue (e.g., wars, recessions, etc.), variation in need should affect both the introduction of legislation and subsequent floor attention to legislation. To explore patterns of attention across early and later stages of the legislative process, I focus on the same three categories of issues used previously – those with the least, medium, and most bipartisanship.

For each Congress, the ratio between the percentage of the roll call agenda and the percentage of introduced bills that include these issues speaks to whether the roll call agenda overstates or understates attention to that set of issues relative to bill introductions. When this ratio is greater than one, bills in this category make up more of the roll call agenda than their share of introduced bills. When this ratio is less than one, bills in this category make up less of the roll call agenda than of introduced bills.

Figure 6.7 (top row) plots the ratio over time for each group. A marker line at one represents the expected ratio if leaders set the agenda randomly based on the distribution of introduced bills. For the least and medium bipartisan categories there is a slight increase in the ratio of the roll call agenda to introduced bills. Generally, the ratio for medium bipartisan bills was just under one prior to the late 1980s, and over one after the 100th Congress (1987–88). A clear decline in the ratio for the most bipartisan category is striking. Not only has this ratio

---

[10] With a few exceptions (e.g., government operations bills in the 1980s), the differences between the proportion of introduced and cosponsored bills in each policy area are slight. As a result, inferences about legislative attention are similar if introduced or cosponsored bills are used as the baseline level of attention.

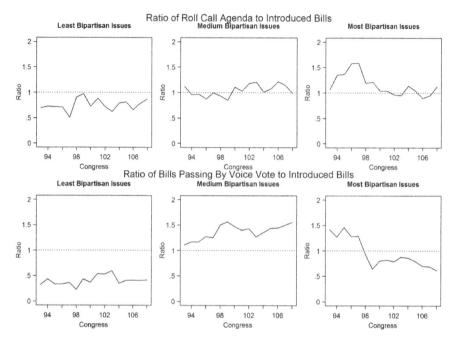

FIGURE 6.7 Ratio of Agenda Attention to Introduced Bills by Policy Category

dramatically declined since the 1970s, but the ratio moved from being substantially above one to at, or less than, one. These patterns imply that the strategic use of agenda-setting has changed the degree of attention that some issue areas receive relative to others. Issues that are likely to garner bipartisan support have changed from being overrepresented on the roll call agenda (relative to bill introductions) to being represented roughly as expected based on their share of bill introductions. In some more recent Congresses, these issues were occasionally underrepresented on the roll call agenda.

Issues on the most bipartisan policies fare no better over time in their attention via voice votes. Figure 6.7 (bottom row) replicates the previous analysis, but compares the ratio of the percentage of bills that pass the House without a roll call vote (i.e., passage with voice vote) to the percentage of bills introduced within each issue category. When this ratio is less than one, bills pass via voice vote less frequently than would be predicted by their introduction rate if selection for voice votes were random. When this ratio is more than one, bills pass via voice vote more often than would be expected if leaders selected bills randomly.

The results clearly indicate that issue attention has changed over time and is not random. Bills in the least bipartisan category never have a ratio above one, nor is there any clear trend in the ratio over time. These bills pass infrequently under voice votes, which is not surprising given their partisan nature. In contrast, bills with a medium level of bipartisanship always have a ratio greater than one, and there is a positive trend over time. Thus, this category of bills, which includes health, law, energy, government, banking, and public lands, passes via voice votes more often than would be expected by the category's frequency of bill introductions. Combined with the trend for attention in roll call votes, this result suggests that these policy areas are increasingly overrepresented on the legislative agenda (relative to bill introductions). The final panel of the figure captures the most bipartisan category, which includes foreign trade, agriculture, international affairs, environment, space and technology, transportation, and defense. This is the one category with a clear negative trend over time. The negative trend of this ratio, moving from above one until the early 1980s when it crossed to below one, suggests that the most bipartisan issues are not overwhelmingly receiving attention and passing via voice votes. Rather, party leaders increasingly left these most bipartisan issues off of both the roll call agenda (Figure 6.7 top row) and the voice vote agenda (Figure 6.7 bottom row).

A stylized exercise comparing legislative attention for bills in the most bipartisan category between the 94th and 108th Congresses reiterates this finding. Whereas the 94th Congress corresponds to the minimum percentage of sorted districts, the 108th Congress corresponds to the maximum, for the period of analysis. As a result, the 108th Congress had a much more partisan legislative agenda than the 94th. Assessing legislative attention for the most bipartisan issues if the agenda of 108th Congress were more like that of the 94th Congress is complicated by the many moving parts of the congressional process – the number of introduced bills, the size of the roll call agenda, and so forth. However, a few simple hypothetical calculations demonstrate the possible effect that a more partisan agenda might have had on attention for bills in the most bipartisan category. All other things being equal, 94 bills in the most bipartisan category would have received roll call votes in the 108th Congress if the proportion of bills introduced for the most bipartisan issues is held at the observed value for the 108th Congress (0.30), but the proportion of the roll call agenda is increased from the observed value (0.34) to that of the 94th Congress (0.36). This is six more bills than actually received roll call votes in the 108th Congress.[11] An even larger number of bills would have received attention in the 108th Congress if the relative benefit between introductions and roll call voting for the most bipartisan bills is held constant between the 94th and 108th Congresses. In this case, an additional 20 bills on bipartisan issues would have received roll call votes in the 108th Congress.[12] If the leadership's agenda in the 108th Congress were more like that of the 94th Congress, attention to the most bipartisan issues

---

[11] In the 108th Congress, 263 House bills received roll call votes. Note that this number is different from the number of roll call votes in total since a single bill may receive multiple roll call votes and not all votes occur on House bills.

[12] This calculation holds the proportion of introduced bills in the most bipartisan category constant at the observed level (0.30) and assesses the needed proportion of the roll call agenda to achieve a ratio of roll call to introduced of 1.38 (equal to that of the 94th Congress).

would also have increased among voice votes. The same calculations as those above for attention via roll call votes indicate that if the agenda of the 108th Congress were more similar to that of the 94th Congress, the number of bills on the most bipartisan issues passing the House via voice vote would have increased by somewhere between 56 and 74. This exercise shows that changes in strategic partisan agenda-setting have very real consequences for the issues that are addressed by government.[13]

CONCLUSIONS

The evidence in this chapter shows that there is variation in bipartisanship among issues and that this variation is important for understanding strategic partisan agenda-setting within and between issues. Although strategic partisan agenda-setting occurs to some extent within all categories of issues, the degree to which party leaders replace bipartisan legislation with partisan legislation varies between issues. The shift from bipartisan to partisan legislation is most pronounced in policy areas with low levels of bipartisan cosponsorship, which largely correspond to policy areas with a large degree of issue ownership. These are the policies where, when partisanship is possible, party leaders opt to pursue these bills rather than bipartisan bills. In contrast, in policy areas that have high levels of bipartisanship, the effect of bipartisan cosponsorship is not significantly different across the percentage of sorted districts. Rather, the effect of bipartisanship is positive and significant for all but the highest percentage of sorted districts. Party leaders nearly always pursue bipartisan bills in these issue areas. Together, these results suggest that the aggregate patterns of strategic partisan agenda-setting reflect some changes in the prioritization of bipartisan legislation within all issues, but that the dominant route of shifting the agenda from bipartisan to partisan legislation occurs on traditionally partisan areas associated with issue ownership and the party brand.

Issue attention has changed as a consequence of strategic partisan agenda-setting and the resulting increase in leaders' focus on partisan legislation over time. Bills in the issue areas that are the most bipartisan receive less attention over time, both in roll call votes and in voice votes. Bills in the least and medium bipartisan issue areas increasingly receive attention in roll call votes (and for medium bipartisan bills, in voice votes as well). This suggests that legislative priorities and the very issues that make up the agenda change as parties move

---

[13] For this concern to be minimized from a policymaking standpoint, we would have to assume that the introduction of bills in this category occurs significantly more often than is "necessary" and that the percentage of unnecessary bills increases over time, in which case the House is just ignoring unnecessary legislation. However, the percentage of introduced bills that fall into policy areas in the most bipartisan third of issues is relatively constant over time. In the 93rd Congress, 28 percent of introduced bills were in the most bipartisan category compared to 30 percent in the 108th Congress. The correlation between the percentage of introduced bills in the most bipartisan category and time is insignificant as well ($r = 0.32, p = 0.23$).

from an agenda-setting strategy that is constrained to be bipartisan to one where partisanship can be pursued.

Overall, the evidence presented in this chapter, along with the evidence from Chapters 2, 4, and 5, suggests that changes in agenda-setting have produced changes in the roll call vote attention given to bipartisan and partisan bills and that, to a lesser extent, these changes are also seen on the broader floor agenda. Party conflict in voting is not just driven by a lack of common ground between members of the two parties, based on ideological differences. It is also driven by an agenda-setting strategy that prioritizes partisan legislation on roll call votes. These partisan bills can help the majority pursue policy goals and party differentiation. The strategic choices that the parties make regarding the agenda, combined with the differences in bipartisanship by issue areas found in this chapter, further attest to the importance of looking beyond roll call votes in understanding party conflict in Congress. When bill cosponsorship coalitions are included, bipartisanship persists over time in the aggregate but declines in policy areas that form the basis of the party brand and issue ownership. These patterns suggest that while it is certainly the case that there have been some areas of declining bipartisan agreement, this pre-agenda decline has been magnified by the partisan agenda-setting strategy of party leaders.

The theoretical framework of strategic partisan agenda-setting has a number of important implications for democratic governance. This chapter focused on the implications of agenda-setting for policy attention. In the next chapter, I turn to the implications of my argument for representation and members' electoral interests. Does the majority party's increasing prioritization of partisan legislation result in less responsiveness to constituent preferences? If so, why do members support a legislative strategy that places them out-of-step and at risk of being voted out-of-office?

7

District Responsiveness and Member-Party Relationships

> [T]he resulting polarization is worrisome. By reducing the space for bipartisanship,
> it can condemn Congress to gridlock. By driving elected officials to the fringe while
> citizens inhabit the center, it can alienate citizens from their government.
>
> ("A Polarized Nation?" 2004)

This excerpt from a 2004 *The Washington Post* editorial captures many of the
concerns members of the public and political commentators share about party
polarization. Beyond expressing alarm about the health of the legislative process
and the risk of inaction on important policy initiatives, comments like these
focus attention on concerns about the consequences of polarization, suggesting
that elected officials are partisan and unresponsive to the public. Rising partisanship damages institutional approval (Ramirez 2009), and high levels of party
unity raise fears that elected officials fail to bend away from the party and
toward constituent interests (e.g., Hacker and Pierson 2005). As a result, there
are concerns that there may be a breakdown in representation. In particular, as
party strategies increasingly focus on partisan over bipartisan legislation in roll
call votes, members produce heavily partisan voting records regardless of the
districts they represent. This signals a decline in responsiveness. This chapter
explores the implications of partisan agenda-setting for representation, exploring potential differences in responsiveness between roll call voting and cosponsorship coalitions.[1]

Despite the large number of scholars who have directly examined representation or have considered the implications of various theories for representation,
few have looked at responsiveness across various stages of the legislative process
or taken into account how the composition of the roll call agenda affects the

---

[1] This chapter focuses primarily on the implications of strategic partisan agenda-setting for dyadic
representation, or how well the actions of an elected official correspond to the interests of his or her
constituency.

measures of representation. The shifts over time in agenda-setting documented in previous chapters suggest that roll call vote-based measures of members' responsiveness to constituent interests may have declined. Yet, given the results discussed elsewhere in this book, it may be that members have nevertheless been able to maintain a greater degree of responsiveness in their cosponsorship behavior. The independence of member behavior at this legislative stage suggests that this may be the case. For instance, Arnold (1990, 269) suggests that "The power of the electoral connection may actually be greater at earlier stages of decision making, when legislators are deciding which problems to pursue and which alternatives to consider, rather than at the final stages, when legislators are voting on particular amendments or on a bill's final passage." Members' choices when voting on bills on the floor are limited, and agenda manipulation can affect the representational relationship (Wilkerson 1990).

Given the shift from a bipartisan to a partisan roll call agenda, I expect to find that member responsiveness has declined over time in vote-based, but not cosponsorship-based, measures. Moreover, this asymmetric shift in responsiveness should correspond to the degree of partisan conflict on the roll call agenda. I also explore whether members' efforts to work across the aisle in cosponsorship coalitions have affected their electoral fortunes, particularly as their voting records have grown more partisan. This chapter examines these two issues in an effort to shed light on the implications of strategic partisan agenda-setting for representation and member-party relationships. To do so, I shift my unit of analysis from bills or votes to House members.

The findings in this chapter suggest that the change in party strategy has mixed consequences for responsiveness. Despite developing increasingly partisan voting patterns, members still maintain records of bipartisanship in cosponsorship coalitions. As a result, legislator responsiveness declines in vote-based measures of legislative partisanship but increases in cosponsorship-based measures. While these two patterns suggest that members might be electorally concerned about a partisan legislative strategy, my analyses of electoral outcomes indicate that the risk of partisanship declines as the electoral coalitions of parties sort and that members can point to their records of bipartisan cosponsorship to highlight their bipartisan behavior. As a result, members can continue to support a partisan legislative strategy while minimizing the electoral consequences. In essence, voting and cosponsorship are partially compensating vehicles for responsiveness, particularly for members in more competitive districts.

RESPONSIVENESS

Scholarly perspectives on congressional representation are quite varied. Scholars have recognized multiple representational role types – trustee, delegate, and politico (Eulau et al. 1959) – as well as various ways of achieving representation, including recruitment and electoral constraint (Mansbridge 2003; Miller and

Stokes 1963).[2] Across perspectives, political representation implies that members are "acting in the interests of the represented, in a manner responsive to them" (Pitkin 1967, 209). Within this view of the representative role, approaches to measuring responsiveness vary. Some approaches to representation focus on policy congruence (e.g., Erikson and Wright 1980; Miller and Stokes 1963), while others consider issue priorities (Sulkin 2011, 2005) or public preferences over process, bargaining, and style (Fiorina and Abrams 2009; Hibbing and Theiss-Morse 2002, 2001). Still others focus on whether legislators respond to constituent inquiries (e.g., Butler and Broockman 2011). Across these approaches, some scholars have stopped short of claiming that members are being constrained by their constituents (Achen 1978; Burden 2007), noting that the recruitment and selection of members may produce the appearance of responsiveness. Other scholars have shown that members are penalized electorally for being unresponsive (Canes-Wrone et al. 2002; Carson et al. 2010b), suggesting that constituents do constrain members and promote representation. Moreover, Sulkin (2005) finds that winning legislators take up the issues raised by their challengers, again suggesting that elections promote representation. The belief that responsiveness is an important component of democratic legitimacy unites much of this research (Pitkin 1967). Rising levels of polarization in Congress raise concerns by scholars, commentators, and members of the general public that this important component of democratic legitimacy is in peril.[3]

The actual connection between polarization and representation is unclear. Differences between Democrats and Republicans are particularly pronounced during periods of high polarization, especially when members represent safely partisan areas of the country (McCarty et al. 2006). The consequence of these differences for responsiveness is ambiguous. Partisan conflict may fulfill dyadic representation between members of Congress and same-party constituents who identify as strong partisans (Harbridge and Malhotra 2011) or among the most engaged (and partisan) segments of the public (Abramowitz 2010). But partisanship is at odds with the preferences of constituents who are weaker partisans or aligned with the opposing party. Moreover, same-party constituency preferences do not entirely account for systematic differences in Republican and Democratic legislators' voting behavior (Clinton 2006). Research has also pointed to a potential decline in responsiveness since the 1960s, with members of Congress responding little to changes in their districts' ideological preferences (Ansolabehere et al. 2000, 2001). These patterns suggest that, over time, members' increasingly partisan voting behavior reflects responsiveness to the interests

[2] While recruitment mechanisms suggest that members whose positions align with district preferences are elected, electoral constraint suggests that regardless of members' own positions, they act in the interests of their constituents in order to be reelected.

[3] These normative concerns over increasing polarization in Congress reflect assumptions that much of the public lacks coherent political ideologies that align with one party (e.g., Converse 1964; Zaller 1992), and that where they do hold positions, the public has more moderate preferences than party elites.

of the most engaged partisans in their district (of their own party), but less responsiveness to constituent interests more broadly (particularly if a district is competitive between the two parties).

The approach to understanding representation in this chapter focuses primarily on characterizing legislative behavior as either bipartisan or partisan, which includes elements of policy, process, and what Eulau and Karps (1977) term symbolic responsiveness. The characterization of legislator behavior as bipartisan or partisan speaks to the policy positions that members hold, the types of legislation they support, and the people who join their coalitions, even if this characterization does not directly assess congruence between legislators and constituents on particular policies. Differences in the degree of bipartisanship or partisanship by members also speak to their willingness to work across the aisle. Finally, building a record of bipartisan coalitions in both voting and cosponsorship can provide the "public gestures that create a sense of trust and support in the relationship between the representative and represented" (Eulau and Karps 1977, 241), particularly for members in more competitive districts.

On the bipartisan–partisan spectrum, I argue that responsiveness is greater when members representing very competitive and very safe districts engage in substantially different levels of bipartisanship. If members of the same party who represent very different types of districts engage in similar or indistinguishable behaviors, then they are not being responsive to their geographic constituencies. This argument is based on the assumption that competitive districts, on average, favor greater bipartisanship, while safely partisan districts favor less bipartisanship (and greater partisanship). Whereas competitive districts are more likely to include a large mix of voters from both parties as well as independents, safely partisan districts are more likely to be dominated by voters who align with one party.

The assumption that voters' party identification aligns with desires for partisanship by members is supported at an individual level by experimental work on evaluations of members' voting behavior. For example, Harbridge and Malhotra (2011) find that weak partisans and independents approve of members more when they engage in bipartisanship, while strong partisans approve of members less when they engage in bipartisanship. The desire for bipartisanship is particularly strong when voters evaluate members of the opposing party (Wolack 2010). In general, if members exhibit behaviors that are too partisan for their district, they risk electoral defeat (Carson et al. 2010b). Moreover, members in competitive districts may be more concerned with district interests than members in safe districts (Eulau et al. 1959, 753), further encouraging bipartisanship as a means of responsiveness. Characterizing legislators as being responsive to co-partisans or to broader district preferences on the basis of their partisanship (at least for members in more competitive districts) necessarily simplifies both the preferences of constituents and the complexities of representation, but it emphasizes key dynamics and differences across time and across individuals.

This chapter works from the premise that the desire for bipartisanship versus partisanship varies across districts, and that this variation is related to the degree of partisan alignment between constituents and their representative. Because I lack a direct measure of preferences for bipartisan cooperation at the district level, I follow other scholars in focusing on presidential voting patterns in the public as a proxy for these preferences. Though imperfect as a measure of district preferences (see Kernell 2009), they capture pertinent information about the voting patterns and partisan alignment of the district. The metric of district preferences – the normal presidential vote – measures the average two-party vote share for the party of the representative in the previous two election cycles. Using two elections downplays the influence of any single landslide election. Given the frequency of presidential elections, this measure typically changes every four years. For instance, the normal presidential vote for members in both the 105th (1997–98) and the 106th Congress (1999–2000) are both based on the votes in the 1996 and 1992 presidential elections. However, when redistricting occurs (e.g., before the 108th Congress (2003–04)), the normal presidential vote in the following Congress is adjusted for the most recent election, allowing the normal presidential vote to vary more frequently.[4] When members represent sorted or safe districts with many co-partisans in their constituency, then they can engage in partisanship while still maintaining responsiveness. However, when members represent unsorted or competitive districts, then responsiveness may require greater bipartisanship. That is, partisanship by the member is less likely to alienate large portions of the district when the normal presidential vote highly favors his party compared to a district whose voting patterns are more evenly split.

Cosponsorship Patterns by Members

Before examining the implications of strategic partisan agenda-setting for member responsiveness in voting versus cosponsorship coalitions, I briefly demonstrate how members' legislative behavior can be captured by their cosponsorship behaviors, and that these, in turn, are generally associated with their district preferences. A relationship between members' voting patterns – whether characterized as ideological or partisan – and district preferences has been shown by other scholars (Canes-Wrone et al. 2002; Carson et al. 2010b). The relationship between legislative behavior and district preferences is less well established for cosponsorship coalitions.

Although some scholars use cosponsorship data to directly estimate members' ideological positions (Aleman et al. 2009; Talbert and Potoski 2002), others have urged caution against applying standard techniques of ideal point estimation to cosponsorship because of a lack of information about the underlying

---

[4] All findings presented in this chapter are similar if the normal presidential vote is based on one election cycle or one past and one future election cycle for districts with substantial redistricting.

data-generation process and the resulting ambiguity in how to treat those members who do not cosponsor a particular bill (Desposato et al. 2011). I avoid this issue by continuing with the focus on bipartisanship used throughout this book, characterizing members' behavior as largely bipartisan or partisan rather than developing an ideal point estimate of ideology. This approach allows me to look at the proactive actions of members in cosponsoring legislation. In particular, I assess the bipartisanship of members by the frequency with which they join bipartisan cosponsorship coalitions, regardless of whether they are from the party of the sponsor or not.[5] Since I am interested in the record that members produce through their cosponsorship, only those bills that they cosponsor are relevant. As with the previous chapters, I omit non-cosponsored bills from the analysis since they are not informative about the coalitions formed by members from the perspective of voters or from an empirical standpoint. As noted by Sulkin (2005, 96), the vulnerability of members is more likely to affect the content of legislative behavior than it is the volume of activity. Since I have no a priori expectations about whether members who engage in more or less cosponsorship in total will be more or less responsive, I focus on the relative frequency of bipartisan and partisan cosponsorship, rather than the frequency of cosponsorship.[6]

Table 7.1 provides general descriptive information on how often members engage in bipartisan cosponsorship.[7] The table lists the members associated with the minimum, mean, and maximum levels of bipartisan cosponsorship in each Congress of my analysis (93rd–108th). In all cases, bipartisan cosponsorship refers to cosponsoring a bill where at least 20 percent of the cosponsors are from the party opposite the party of the sponsor (the same measure used to capture bipartisan coalitions in earlier chapters). For each member, I calculate the percentage of bills that a member cosponsors that are bipartisan;

---

[5] While there could be variation across members in their opportunities to join bipartisan coalitions – with members in cross-party delegations, regions with more members from both parties, and entering classes of Congress that were more mixed between parties having more "natural" opportunities for bipartisan coalitions – the full list of reasons why members join cosponsorship coalitions is beyond the scope of this analysis. Moreover, regardless of why members cosponsor with particular groups, it still builds a record that members can point to, which is the focus of this chapter. In particular, I am interested in whether this record is bipartisan or partisan.

[6] Overall, there is a positive correlation between the normal presidential vote and the frequency of cosponsorship ($r = 0.19$, $p < 0.001$). However, when calculated by Congress and by party, this correlation ranges from 0.06 to 0.42 among Democrats but from –0.29 and –0.04 among Republicans. Whereas Democrats in safely partisan districts cosponsor more frequently, Republicans in more competitive districts cosponsor more frequently. Even with these correlations, however, I have no a priori reasons that members who cosponsor more or less frequently will be more responsiveness to constituent preferences. While members who cosponsor less may be more purposeful in building a record of bipartisanship, this need not be the case. Regardless of whether members join many or few cosponsorship coalitions, the key feature for this chapter is the record they produce in terms of bipartisanship.

[7] Summary statistics for the frequency of cosponsorship by members are presented in Table A7.1.

TABLE 7.1 *Summary Statistics of Bipartisan Cosponsorship by Members*

Congress	Minimum Bipartisanship	Mean Bipartisanship	Maximum Bipartisanship
93	20.0%	66.9%	100%
	P. Burton (D-CA)	G. Davis (R-WI)	J. Jarman (D-OK)
94	13.3	53.8	100
	W. Randall (D-MO)	E. Jones (D-TN)	S. Hall (D-TX)
95	0.00	63.8	96.2
	J. Young (D-TX)	J. Hightower (D-TX)	C. Wylie (R-OH)
96	23.6	69.6	93.5
	B. Stewart (D-IL)	C. Zablocki (D-WI)	J. Hammerschmidt (R-AR)
97	38.1	77.8	97.9
	P. Burton (D-CA)	P. McCloskey (R-CA)	L. Fountain (D-NC)
98	15.4	64.2	95.7
	P. Burton (D-CA)	J. Jeffords (R-VT)	W. Broomfield (R-MI)
99	26.8	64.1	91.8
	A. Wheat (D-MO)	F. Sensenbrenner (R-WI)	M. Snyder (R-KY)
100	29.9	64.7	93.2
	R. Dellums (D-CA)	R. Smith (R-OR)	B. Shuster (R-PA)
101	34.5	65.4	94.5
	W. Clay (D-MO)	D. Bosco (D-CA)	J. Whitten (D-MO)
102	22.6	60.5	95.3
	M. Waters (D-CA)	D. Rostenkowski (D-IL)	B. Shuster (R-PA)
103	16.1	56.3	87.7
	X. Becerra (D-CA)	J. Bachus (R-AL)	J. Tanner (D-TN)
104	22.4	56.7	87.9
	R. Armey (R-TX)	G. Studds (D-MA)	C. Edwards (D-TX)
105	28.9	56.4	87.7
	R. Armey (R-TX)	J. Moran (D-VA)	L. Hamilton (D-IN)
106	30.9	60.5	83.3
	M. Waters (D-CA)	W. Pascrell (D-NJ)	R. Frelinghuysen (R-NJ)
107	26.1	58.6	87.7
	R. Gephardt (D-MO)	V. Hilleary (R-TN)	D. Sherwood (R-PA)
108	26.5	55.6	84.8
	B. Lee (D-CA)	D. Rohrabacher (R-CA)	B. Young (R-FL)

the remainders are classified as partisan. The data suggest that there has been a slight decline in both the mean and maximum levels of bipartisanship, but that the average member engages in bipartisanship more than half of the time.

A cursory glance at Table 7.1 suggests that district preferences may be an important factor in understanding members' use of bipartisan cooperation. For instance, in the 108th Congress, Representative Barbara Lee (D-CA) is at the lower tail of bipartisanship. Her highly partisan behavior makes sense given her district: she represents the Berkeley and Oakland areas of California, a highly Democratic area. In contrast, Representative Bill Young (R-FL), the member at the top end of the distribution of bipartisanship, represents the St. Petersburg area of Florida, which is a much more competitive area at the national level between Democrats and Republicans. A significant relationship between the normal presidential vote and members' bipartisan cosponsorship behavior, both in general and within a member's record as the normal presidential vote in his district changes, captures this pattern more systematically (Harbridge and Malhotra 2011).[8] For instance, bipartisan cosponsorship increases by 6.1 percentage points between a competitive district with a normal presidential vote near 50 percent and a more safe district with a normal presidential at 60 percent (Harbridge and Malhotra 2011, 498–9). This relationship suggests that bipartisan cosponsorship during these Congresses is related to district preferences.

Responsiveness by Members Over Time: Roll Call Voting and Bill Cosponsorship

Since bipartisan cosponsorship behavior appears related to district preferences in general, the next step is to assess district responsiveness over time and across measures. To better understand the implications of partisan agenda-setting for representation, I focus primarily on two summary measures of member behavior as bipartisan or partisan – one from roll call behavior (party unity support scores) and one from bill cosponsorship behavior (bipartisan cosponsorship). For the vote-based measure, greater bipartisanship reflects votes by a member against the majority of his party on party unity votes, while greater partisanship reflects votes with his party. Party unity support scores capture the frequency of members voting with their party on these party unity votes. I also consider the frequency of members voting with their party on party unity votes relative to all votes cast, to account for the frequency of party unity votes across time. Even though the standard party unity support score does not capture the frequency of partisan bills on the agenda, it is one of the more visible measures of legislative behavior to constituents, advertised both by interest groups and challengers.[9] The extremity of members' DW-NOMINATE score offers an additional measure of vote-based partisanship. For the cosponsorship-based measure, greater bipartisanship reflects cosponsoring bills with mixed coalitions of Democrats and Republicans, while greater partisanship reflects joining coalitions of predominantly same-party members. Both the vote and cosponsorship-based measures capture important aspects of responsiveness.

---

[8] Harbridge and Malhotra (2011) examine this relationship between the 103rd and 109th Congresses.

[9] For instance, in the 2008 Senate race, Elizabeth Dole (R-NC) was criticized in an ad by the Democratic Senatorial Campaign Committee for voting with President Bush 92 percent of the time (2008).

For both types of measures, variation within parties is critical for evaluating responsiveness. As noted by other scholars (e.g., Burden 2007, 32), variables like the normal presidential vote may increasingly explain much of the difference in voting patterns *between* parties, but does less to explain variation *within* parties. This may be particularly true if Democrats work (and vote) only with Democrats, and Republicans work (and vote) only with Republicans. Since my interest in responsiveness stems from an effort to understand the consequences of strategic partisan agenda-setting and whether members are put at risk by a partisan strategy, I am concerned with whether members appear too partisan for their district, not simply whether Democrats and Republicans behave differently from one another. As a result, I focus on member behavior on a scale of bipartisan to partisan that captures variation across members, including within-party variation.

In terms of electoral responsiveness, members in competitive districts should have lower party unity support scores than members in safe districts. Since larger values of all of these measures reflect greater partisanship, the relationship between these measures and the normal presidential vote should be positive. When members' legislative behavior is captured by their cosponsorship behavior, the expectation is that members in more competitive districts will engage in greater bipartisanship, while members in safely partisan districts will engage in less bipartisanship. The relationship between bipartisan cosponsorship and the normal presidential vote should be negative.

Since party leaders have shifted from prioritizing bipartisan bills on the roll call agenda to prioritizing partisan bills, I expect that members' roll call records should also show increasing partisanship over time. This increasing partisanship reflects a lack of responsiveness if members from all types of districts engage in high levels of partisanship. The same decline in responsiveness need not be true in members' cosponsorship coalitions. As a result, members who appear out-of-step in their voting patterns may appear more in-step in their cosponsorship coalitions. The impression that constituents have of their members may be different depending on whether they hear about their voting or cosponsorship records.

Consider the example of Representative Marge Roukema, a Republican who represented northern New Jersey for over 20 years. Between the 104th and 107th Congresses (1995–2002), when she was in the majority party, Roukema's party unity support score increased from 70 percent to 83 percent. Likewise, her DW-NOMINATE score (capturing her estimated ideological position on a liberal to conservative scale ranging from −1 to 1) increased from 0.17 to 0.20. While these metrics still make her more of a moderate than many of her Republican colleagues, they nonetheless paint a picture of a member who became increasingly partisan over time. The normal Republican presidential vote in her district, however, decreased from 63 percent to 53 percent over this same period, suggesting that her district became more competitive between the two parties and that her constituents were less heavily aligned with the

Republican Party. By vote-based measures, Roukema appears increasingly out-of-step with her district, becoming more partisan as the district became less heavily Republican. Her bill cosponsorship coalitions, however, paint a different picture. Between the 104th and 107th Congresses, the percentage of Roukema's cosponsorship coalitions that were bipartisan increased from 55 percent to 71 percent, pointing to changing behavior that aligned with changes in district preferences, suggesting greater responsiveness.

Similar differences in responsiveness arise among members who served across the earlier period of increasingly partisan floor strategies. For instance, the voting record of Democrat Jack Brooks, who represented the 9th district of Texas from 1967 to 1994, grew increasingly partisan during this period. From 1973 (when my data collection began) until the end of his tenure, the normal presidential vote in his district averaged 51 percent, ranging from 49 percent in the period from 1975 to 1976, to 55 percent in the period from 1981 to 1984, before declining again. However, his party unity support score increased from roughly 70 percent to 90 percent over the same period. Weighting this measure by the percentage of party unity votes in each year yields similarly large increases in partisanship. Party support on this metric increased from 25 percent to 54 percent. Likewise, Brook's DW-NOMINATE score became somewhat more liberal, moving from –0.36 in the 93rd Congress to –0.43 in the 103rd Congress. These vote-based measures suggest that this long-serving member became increasingly partisan and more liberal, despite the fact that he represented a fairly competitive district between the two parties at the national level. However, Brook's cosponsorship record suggests a greater degree of bipartisanship than his voting record. Between the 93rd and 103rd Congresses, the average percentage of Brook's cosponsored bills that were bipartisan was 63 percent. Although the number varies from year to year, there is no downward trend over time that would suggest he was becoming more partisan or less responsive to district interests. In both the 93rd and 103rd Congress, 68 percent of his cosponsored bills had bipartisan coalitions.

These examples highlight two important issues. First, at any given point in time, vote-based measures of behavior for a member may point to high levels of *partisanship* that obscure the relatively high levels of *bipartisanship* that are found in bill cosponsorship coalitions. Second, vote-based measures may show increasing partisanship over time even if district preferences remain fairly constant or become more evenly split between the two parties. However, including cosponsorship measures of legislator behavior often tempers any conclusions about a member becoming increasingly partisan and out-of-step with his district. Members who are responsive to only co-partisans in voting (i.e., engaging in relatively high levels of partisanship) may demonstrate greater responsiveness to their broader constituencies in cosponsorship. In order to assess whether these examples are illustrative of systematic patterns, I now turn to evaluations of responsiveness over time, using both voting and cosponsorship measures of legislative behavior. I begin by looking at patterns of responsiveness over time, and then connect those patterns to changes in agenda-setting.

The correlation between legislative behavior and district preferences provides a simple exploration of whether or not responsiveness has changed over time. Although the correlational measure is not ideal for capturing all facets of representation (Achen 1978), it provides a first step toward assessing overall levels of responsiveness (Converse and Pierce 1986, 507–11; Wright 2007, 264). The correlation between the normal presidential vote in the district and cosponsorship or vote-based measures of legislative behavior suggests evidence of changes in representation over time (see Table 7.2).

While all of the measures of legislative behavior are correlated with the normal presidential vote, the magnitude of these correlations changes over time. Although initially exhibiting a relatively strong correlation with the normal vote, party unity support scores show a weakening relationship from the 96th to 102nd Congresses. This is precisely the period in which party strategies changed from prioritizing bipartisan bills to prioritizing partisan bills on the roll call agenda. A similar pattern is seen if party unity votes are measured relative to all

TABLE 7.2 *Correlations of Legislative Behavior and the Normal Presidential Vote*

Congress	Bipartisan Cosponsorship	Party Unity Support Score	Percent Party Unity Votes Out of All Votes	Absolute Value of DW-NOMINATE
93	0.022	0.441	0.385	0.384
94	0.108	0.444	0.389	0.361
95	0.005	0.452	0.366	0.402
96	−0.170	0.409	0.338	0.415
97	−0.223	0.268	0.178	0.431
98	0.016	0.148	0.096	0.411
99	0.049	0.110	0.076	0.459
100	0.082	0.086	0.075	0.463
101	−0.167	0.153	0.097	0.543
102	−0.161	0.293	0.102	0.547
103	−0.544	0.443	0.325	0.589
104	−0.425	0.416	0.248	0.481
105	−0.549	0.363	0.148	0.429
106	−0.651	0.396	0.286	0.398
107	−0.631	0.362	0.190	0.449
108	−0.605	0.394	0.197	0.373

Note: Bipartisan cosponsorship measures the percentage of bills that a member cosponsored where the bill had at least 20% of the cosponsors from the party opposite the party of the bill's sponsor. Party unity support scores measure the percentage of party unity votes on which a member voted with the majority of their party. The percentage of party unity votes (out of all votes) measures the percentage of votes a member cast in which he or she voted with a majority of their party against a majority of the other party. The absolute value of DW-NOMINATE measures the extremity of the ideal point estimate.

of a member's votes. Although the timing is somewhat different, the correlation between the normal presidential vote and the absolute value of members' DW-NOMINATE scores declines slightly from the 103rd to 108th Congresses. In contrast, the bipartisan cosponsorship measure shows little to no relationship with the normal presidential vote for the first part of the series, but a growing correlation from the 101st Congress on. Since the 103rd Congress, the correlation between the normal vote and members' bill cosponsorship coalitions has generally been larger in magnitude than the correlation between the normal vote and members' party unity support scores. Combined, these patterns offer suggestive evidence that between the 93rd and 108th Congresses, members exhibited declining responsiveness in voting but increasing responsiveness in cosponsorship coalitions.

Moreover, these patterns suggest that, in the early period of analysis, members did not have to rely on cosponsorship to differentiate themselves, as voting already did this. In the more recent period, members may have used cosponsorship to differentiate themselves and compensate for partisan voting records. The anecdotes in the introductory chapter about members referencing bipartisan cosponsorship in newsletters and in their communication with local newspapers reinforce this contention. In recent years, members have continued to reference their patterns of cosponsorship, emphasizing places of bipartisanship. For example, a 2004 newsletter by Representative John Kline (MN-2) discussed four bills he cosponsored (Kline 2004). Similarly, in his response to the *Chicago Tribune* editorial board in 2010, Representative Dan Lipinski (IL-3) noted that he is a "proud cosponsor of the bipartisan Currency Reform for Fair Trade Act, H.R. 2378, which would require the administration to impose countervailing or antidumping duties on goods from nations that undervalue their currency" (Lipinski 2010).

While suggestive of a changing degree of member responsiveness between voting and cosponsorship coalitions, the correlation measures fail to explain *how* members' behavior changed over time. In particular, they miss whether the changes over time reflect all members becoming more partisan (i.e., an intercept shift), members in competitive and safe districts behaving in more similar ways over time (i.e., a slope shift), or both. In order to capture these changes in responsiveness, an approach that considers the distribution of members' bipartisanship both within and between Congresses is needed.

By examining members' legislative records as a function of district preferences, and allowing this relationship to vary in each Congress, I capture whether members in competitive districts behave similarly to or differently from members in very safe districts. The dependent variable of these analyses captures the likelihood that a member engages in partisan (or bipartisan) behavior.[10] I use a binomial model rather than a linear model to include the number of votes or total cosponsorship coalitions in the analysis. When members participate in very

---

[10] More details on the model and the complete regression results are included in the Appendix.

few votes or cosponsorship coalitions, I want to make only limited inferences about their record of bipartisanship. The resulting dependent variable is made up of two components – the number of "successes" and the number of "failures." In the case of party unity support scores, votes with the party are defined as "successes" and votes against the majority of the party are defined as "failures." In contrast, in the case of bipartisan cosponsorship, bipartisan cosponsorship coalitions are defined as "successes" and partisan cosponsorship coalitions are defined as "failures." Thus, the expected effect of district preferences is in the opposite direction for models of voting and cosponsorship behavior.

The primary independent variable in this model is the normal presidential vote in the district. This effect, as well as the intercept, varies by Congress. Allowing the effect of the normal presidential vote to vary by Congress lets me capture whether members in both competitive and safe districts behave more similarly over time. Allowing the intercept to vary by Congress enables me to capture whether all members have, on average, become more partisan over time. Finally, I include a number of individual-level covariates – member of the majority party, gender, age, tenure, and whether the member holds a leadership post (Speaker, Majority or Minority Leader, or Whip) – as control variables. For each of these control variables, the effects are constrained to be constant across time.

The predicted probability of partisan voting (or bipartisan cosponsorship) over the range of the normal presidential vote for each Congress captures the degree of responsiveness over time. When members are relatively responsive to constituent preferences, members in districts with low levels of the normal presidential vote should behave very differently from members in districts with high levels of the normal presidential vote. The extent of this responsiveness is captured by the slope of each line. The intercept of each line (i.e., the predicted behavior for members with the lowest normal vote) captures the extent to which members engage in partisanship (or bipartisanship) when they represent the most competitive districts.

The results yield a striking asymmetry. Figure 7.1(a) presents the predicted probability of a member voting with his party on party unity votes for each Congress in the analysis. Over time, the intercept shifts upward, reflecting greater party support, and the slope decreases, with the flattest line occurring around the 101st Congress. These patterns suggest that regardless of district preferences, members became increasingly partisan over time. Members in even the most competitive districts were increasingly likely to vote with their party, and members in competitive and safe districts had increasingly similar voting patterns to one another (see Table A7.2 for full model results). These patterns further suggest that members' responsiveness has declined; members increasingly represented co-partisans rather than their broader district.

Members' bill cosponsorship behavior shows a different pattern. Figure 7.1(b) presents the predicted probability of joining a bipartisan cosponsorship coalition for the same set of Congresses. As expected, the slope of the line is in the opposite direction than in the previous figure, since the analysis looks at bipartisanship (rather than partisanship). More important, however, is the pattern of responsiveness over time. Here, the intercept changes little over time and the slope shows increasing steepness, suggesting greater differentiation across types of districts. This figure shows that not only have members representing competitive and safely partisan districts become more distinct from one another over time, but members in competitive districts continue to engage in very high levels of bipartisanship. Both patterns speak to increased responsiveness at the cosponsorship level.

The asymmetries of these patterns suggest that whereas members' responsiveness to their districts declined in the roll call-based measure, their responsiveness increased over time in the bill cosponsorship-based measure.[11] I note that these patterns hold even when I look at the raw data on member behavior, without any additional control variables or assumptions about modeling. There is a general decline in responsiveness for party unity voting and an increase in responsiveness for cosponsorship behavior, with the timing of increasing responsiveness in cosponsorship occurring when the roll call agenda became increasingly partisan. Members of Congress may have realized that their roll call behavior placed them out-of-step with their districts, potentially because of the types of bills that were selected to face roll call votes, and thus turned to other forms of legislative behavior to show their responsiveness.

Not only do patterns of responsiveness change over time within voting, but these changes are closely related to the content of the roll call agenda. Although the extent of partisan agenda-setting is correlated with time, the partisanship of the agenda did not change linearly. Rather, leaders shifted the agenda from highly bipartisan in the 1970s to highly partisan in the mid-1990s and then returned to crafting a somewhat more bipartisan agenda before pursuing partisan legislation again. Systematic analysis of responsiveness as a function of the extent of partisan agenda-setting affirms that agenda-setting has implications for representation, and that there are asymmetric patterns for vote and cosponsorship-based behaviors. Focusing again on the dependent variable as either voting with one's party on party unity votes or joining bipartisan cosponsorship coalitions, I allow the effect of the normal presidential vote to vary with the percentage of party unity votes in a given Congress. The later measure captures the degree of partisan agenda-setting. For ease of interpretation, the effects of the normal vote across the observed values of party unity voting are presented in Figure 7.2, with full model results presented in Table A7.3.[12]

---

[11] These results are robust to measuring district preferences by the normalized presidential vote, which captures district voting relative to the national average, adjusting the normal vote for redistricting, and to using either the 30 percent or 40 percent thresholds for bipartisan cosponsorship.

[12] Since the resulting interaction is between a member-Congress-level variable (normal presidential vote) and a Congress-level variable (percentage of party unity votes), a multi-level model captures

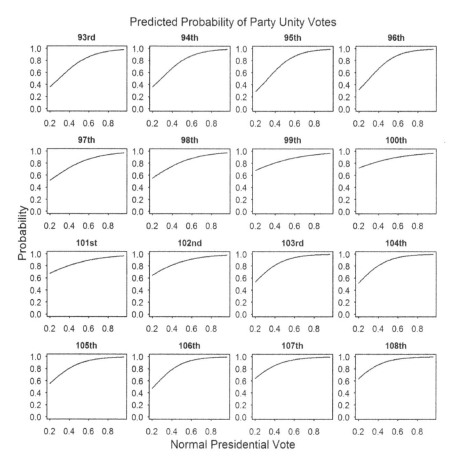

FIGURE 7.1(A) Predicted Probability of Legislative Behavior
Note: For panel (a), representing voting behavior, the y-axis is the predicted probability of voting with a majority of one's party on party unity votes. For panel (b), representing cosponsorship behavior, the y-axis is the predicted probability of joining as a cosponsor on a bipartisan bill. Full regression models available in Table A7.2.

Figure 7.2 summarizes the patterns of responsiveness somewhat differently than Figure 7.1. Whereas the predicted probabilities displayed in Figure 7.1 speak to how members' behavior changes with the normal presidential vote in the district, those depicted in Figure 7.2 show how the effect of the normal presidential vote on members' behavior changes with the extent of partisan

the nested structure of the data (see Appendix for more details). The resulting estimated effects come from bootstrapping the model, drawing 1,000 samples of the data, and allowing the values of the normal vote and the frequency of party unity voting in each Congress to vary in the model predictions.

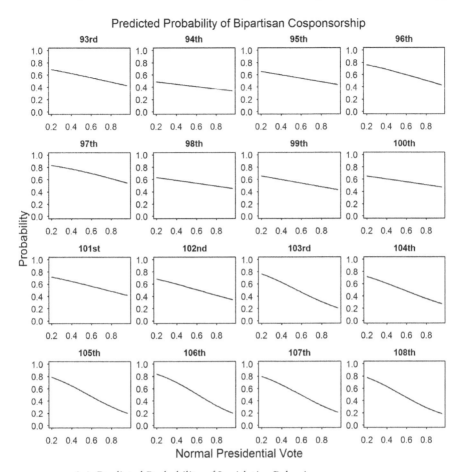

FIGURE 7.1(B) Predicted Probability of Legislative Behavior

agenda-setting. Figure 7.2 plots the average effect of moving from one standard deviation below the mean in the normal presidential vote to one standard deviation above the mean.[13] This effect captures whether members in competitive districts behave differently than members in safe districts. Given the previous patterns of responsiveness, as the percentage of party unity votes in Congress increases, I expect the effect of the normal presidential vote to decline in magnitude for voting but to increase in magnitude for cosponsorship coalitions.

The left-hand side of Figure 7.2, which captures members' voting behavior, shows that the effect of the normal presidential vote declines in magnitude by

[13] The mean value of the normal presidential vote is 55.3 and the standard deviation is 11.3.

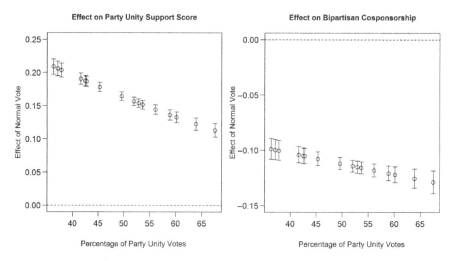

FIGURE 7.2 Member Responsiveness Varies Across the Extent of Partisan Agenda-Setting
Note: Average effect of moving from one standard deviation below the mean of the normal presidential vote to one standard deviation above the mean. Full regression models are available in Table A7.3.

nearly 50 percent as the percentage of party unity votes in Congress increases. The positive effect indicates that members in more safely partisan districts engage in more partisan voting. However, the declining magnitude of the effect indicates that the difference in voting behavior between members in more competitive and safer districts is smaller when there are many partisan roll call votes compared to periods when there are few.

In contrast, the right-hand side of the figure, which captures members' cosponsorship behavior, shows that the effect of the normal presidential vote grows in magnitude as the percentage of party unity votes in Congress increases. Here, the negative effect indicates that members in more safely partisan districts engage in less bipartisanship. As party leaders increasingly focused the roll call agenda on partisan legislation, members' voting became less responsive to district preferences and their cosponsorship records became more responsive to district preferences. These results suggest that House members increasingly represent co-partisans in their voting regardless of the type of district they represent. Members' cosponsorship behavior reveals much greater potential for representation of the interests of their broader constituency.

This shift toward members responding to co-partisans in their voting patterns is visible in a plot of the legislative behavior of Democratic and Republican members across Congresses. At both the national and state levels, vastly different voting records from members of different parties who represent similar types of districts indicate partisan polarization (McCarty et al. 2009; Shor and

McCarty 2011). For a fixed level of Democratic presidential support, differences in the behavior of Democrats and Republicans, each engaging in partisanship on their side of the aisle, may produce a disconnect in representation. In this case, differences between members of the two parties are of interest, rather than differences across members, irrespective of party.

This analysis of responsiveness shifts the measure of district preferences from the normal presidential vote to the normal *Democratic* presidential vote, and assesses district preferences relative to actions by members in support of the Democratic position. For voting, the percentage of party unity votes on which a member takes the Democratic position captures his legislative behavior.[14] For cosponsorship, the percentage of bills a member cosponsors where the original sponsor was a Democrat captures his legislative behavior. In both cases, higher values reflect greater consistency in taking the Democratic position. For each Congress, panel (a) of Figure 7.3 plots the relationship between district preferences and Democratic positions on party unity votes, while panel (b) plots the relationship for cosponsoring Democratic bills. In each plot, dark gray "D's" denote Democrats and lighter gray "R's" denote Republicans. While voting and cosponsorship measures are not directly comparable, the patterns over time within each measure are illuminating.

Voting patterns point to increasing partisanship and responsiveness to co-partisans rather than to the broader district. In the 1970s, there was substantial overlap between the voting patterns of Democratic and Republican members who represented fairly competitive districts (measured as those with a normal Democratic vote around 0.50). While variation occurred in members' voting patterns and Democrats tended to vote more often with Democrats than Republican members did, there was quite a bit of overlap between members of the two parties during this period. This overlap suggests that members from both parties responded in similar ways to their constituents. In contrast, there was essentially no overlap in voting after the 102nd Congress (1991–92). By the 105th Congress (1997–98), a large number of Democrats voted with their party (and against the other party) over 80 percent of the time, regardless of the type of district they represented. Republicans rarely voted with the Democratic Party more than 20 percent of the time. During the most recent Congresses, there was no overlap between the voting behavior of Democrats and Republicans.[15]

While the cosponsorship measure also shows growing partisan differentiation, the gap between Democrats and Republicans is never as stark as in their voting behavior. On average, Democrats were more likely to cosponsor Democratic sponsored bills than were Republicans at all levels of the normal

---

[14] For Democrats, this number is equal to the party unity support score. For Republican members, this number is equal to 100 percent minus the party unity support score.

[15] Not surprisingly, there is greater variation in most Congresses among Democratic members than among Republican members, consistent with findings about the heterogeneity of Democratic districts and members (Erikson and Wright 2005).

Roll Call Voting

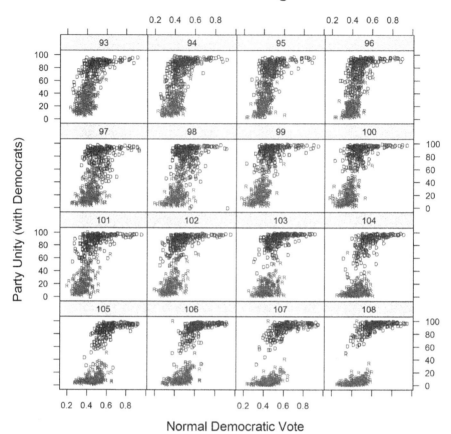

FIGURE 7.3(A) Differences in Legislative Behavior for Democrats and Republicans
Note: In panel (a), which captures voting behavior, the y-axis measures the percentage of party unity votes where the member votes with a majority of the Democratic Party. In panel (b), which captures cosponsorship behavior, the y-axis measures the percentage of cosponsorship coalitions a member joined where the bill sponsor was a Democrat. The x-axis measures the average two-party vote share for the Democratic presidential candidate in each district.

Democratic vote. Even though the extent of overlap between the cosponsorship records of Democrats and Republicans declined over time, some overlap in their behavior remained in the 1990s and 2000s. For instance, in the 104th Congress (1995–96), there were a number of Democrats and Republicans representing districts with a Democratic presidential vote near 0.50 who regularly cosponsored bills sponsored by Democrats (roughly 40 percent for members of both parties). While these patterns certainly show partisan differences in behavior, as

Cosponsorship

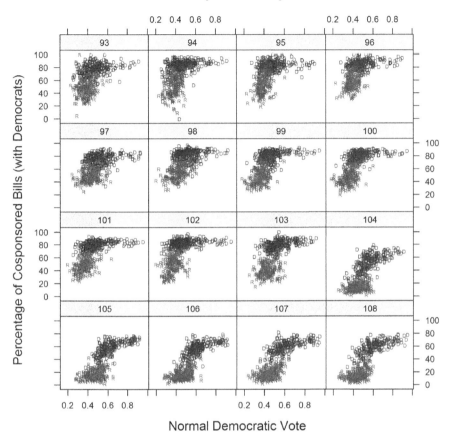

FIGURE 7.3(B) Differences in Legislative Behavior for Democrats and Republicans

some Democrats and Republicans engaged in highly partisan behaviors that were representative of co-partisan interests in the electorate, there were still many members who worked across the aisle and showed greater responsiveness to their broader constituencies.[16]

In sum, member responsiveness – as gauged by differences in the behavior of members in competitive and safely partisan districts – has declined on vote-based measures while increasing on cosponsorship-based measures. These patterns of responsiveness over time are important for at least two reasons. First, representation is important in a normative sense. Responsiveness speaks to whether constituent interests are reflected in policymaking and whether increases in

---

[16] Another pattern to note in the cosponsorship behavior is that the percentage of cosponsored bills with Democratic sponsors is sensitive to which party is in the majority.

partisan agenda strategies have damaged the representative nature of our government. Second, responsiveness is important for understanding the consequences of a partisan agenda strategy, which ties back to the question of why members work together as partisan teams. Since the support of members is crucial for party leaders to pursue a partisan legislative strategy, the next section of this chapter explores the electoral costs of partisanship in voting, the electoral benefits of bipartisan cosponsorship, and whether these costs and benefits vary across contexts and across districts.

ELECTORAL COSTS AND MEMBER-PARTY RELATIONSHIPS

The combination of rising levels of party unity votes in Congress and increasingly partisan voting records by members support the contention that rising partisanship in Congress is associated with declining responsiveness by members. On its own, this finding suggests that by supporting a partisan floor strategy, members may be at risk of putting themselves out-of-step and thus out-of-office (Canes-Wrone et al. 2002; Carson et al. 2010b; Koger and Lebo 2012). The potential electoral costs associated with rising partisanship in Congress highlight the importance of exploring the member-party relationships that sustain the pursuit of partisan legislative strategies and the trade-offs that members and their leadership face in balancing individual and collective goals.

Members of Congress care about both policy influence and reelection (see Chapter 3). Partisan legislative agendas help members pursue policy goals and may also help develop the party brand, which can help their party electorally (Grynaviski 2010). On the other hand, partisan agendas can be costly for members whose constituents are not aligned with the party (Snyder and Ting 2002, 91). There is consensus among scholars that members believe that their activities in office impact upon their electoral prospects (Fenno 1978; Mayhew 1974), and empirical evidence indeed shows that legislative behavior affects vote shares and the probability of reelection, particularly among more vulnerable legislators (Canes-Wrone et al. 2002; Sulkin 2005). If a partisan floor strategy leads to members being out-of-step as individuals, why do they support this strategy? One possibility is that an increase over time in the percentage of sorted districts has made partisan voting less costly. Another possibility is that joining bipartisan cosponsorship coalitions can provide an electoral benefit, mitigating the costs of partisan agendas and partisan voting.

While some members are cross-pressured between their party and constituency, other members see greater alignment between the two. I refer to members in the former category as those in unsorted districts, and those in the latter as falling in sorted districts. If members in sorted districts face less electoral punishment for partisanship than members in unsorted districts, changes in district sorting over time (through member replacement, redistricting, geographic segregation, and individual-level sorting of party and issue positions) should make it possible for members to support partisan agenda-setting with fewer electoral risks.

My analyses of how partisan voting affects the electoral interests of members begin with models similar to those in Canes-Wrone et al. (2002).[17] To assess whether the electoral costs of partisanship in voting vary between sorted and unsorted congressional districts, the first analysis pools together contested House elections from 1974 to 2004. The dependent variable is the incumbent's two-party vote share. The primary independent variables are vote-based measures of ideological or partisan extremity, an indicator for whether the district is sorted or unsorted, and an interaction between the measure of voting extremity and whether the district is sorted. This interaction captures whether the effect of voting behavior is different in sorted and unsorted districts; as in previous analyses, I define sorted districts as those where the normal presidential vote is greater than or equal to 50 percent. I use four different measures of voting behavior – the extremity of the member's Americans for Democratic Action (ADA) score (as in the original Canes-Wrone et al. analysis), the absolute value of the member's first dimension DW-NOMINATE score, the member's party unity support score, and the member's party unity support score weighted by the percentage of party unity votes in that Congress. Additional control variables include the normal presidential vote in the district; differences in challenger and incumbent spending; indicators for quality challengers, freshman members, and whether or not the member is in the president's party; and interactions between the president's party and the variables capturing change in real income per capita in the year prior to the election, presidential popularity, and midterm election years.[18]

Figure 7.4 presents the average effect on the two-party vote share of moving from one standard deviation below the mean to one standard deviation above the mean for each vote-based measure of legislative behavior.[19] This average effect captures the impact of partisan behavior on a members' vote share. Since partisanship hurts members' vote shares, the effects are negative. Larger magnitudes (i.e., absolute values) indicate greater electoral punishment for partisanship. In three of the four panels of the figure, the interaction between voting behavior and whether a district is sorted is highly significant. The only exception is members' ADA scores, where the 90 percent confidence intervals overlap

---

[17] Since their analysis ended in 1996, the key variables for the analysis were re-calculated using Gary Jacobson's data on House elections for the full 1974–2004 period of analysis. Races are omitted from analysis if the incumbent in a district changed as a result of redistricting.

[18] I model the effect of members' voting behavior on their vote share using a linear multi-level model with random effects by election year for the intercept and for the indicator for the president's party. This model helps to capture the nested structure of the data since elections for individual members fall within years.

[19] These predictions are based on bootstrapping simulations of the model with 90% confidence intervals. The mean and standard deviation for each measure are as follows: extremity of ADA score (mean 77.0, SD 22.4), extremity of DW-NOMINATE (mean 0.350, SD 0.170), party unity support score (mean 83.4, SD 15.0), and weighted party unity support score (mean 42.2, SD 11.9). Full regression models are available in Table A7.4.

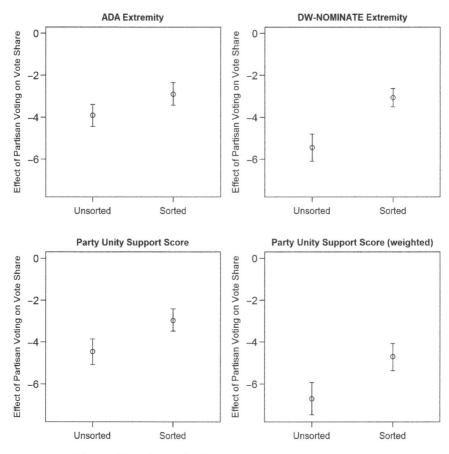

FIGURE 7.4 Electoral Punishment for Partisan Voting

slightly. In general, the electoral costs of partisanship are larger in unsorted districts than in sorted districts. While members in both types of districts are punished for partisanship, the magnitude of the effect is significantly larger for members in unsorted districts.

These results are important for two reasons. First, they suggest that a member's support for a partisan floor strategy and, ultimately, voting with the party may not be likely to cost him his seat, particularly if he is in a sorted district. As noted by Wright (2007, 264), many studies of electoral punishment for being out-of-step yield effect sizes of 3 to 6 percentage points, which may allow members, particularly in safe districts, to keep their seats. Thus, any benefits from working as a partisan team and developing a brand that could help members of a party achieve majority status may outweigh the relatively small decreases in vote share that accompany that behavior. While not captured by the treatment effects above, the average two-party vote share is larger for members in sorted districts than for members in unsorted districts, meaning that a punish-ment of a few percentage points is unlikely to result in electoral loss.

Second, and perhaps more important, these results shed light on why parties were able to pursue increasingly partisan floor strategies between the 1970s and 2000s. Over this time period, as more House seats fell into the sorted category, the electoral costs of a partisan strategy decreased. Whereas just over half of all districts were sorted in the 94th Congress, by the 107th Congress over 80 percent were sorted. Over time, fewer and fewer members represented unsorted districts where the costs of partisanship were high.

Out-of-Step, but Keeping Your Office

A second possible answer to the question of why members work with their party to pursue a partisan agenda, even though it leads them to appear unresponsive to constituent preferences, is that bipartisanship in cosponsorship coalitions helps mitigate the electoral damage of partisan voting. Bipartisan cosponsorship behavior may be particularly beneficial to members if they are able to highlight their efforts at reaching across the aisle in this domain during elections.

Replicating the previous analysis of electoral punishment/reward for legislative behavior in unsorted and sorted districts emphasizes that bipartisan cosponsor-ship is most useful in unsorted districts. Here, the average effect on the two-party vote share of moving from one standard deviation below the mean of bipartisan cosponsorship to one standard deviation above the mean is 3.87 in unsorted districts (90 percent confidence interval from 3.24 to 4.48), but only 1.23 in sorted districts (90 percent confidence interval from 0.69 to 1.74).[20] Thus, cosponsorship can help members in those unsorted districts where a partisan voting record hurts most.

Perhaps cosponsorship allows members, particularly in competitive districts, to build a record of symbolic responsiveness that mitigates the electoral costs of partisanship by creating a "sense of trust and support in the relationship between the representative and the represented" (Eulau and Karps 1977, 241). For members in competitive districts who may be most concerned about the general election (rather than primary elections), bipartisan cosponsorship offers one means of insulation (Kanthak et al. 2010). Although it is impossible to isolate the effects of cosponsorship and voting in observational studies, I explore whether members who are at risk of appearing out-of-step with their constitu-ents in their voting records can benefit electorally by engaging in bipartisan cosponsorship.

These analyses leverage two different ways of considering how bipartisan cosponsorship can help members who are at risk of being out-of-step in voting. The first captures the relative risk between members within a given year – in other words, whether records of bipartisan cosponsorship systematically help

---

[20] The mean value of bipartisan cosponsorship is 61.7 and the standard deviation is 15.3.

members in competitive districts more than they help members in less competitive districts. The second analysis captures the legislative behavior and electoral benefits of bipartisan cosponsorship for the most vulnerable members over time. Bipartisan cosponsorship may have become increasingly beneficial to members in the most competitive districts as partisan voting has increased, thereby mitigating the costs of supporting a partisan agenda. Thus, I consider how the frequency of party unity votes on the House floor affects the benefits of bipartisan cosponsorship for members in the most competitive districts.

To examine both perspectives of risk for being out-of-step, I separate members into two categories – those at a high risk of being out-of-step in voting (competitive districts) and those at a lower risk of being out-of-step in voting (non-competitive districts). I define competitive districts as those where the normal presidential vote is less than the median (by election year). I define non-competitive districts as those where the normal presidential vote is greater than or equal to the median. This binary measure of competitive seats is used in place of the sorted–unsorted distinction to ensure that there are similar numbers of members in each category for each election year, providing greater power for the analysis. For each election year between 1974 and 2004, I analyze the incumbent two-party vote share as a function of members' bipartisan cosponsorship coalitions and each of the individual-level control variables mentioned previously. An interaction term between the percentage of bipartisan cosponsorship coalitions by members and an indicator for whether they represent competitive districts captures whether the benefits of bipartisanship are greater for members in more competitive seats.

Figure 7.5 shows the effect of the percentage of bipartisan cosponsorship coalitions on the incumbent vote share for members in non-competitive and competitive districts (full model results are presented in Tables A7.5 and A7.6).[21] The effect of bipartisanship is calculated as the difference in the predicted vote share for members with bipartisan cosponsorship behavior one standard deviation above the mean and those with bipartisan cosponsorship one standard deviation below the mean. Larger (positive) effects indicate that members receive greater electoral benefits from greater bipartisan cosponsorship. Among members in the least competitive half of districts, the effect of bipartisan cosponsorship is significant in only five elections, with one of these being a negative effect. In contrast, among members who are in the most competitive half of districts, the effect of bipartisan cosponsorship is positive in all cases and significant in 14 of the 16 elections. Thus, for members who are at greater risk of being out-of-step with district preferences through vote-based partisanship, engaging in bipartisan bill cosponsorship coalitions provides a significant electoral benefit. As a result,

---

[21] The analysis is restricted to races with two or more candidates and those without substantial redistricting that affected incumbent status. The dependent variable is the incumbent two-party vote share.

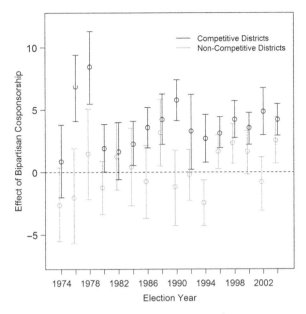

FIGURE 7.5 Electoral Benefits for Bipartisan Cosponsorship

these members may be able to balance their support for a more partisan roll call agenda with bipartisan cosponsorship.

A second test directly captures whether or not the benefits from bipartisan cosponsorship have changed as the roll call agenda has prioritized partisan legislation. This test also explores whether bipartisan cosponsorship can help members even when controlling for their voting behavior. Since the majority party needs the support of members in competitive districts to pursue a partisan agenda, but also must balance the electoral risks for these members resulting from that agenda, the analysis focuses on just those members in the most competitive half of districts within each election. Results are similar when analyzing members in unsorted districts and the same logic applies – the support of members in more competitive or less well-sorted districts is needed to pursue a partisan roll call agenda, but they face greater electoral risk for supporting the party.

The evidence suggests that when the roll call agenda is very partisan, bipartisan cosponsorship provides members with an electoral benefit. The analysis pools election results from 1974 to 2004, with the incumbent two-party vote share as the dependent variable. The key independent variables of interest are the percentage of cosponsorship coalitions by a member in the previous Congress that are bipartisan, the percentage of party unity votes in the previous Congress, and an interaction between bipartisan cosponsorship and the percentage of party unity votes. Other control variables from the pooled models above are

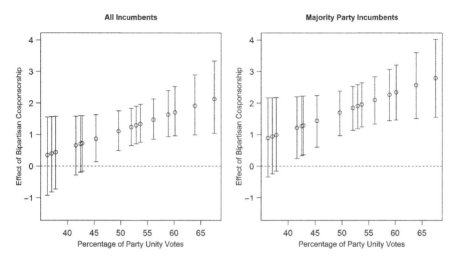

FIGURE 7.6 Electoral Benefits for Bipartisan Cosponsorship as Risk of Being Out-of-Step in Voting Increases for Members in Competitive Districts

also included, with the addition of a variable for the member's own party unity support score. Figure 7.6 plots the average effect on the two-party vote share of moving from one standard deviation below the mean of bipartisan cosponsorship to one standard deviation above the mean across the range of the percentage of party unity votes.[22] As in previous analyses, larger values of this effect indicate that greater bipartisan cosponsorship by members is associated with higher vote shares.

The left-hand panel of the figure shows that bipartisan cosponsorship has an insignificant effect on member's vote share when there are very few party unity votes. In contrast, when there are many party unity votes, bipartisan cosponsorship has a positive and significant effect. The large confidence intervals limit inferences about significant differences between the effects of bipartisan cosponsorship across the range of party unity votes. However, the patterns suggest that when party leaders pursue partisan agendas and members are more out-of-step in voting, bipartisan cosponsorship offers members a means of being in-step and reducing the risks of supporting a partisan roll call strategy. The right-hand

---

[22] The analysis is restricted to races with two or more candidates, those without substantial redistricting that affected incumbent status, and to the most competitive half of districts in each election (based on the normal presidential vote). Full model results are available in Table A7.7. The effects in Figure 7.6 are based on bootstrap simulations that vary bipartisan cosponsorship and the percentage of party unity votes across the observed values, with all other variables held at their observed simulation values. The mean value of bipartisan cosponsorship among members in competitive districts is 61.5 and the standard deviation is 13.3. Among majority party incumbents in competitive districts, the mean is 60.3 and the standard deviation is 13.3.

panel of the figure shows the analysis for just majority party incumbents in competitive seats. The resulting pattern is similar to that for all members in competitive seats, but demonstrates slightly larger effects of bipartisan cosponsorship. Since bipartisan cosponsorship provides a significant electoral benefit when the roll call agenda is partisan, members can support a partisan roll call agenda and even vote with the party while nonetheless building a record of bipartisan cooperation that limits the electoral costs of partisanship.

Combining partisanship in voting with bipartisanship in cosponsorship coalitions offers one route for members to achieve the policy goals of their party without sacrificing their reelection. Since constituents imperfectly monitor the behavior of their congressmen, members may be able to emphasize areas of bipartisanship when communicating with their districts. Both direct communication with constituents and mediated communication via local news coverage allows members to convey information about their positions and their actions (Arnold 2004), including their roll call votes, bill introductions, and cosponsorship coalitions. Members in more competitive seats may have greater incentives to cultivate (and transmit) their personal records of bipartisanship rather than the party brand (Grynaviski 2010, 157). For instance, candidates in districts where the balance of partisanship is against them (i.e., the normal presidential vote is low) are less likely to use their party label in political advertising (Neiheisel and Niebler 2013) and on campaign websites (Druckman et al. 2009) compared to those members in more well-sorted environments.

The examples referenced in the introductory chapter, from constituent newsletters in a handful of Congresses in the late 1990s and from the *Chicago Tribune* during the 2010 election, point to members' ability to manage their image as either partisan or bipartisan by referencing cosponsorship behavior. These types of communications may influence voters' affective evaluations of the incumbent, even if they are unable to identify specific cosponsorship coalitions. Thus, members' efforts to highlight their bipartisan activities in cosponsorship coalitions may help them build a positive individual brand that increases the trust and goodwill of their constituents.

CONCLUSIONS

This chapter explored the implications of increasingly partisan agenda-setting for representation and responsiveness. The primary findings of this chapter suggest that although dyadic responsiveness to members' constituents has declined in voting, responsiveness has grown in bill cosponsorship behavior. The results are important from both a normative perspective on representation and a theoretical perspective for understanding the member-party relationships that sustain partisan agendas in Congress. Just as many of the criticisms of polarization suggest, rising partisan conflict in the House has affected representation. In voting, members increasingly represent the interests of co-partisans but not those of their broader constituency. Declining responsiveness in voting, however, is countered by increasing responsiveness in cosponsorship behavior. While these differences are important and speak to continued efforts by members to respond to their constituents, vote-based partisanship remains worrisome because policy outcomes, not just members' actions, affect the end-stages of democratic representation. Members' votes are much closer than their cosponsorship coalitions to House policy outcomes. In their voting record, members increasingly respond to the interests of like-minded partisans in the public.

The fact that members support a partisan roll call agenda and increasingly vote with the party on party unity votes suggests that, in recent decades, a partisan legislative strategy has not been particularly costly for most members. Across measures of vote-based legislative behavior, the electoral costs of being out-of-step in voting are lower when a member represents a sorted rather than an unsorted district. The same holds for cosponsorship, with a greater electoral benefit for bipartisan cosponsorship in unsorted districts relative to sorted districts. In recent decades, increasing numbers of sorted House districts allow members to support a partisan legislative strategy without substantial risk. For those members that remain in more competitive districts, bipartisan cosponsorship provides one way to mitigate the costs of being out-of-step in voting. Through this behavior, they can promote an individual record of willingness to work across the aisle.

These findings point to the ways in which district sorting not only opened the door for House parties to pursue greater partisanship in their legislative agenda, but continued to reinforce partisanship through their impact on members' electoral fortunes. Even though members have grown increasingly partisan in their voting – representing co-partisans rather than the full district – those in sorted districts receive relatively little electoral punishment. Even if the public does not want partisanship from Congress as a whole (Harbridge and Malhotra 2011), they provide the incentives for individual members to support a partisan strategy. As a result, members can focus on coordinating actions with others in their party while not risking electoral defeat. For those members in unsorted and competitive districts, where the costs of partisanship are higher, members boost their electoral fortunes by balancing support for a partisan agenda with bipartisan cosponsorship.

8

The Past, Present, and Future of Bipartisanship

The extent to which political conflict falls along party lines has waxed and waned over the years. Studies of roll call voting patterns in Congress indicate that partisan conflict has risen steadily over the last several decades (e.g., McCarty et al. 2006; Theriault 2008). Despite a previous generation of scholars' claims that strong, conflictual parties were a desirable part of a functioning democracy (APSA 1950; Schattschneider 1942), recent assessments of partisan conflict have been far from positive. Rather, the resurgence of partisan conflict raises concerns about the legislative process itself, as well as concerns with representation, suggesting that elected officials are increasingly partisan and unresponsive to the public (Hacker and Pierson 2005; Mann and Ornstein 2006, 2012).

As Congress has shifted toward greater partisan conflict, political scientists have studied many facets of rising polarization. However, few scholars have sought to systematically separate substantive disagreement between members of opposing parties, agenda control, and voting patterns. Much of the research on polarization has focused on estimates of members' ideological positions based on their roll call voting; this work shows a linear increase in polarization since the early 1970s (McCarty et al. 2006; Poole and Rosenthal 1984, 1997; Theriault 2008). Although many scholars assume that this increase reflects growing ideological differences, Lee's (2009) research on Senate partisanship suggests that not all partisan conflict is ideological. And while many scholars have emphasized the importance of agenda-setting in the House (e.g., Aldrich 1995; Cox and McCubbins 2005; Lawrence et al. 2006; Lebo et al. 2007; Rohde 1991), little research has systematically examined the selection of legislation for the agenda or how the content of the agenda has changed over time (for an exception, see Roberts and Smith 2003). As a consequence, existing work examining partisan conflict remains incomplete because it has focused either on the polarization of member preferences or on party influence over time, but not on the connection between party control over the agenda, the roll call votes of members, and resulting level of partisan conflict. In many ways, the near-exclusive focus on roll call votes has limited the resulting insights about the extent of partisan conflict versus bipartisan agreement.

This book has provided a new perspective on partisan conflict by focusing attention on the degree of bipartisanship in voting and cosponsorship coalitions, and on what bills party leaders select to receive floor attention or roll call votes. This focus on agenda-setting by the majority party sheds light on the decline of bipartisanship in voting. Whereas the agenda of the majority party in the 1970s prioritized places of bipartisan agreement, their agenda in the 1990s and 2000s prioritized partisan disagreement, with a low point for bipartisanship in the 104th Congress (1995–96). This shift is mirrored by the patterns in roll call voting itself: the percentage of votes with bipartisan coalitions fell from over 70 percent in 1974 to only 27 percent in 1995, before rebounding some in subsequent years. Bipartisanship has clearly declined on the roll call agenda and in roll call voting.

I was surprised, at the beginning of this project, to find that bipartisanship in cosponsorship persisted between 1973 and 2004 even as the roll call agenda grew more partisan. My findings from this era, and even through 2006, conveyed a relatively optimistic picture about bipartisan agreement and the ways in which parties balanced partisan differentiation and governance. But recent developments in American politics, particularly during the Obama administration, offer a less sanguine assessment. This chapter therefore attempts to grapple with the legacy of partisan agenda-setting in the House of Representatives, focusing first on the important insights from the period from 1973 to 2004, then considering recent developments in bipartisanship, and finally exploring reasons why bipartisan legislation may be more important again in the future.

BALANCING PARTISANSHIP AND GOVERNANCE: 1973–2004

Even in the face of partisan disagreement in roll call voting, bipartisanship is not dead. Not only did bipartisan cosponsorship of legislation persist from 1973 to 2004, even as roll call voting became less bipartisan, but bipartisan legislation was consistently advantaged among legislation receiving voice votes. These voice votes addressed a range of legislative issues, including substantively important bills. Among bills becoming public law, bipartisanship also remained the norm. However, the degree of bipartisanship in legislative outputs was related to the degree of bipartisan legislation on the roll call agenda. Thus, while legislative outputs remained bipartisan, the extent of bipartisanship was affected by the agenda, which became much more partisan. Moreover, members' responsiveness to their districts increased over time in the form of bipartisan cosponsorship coalitions, despite declining patterns of responsiveness in roll call voting. These findings point to a complex picture of partisan conflict in the House of Representatives – one in which the leadership's selection of bills for the floor and, in particular, for the roll call agenda magnifies the substantive differences between members. Not only does Washington incentivize partisanship, but it manufactures vote-based disagreement via agenda-setting.

The theoretical framework of the book – strategic partisan agenda-setting – points to how party leaders balance their members' electoral goals with collec tive goals of governance and emphasizing partisan differences. Since variation in district sorting, divided government, and majority seat shares all affect whether bipartisan or partisan legislation best helps the party leader achieve these goals, the degree to which the legislative agenda prioritizes bipartisan legislation varies across these contexts. By focusing on leaders' constraints in pursuing partisan legislation, this approach not only explains why partisan conflict has risen in recent decades (as conditions have become more favorable), but it also suggests that the post–World War II era of bipartisanship should not be idealized as a time when politicians necessarily put country above party (Brownstein 2007, 25). Although the empirical analyses of this book begin with 1973, the argument and findings point to constraint, not virtue, as having been responsible for leaders' focus on bipartisanship in this earlier era. The same is true in more recent periods. Republican leaders in the 105th Congress (1997–98) backtracked from a partisan agenda toward a more bipartisan agenda when they were confronted with legislative failure and electoral risks.

My findings provide important insights and implications for scholarly research as well as for a broader understanding of American politics during this period of history. First, this research adds to the growing body of literature that suggests that researchers need to better understand the biases and limita- tions of roll call data (Carrubba et al. 2008; Clinton 2007, 2012; Loewenberg 2008; Noel 2013; Roberts 2007; Rosas and Shomer 2008). By looking beyond roll call votes, this book highlights the continuation of bipartisanship in the form of bill cosponsorship coalitions across the period from 1973 to 2004. The evidence also shows that the content of the roll call agenda has changed over time, increasingly prioritizing partisan legislation relative to bipartisan legisla- tion. A greater focus on congressional agenda control is necessary to provide a better understanding of the implications of this agenda for the growth in party cohesiveness since the 1970s. To assess the effects of agenda-setting on which bills receive votes, future research should combine the insights from this book – specifically the pursuit of bipartisan versus partisan legislation – with attention to additional factors that can drive legislative attention to particular policies or laws. These factors include expiring authorizations (e.g., Adler and Wilkerson 2013) and shifts in coalitions since laws were initially enacted (e.g., Berry et al. 2010; Maltzman and Shipan 2008).

Second, these findings shed light on democratic governance, especially during periods of partisan conflict in roll call voting. An effective legislature must be able to communicate with its citizens, respond to their concerns, and shape laws and policies that reflect both national and constituent interests (National Democratic Institute 2013). Thus, both the government's ability to pass legislation and the degree to which the outputs of government are commensurate with public preferences are important (Bessette 1994). Of course, no evaluation of democratic governance can fully capture all relevant aspects of policymaking, and any evaluation of "good" policies will be reliant on personal judgment. Here, I have simplified the issue of governance by focusing on the degree to which outputs are bipartisan, both because legislation enacted with wide bipartisan coalitions may be more stable over time (Maltzman and Shipan 2008) and because bipartisan legislation may be more commensurate with collective public preferences (Fiorina and Abrams 2009). The findings in this book provide cautious optimism that bipartisanship in governing approaches and outputs continues across this period of American politics, even as traditional polarization measures have increased.

The absence of purely partisan agenda strategies provides one basis for optimism. Even on the roll call agenda, partisanship never fully replaced bipartisanship, and the frequency of bipartisan roll call votes dropped below 40 percent in only three of the Congresses examined. Moreover, the broader floor agenda, which includes the passage of legislation by voice votes, was even more bipartisan during this time. Since bipartisan bills are more likely to be enacted into public law than partisan bills once they have passed the House, the record of public laws remains overwhelmingly bipartisan across the period of analysis. On average, 77 percent of cosponsored bills passed into law originated from bipartisan coalitions. Even at the low point in the 103rd Congress during unified government under Clinton (1993–94), 66 percent of public laws originated from bipartisan coalitions. This suggests that bipartisan legislation continues to be a central part of governance.

Just how much bipartisanship is necessary for governance hinges on how governance is defined. On the one hand, governance entails a baseline ability to address the reoccurring issues that face Congress – budgets, appropriations, reauthorizations – and to enact new laws to address problems that face the country (Adler and Wilkerson 2013). Under this view, party leaders only need to pursue bipartisan legislation if the electoral risks for members or their need to achieve legislative success prohibits their pursuit of partisan legislation. On the other hand, governance can entail the crafting of legislation that weathers the test of time and is viewed as legitimate by the public (and not just those from one party). Here, more bipartisan legislation may be needed regardless of the political context.

Despite the continued presence of bipartisan legislation in the legislative process and in policy outputs, there are some reasons to be concerned that increasingly partisan roll call agendas do damage governance. First, when party leaders pursued more partisan bills on the roll call agenda, fewer bills that passed the House were enacted into public law and fewer laws had bipartisan support (see Chapter 4). Second, there have been times when the majority party appears to have over-stepped in a partisan direction, leading to gridlock and a failure to govern. The case of the 104th Congress under Gingrich fits this description (see Chapter 5). Third, partisan agenda-setting has implications for issue attention (see Chapter 6). When leaders pursued a more partisan agenda, bills on policies that are traditionally bipartisan (for instance, defense, transportation, and agriculture) received less legislative attention than when leaders pursued a more bipartisan agenda. This raises concerns about the extent to which Congress responds to various policy areas at different points in time.

On the whole, these results point to how American parties have balanced efforts to govern effectively with efforts to pursue partisan policy goals and party differentiation. As a result of these competing factors, leaders do not always pursue places of bipartisan agreement, even when it exists, and policy outputs are shaped by their decisions. When leaders pursue more partisan agendas, places of bipartisan agreement may be ignored. Even though policy outputs continue to be largely bipartisan, the extent to which this is true varies over time. Future work should explore policy outputs more thoroughly, examining differences in bipartisanship between major and minor legislative initiatives and the extent to which bipartisan versus partisan outputs are seen as legitimate by the public.

Third, this book speaks to the relationship between rising partisanship in roll call voting and congressional responsiveness. Members, particularly those in more competitive districts, seek to be bipartisan and these efforts are seen in their cosponsorship coalitions. The agenda-setting process of the House, however, has increasingly limited members' opportunities for taking a bipartisan position on the floor, with roll call voting becoming increasingly partisan as a result. Even though partisan agenda-setting affects members' legislative records and paints them as highly partisan, members nonetheless appear to support these more partisan agendas; they are not simply imposed by the party leadership.

The pursuit of partisan legislation in House roll call votes comes at the expense of member responsiveness in voting: members develop an increasingly partisan record regardless of the type of district they represent. While members may align with their district in terms of the party receiving the majority of the normal presidential vote, members have become increasingly unaligned *within* parties. That is, members of Congress increasingly vote with their party regardless of whether they represent a district that overwhelmingly favors their party or only slightly favors their party. While individual districts may be better sorted, and constituents may not punish their own member substantially for partisanship (and the most engaged partisans may actually like partisanship (Abramowitz 2010), the recent patterns of member behavior are notably different from earlier eras (or current cosponsorship patterns) wherein members from safe and competitive districts engaged in very different behavior. This finding suggests not only that members may be looking out for district interests rather than national interests (Doherty 2013), but also that members are increasingly looking out for co-partisan interests rather than the interests of all of their constituents. Thus, there is reason to worry that, when it comes to voting, members are moving inward on the scale of Fenno's (1978) nested constituencies – that is, moving away from geographic constituencies and toward general election and perhaps even primary election constituencies. Ultimately, partisan agenda-setting may damage legislative responsiveness as members produce representation that is "good enough" to allow them to be reelected, but is nonetheless more partisan than we would expect given constituent partisanship and members' cosponsorship.

Fourth, this book has addressed the role that political parties play in mediating the relationship between the public, elected officials, and policy outcomes. Representative democracy is designed to mediate the public voice. To the extent that members' sponsorship and cosponsorship of legislation captures the preferences of their constituents, party strategies over which bills receive floor and roll call attention affects which constituent preferences are represented in policy outputs. Political parties affect the distribution of bipartisan and partisan bills on the agenda, which, in turn, affects whether policy outputs are bipartisan or partisan. Importantly, partisan agenda-setting varies over time, even as the level of bipartisan cosponsorship coalitions does not change substantially. Thus, parties as a collective group, and not just as the sum of the preferences of their members, contribute to the rise of partisan conflict. As was noted by Arnold more than two decades ago, "responsiveness by itself does not guarantee citizens' control over policy outcomes. If the agenda is controlled by other forces, then citizens' influence over the final stage in decision making may offer them little real influence over the important decisions in society" (Arnold 1990, 268).

In sum, across the period from 1973 to 2004, there *was* common ground between members, but the roll call agenda increasingly exploited places of partisan division. In essence, this crucial period of American politics represents a moment of shifting equilibrium, loosely defined, from bipartisan to partisan agenda-setting, as House parties sorted and fewer members faced cross-pressures between their constituents and their party. Nonetheless, there remained a delicate balance between partisanship and governing, as evidenced by the back-tracking of the GOP after seeing partisan legislation fail to become law during divided government in the 104th Congress.

PARTISANSHIP AND GOVERNANCE IN THE OBAMA ERA

Contemporary accounts of the last few years suggest that little bipartisanship remains in policymaking. The shift to Democratic House control in 2006 ended 12 years of Republican control and brought back divided government in the waning years of the George W. Bush presidency. With both parties actively contesting for the majority, the parties appeared to engage in endless rounds of positioning and differentiation. The percentage of roll call votes with bipartisan support fell after the 108th Congress, dropping from 50 percent to 41 percent by the 110th Congress. The 2008 election of Barack Obama brought back unified control and a sweeping Democratic legislative agenda in the face of the Great Recession. Major legislative initiatives including The American Recovery and

Reinvestment Act of 2009 and The Affordable Care Act passed without Republican support. The percentage of roll call votes with bipartisan support increased somewhat, rising to 53 percent, but was still lower than the levels in either the 106th or 107th Congresses.

Partisanship in policymaking accelerated with the 2010 election, which brought back Republican control of the House, along with a new breed of members in the form of the Tea Party Caucus. Those who identified with the Tea Party "would not hear of compromise, and pushed GOP officials to act quickly and unremittingly: to reduce taxes, slash public spending, curb public sector unions, and clear away regulations on business" (Skocpol and Williamson 2012, 4). Despite tiny margins of control, they were expected to "ram through maximalist programs" (Skocpol and Williamson 2012, 156), an approach that has put them in a bind with respect to governance (or even balancing governance with partisan differentiation). Bipartisanship in roll call voting fell to record lows, with only 25 percent of votes in the 112th Congress garnering bipartisan support. With divided government and a failure to compromise or find places of common ground, legislation stalled on issues such as immigration, job creation, and drought relief (Dodd and Oppenheimer 2012). The 112th Congress was ultimately decried as the "Worst. Congress. Ever" (Ornstein 2011), in large part because of the partisan conflict which was seen as coming at the expense of policymaking and governing. News coverage emphasized that both parties were using bills to hurt the other party rather than to govern. With each side taking seemingly popular measures and adding language that infuriated the other side, much legislation died on the floor (Fram 2012). Ultimately, efforts to raise the debt ceiling came down to the last minute in 2011, and failure to reach agreement on spending legislation in 2013 led to a 16 day government shutdown that encapsulated the partisanship in Washington and the inability of the two sides to find agreement.

The framework of strategic partisan agenda-setting emphasizes the tension that House majorities face between pursuing policy objectives and partisan differentiation, and producing a record of legislative success. While the former goals may be best achieved by pursuing partisan legislation, the latter is achieved more easily by pursuing bipartisan legislation. The framework suggests that, while the degree to which members are cross-pressured is a primary factor driving partisan or bipartisan agenda-setting, extreme partisanship in agenda-setting must be tempered during periods with divided government and small seat shares if parties prioritize governance over party branding (or even seek to balance these two goals). During the first term of the Obama administration, House leaders could have pursued partisan legislation in the 111th Congress (2009–10) even while balancing governance and partisan differentiation. However, with the shift to divided government and a smaller majority seat share in the 112th Congress (2011–12), leaders would have needed to temper their pursuit of partisan legislation if they were concerned with legislative success.

The recent accounts of partisan conflict raise two obvious questions: First, how do the patterns of policymaking in the last few years align with the empirical patterns of the previous decades and the theoretical framework of strategic partisan agenda-setting? Second, what do these patterns tell us about how the majority party is balancing goals of governance against individual electoral goals and collective goals of party differentiation? The answers to these questions emphasize how political conditions continue to affect party leaders' incentives to pursue bipartisan versus partisan legislation. With few constraints on partisan agenda-setting and many incentives to focus on partisan legislation, there is little bipartisanship on the House floor.

Although bill cosponsorship remained common in the post-2004 period, bipartisan cosponsorship became less common. The percentage of cosponsored bills with a bipartisan coalition (20 percent or more of cosponsors from the party opposite the sponsor) declined after the 109th Congress, falling from 47 percent (which was on par with the levels in the 94th, 103rd, and 108th Congresses) to 37 percent in the 111th Congress and 38 percent in the 112th. This shift suggests that the underlying level of policy agreement that had remained fairly constant over the previous three decades declined by a full ten percentage points (or by 20 percent of the previous all-time low level) from 2005 to 2012.[1]

Figure 8.1 captures this shift, comparing a trend line of bipartisan cosponsorship derived from the 1973–2004 period with the observed rates for the 2005–12 period. The patterns show that the degree of bipartisan agreement in recent years is substantially below that of previous years, and even below the level that would have been expected if bipartisanship continued to decline at a rate similar to the past 30 years. If the linear trend line through the observed data for the 93rd to 108th Congresses were extrapolated into the most recent Congresses, the percentage of cosponsored bills with bipartisan agreement would have only fallen from 49.2 percent to 47.9 percent. Instead, bipartisan agreement dropped from 47 percent to 37 percent. Partisan conflict over policy accelerated substantially after 2007. In recent years, district-party sorting is at its maximum and policy agreement is at an all-time low.

The drop-off in bipartisan policy agreement in recent years emphasizes an important contribution of this book's approach to our understanding of polarization. Whereas the conventional wisdom on polarization emphasized the nearly linear increase in vote-based polarization since the early 1970s, the pattern of cosponsorship coalitions tells a different story. Cross-party agreement fluctuated from the 1970s to the mid-2000s, declining some but not a lot. However, agreement tumbled between 2007 and 2012, falling to levels unseen in the earlier period.

---

[1] Over 16 Congresses, bipartisan cosponsorship varied between 47 percent and 61 percent, over a range of 14 percentage points, but had only a weak relationship with time. Over the next four Congresses, bipartisanship declined by 10 percentage points.

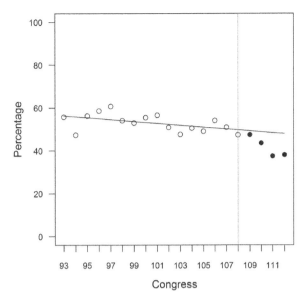

FIGURE 8.1 Shifts in Bipartisan Cosponsorship in the 111th and 112th Congresses
Note: Points indicate the observed percentage of cosponsored bills with bipartisan cosponsorship coalitions. The trend line indicates the trajectory of bipartisan cosponsorship between the 93rd and 108th Congresses, predicting the levels that would have been seen in the 109th–112th Congresses if the decline followed the pattern of the previous decades.

In the most recent Congresses, bipartisanship declined not just in bill cosponsorship coalitions but also in agenda-setting. Figure 8.2 extends the analysis from Chapter 4 by adding measures of bipartisan agenda-setting for the 109th–112th Congresses.[2] A vertical line at the 108th Congress shows where the analyses in previous chapters ended. After the 108th Congress, the percentage of bipartisan bills on the roll call agenda declined, falling to levels on par with those in the 103rd (1993–94) and 104th (1995–96) Congresses. This decline is even more apparent among bills that were not considered under suspension of the rules (as bills brought forward under suspension procedures continue to be bipartisan). For those bills, the 112th Congress eclipsed the previous low of

---

[2] Data for these measures were collected from govtracks.us. Data on sponsorship, cosponsorship, and passage were collected in a way to mirror the data from James Fowler used earlier in the analyses. Data on roll call votes was collected from govtracks.us by using their assessment of the bill underlying each vote. Given differences between this approach and that taken by the Policy Agendas Project (especially on amendment votes), there may be some discrepancies on specific votes. However, since bills that receive amendment votes are also likely to receive other votes (either procedural or passage), the data here about whether a bill receives a roll call vote are unlikely to be significantly different from that in the Policy Agendas Project.

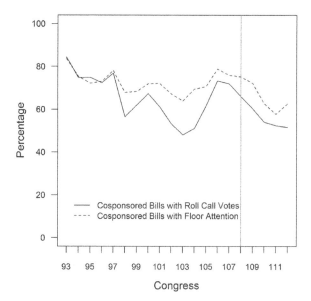

FIGURE 8.2 Recent Patterns of Bipartisan Agenda-Setting
Note: Y-axis represents the percentage of cosponsored bills with bipartisan coalitions. Bipartisan cosponsorship is defined as those bills with at least 20 percent of the cosponsors from the party opposite the sponsor.

31 percent bipartisan bills, falling to only 23 percent bipartisan. When accounting for the decline in the percentage of bipartisan cosponsorship coalitions from which leaders can select bills for the agenda, the roll call agenda in these two Congresses either favored partisan bills or treated partisan and bipartisan bills similarly.[3]

Bipartisan agenda-setting also declined on the broader floor agenda (consisting of both roll call votes and voice votes). Here, the low point for bipartisanship occurred during the 111th Congress. There was a slight increase in bipartisanship during the 112th Congress, but the degree of bipartisanship in this Congress was still the second lowest on record since the 93rd Congress. When accounting for the decline in the percentage of bipartisan cosponsorship coalitions, party leaders prioritized bipartisan bills over partisan bills on the broader floor agenda in the 112th Congress but to a lesser extent than in the 111th Congress.[4] These findings point to increasingly partisan legislative agendas over this period and a

---

[3] The difference in the conditional probability of a roll call vote for bipartisan minus partisan bills was slightly positive in the 110th and 111th Congresses (and similar in size to the those in the 106th Congress) but negative in both the 109th and 112th Congresses.

[4] The difference in the conditional probability of floor attention for bipartisan minus partisan bills is positive in both the 111th and 112th Congresses but declines from 0.096 to 0.062.

limited dedication to pursuing more places of bipartisan agreement, even when the political environment shifted from unified to divided government.

Combined, these patterns suggest that not only did members exhibit less bipartisan agreement on policy in the 111th and 112th Congresses, but that party leaders focused the floor and roll call agendas around places of partisan disagreement rather than bipartisan agreement. Even where some cross-party agreement was possible, the leadership did not pursue these legislative proposals. For instance, leaders did not pursue bipartisan legislation to address Medicare fraud (H.R. 675) despite a bipartisan cosponsorship coalition of 15 Democrats and 15 Republicans. The legislation had passed the House on voice vote in a previous Congress (Herger and Stark 2011). When given the chance to pursue this legislation again in the 112th, the GOP majority did not. Likewise, a proposal by Charlie Dent (R-PA) and Ron Kind (D-WI) to re-open the government in 2013 with a six-month continuing resolution that included a repeal of the medical device tax and payments from a pension-smoothing provision had "critical bipartisan mass" (Huntsman and Manchin 2014, location 294) in the House but was not embraced by the leadership as part of their agenda.

The framework of strategic partisan agenda-setting suggests that partisan agendas help the majority party meet members' electoral and policy goals as well as their collective party branding goals when the congressional parties are well sorted and there are few cross-pressured members. The current period meets this condition. In the 2008 and 2010 elections, only 13 percent of incumbents running for reelection came from unsorted districts.[5] The Democratic majority in the 111th Congress encountered the perfect conditions for pursuing a partisan agenda. In this case, partisan legislation could simultaneously achieve members' electoral, governance, and partisan differentiation goals. However, despite high levels of district-party sorting when the GOP regained majority status, divided government and smaller majority seats shares in the 112th and 113th Congresses yielded conflict between partisan policy goals and producing a record of legislative success. Rather than balancing the needs of governance and partisan differentiation, however, the majority party in the 112th Congress emphasized the latter.

Consistent with my assumption that bipartisan bills offer leaders an easier route to pass bills into law, available evidence suggests that the Republicans' pursuit of partisan legislation resulted in dismal legislative productivity. In fact, the 112th Congress was ranked as the least productive ever by the *Washington Times* (Dinan 2013). Before the August recess of 2011, only 28 bills were passed by Congress and sent to the president for his signature. This number matches the previous low from the 104th Congress when Clinton held the presidency and Republicans

---

[5] This number reflects sorting only among those districts where incumbents ran for election. Strategic retirement by members wary of tough general election campaigns means that, on average, the level of sorting among running incumbents is higher than the level of sorting among all members.

controlled Congress. The 113th Congress appears to be continuing this pattern, with only 22 bills cleared before the August recess in 2013. In contrast, more than 60 bills were cleared in the same period of the 111th Congress (Weiner and O'Keefe 2013). Ultimately, only 283 public laws were enacted in the 112th Congress, compared to 383 public laws in the 111th Congress.

The pursuit of partisan legislation on the agenda is at the root of these legislative failures. Among cosponsored bills that received roll call votes, party leaders in the 112th Congress were able to pass both bipartisan and partisan bills within the chamber.[6] Outside of the chamber, however, partisan bills fared more poorly. Among bills that received a roll call vote and passed the House, 19 percent of partisan bills became public law compared to 59 percent of bipartisan bills ($p < 0.001$). This dramatic difference in success rates for bipartisan and partisan bills in the 112th Congress stands in contrast to the success rates of bills in the 111th Congress. Not surprisingly, unified government in the 111th Congress allowed Democrats to convert nearly a third of partisan bills that passed the House into law. This rate was not significantly different from the success rate for bipartisan bills. Thus, partisan agenda-setting was not at odds with governance in the 111th Congress, when unified government allowed partisan priorities to be enacted. In contrast, for those bills that received a roll call vote and passed the House in the 112th Congress, only one partisan bill in five became law, pointing to the tension between partisanship and governance during divided government.

The importance of the sorting of congressional districts, combined with the ways in which partisan legislation achieves party branding and policy goals, suggests that reining partisanship back in the House is no easy feat. Congressional districts are as well sorted as ever. However, the extent to which partisan conflict has resulted in legislative inaction suggests that governing incentives are not trumping partisan goals – either for policy or partisan differentiation – and that institutional constraints are not encouraging party leaders to pursue places of bipartisan agreement. In past years, even when the majority leadership over-stepped in their partisan agenda-setting, concerns about governance reined back partisanship after the party confronted legislative defeat. Between the 104th and 105th Congresses during the 1990s, the Republican majority backtracked on its partisan agenda after being faced with legislative failures and a (then) record low number of bills being enacted into law. The 112th Congress produced a new record low in the number of bills becoming law. Why hasn't the Republican majority been constrained by governance concerns? Should we expect the GOP to backtrack again and craft a more bipartisan agenda if they remain in power?

---

[6] Across the 109th–112th Congresses, 98 percent of bipartisan bills that received a roll call vote passed the House compared to 94 percent of partisan bills ($p = 0.001$). In the 112th Congress there was no significant difference between the success rates of the two types of bills: 97 percent of bipartisan bills passed the House, compared to 96 percent of partisan bills ($p = 0.64$).

At least three factors that have changed in recent years may explain why the GOP has pursued partisan legislation despite the negative consequences for legislative success. These factors include a substantial decrease in bipartisan policy agreement in recent years relative to previous decades, the costs of inaction, and the electoral interests of Republican members. I have argued that House leaders seek to minimize the costs to members and balance the opportunity to enact legislation with efforts to build the party brand when they set the agenda. All three of these changes appear to have affected the way leaders make this calculation, causing them to prioritize partisan legislation over bipartisan legislation on the agenda.

First, the extent of policy agreement between members from the two parties declined dramatically after 2008 (as captured by the steep decline in bipartisan cosponsorship coalitions during the Obama administration). In contrast to my findings of significant areas of bipartisan policy agreement during the period from 1973 to 2004, there is substantially less bipartisan agreement since 2008. That is, 2009–12 reflects a period of politics with less common ground than in any other period in the modern Congress. With more partisan bills and fewer bipartisan bills, party leaders are more likely to pursue partisan legislation on their agenda.

This drop-off in bipartisan agreement may have a number of causes that are related to the incentives that leaders have to pursue bipartisan legislation. The timing of the decline in bipartisan agreement corresponds to the period of greater competition for majority control and greater electoral parity between the two parties. When majority status began to change more regularly, bipartisan agreement became harder to find. One possible explanation is that when members of both parties believe that the next election might produce a change in majority status, partisan differentiation may be a dominant driver of legislative behavior, trumping members' interests in finding places of common ground. With previous periods of the modern Congress dominated by infrequent change in majority control – the House majority was held by Democrats from 1955 to 1994 and by Republicans from 1995 to 2006 – the impact of, or just the threat of, change to majority control on legislative behavior is difficult to assess. However, the timing of this decline in bipartisan agreement suggests that competition for the majority is a possible explanation for why bipartisan agreement has declined and why leaders have focused more on partisan legislation.

Moreover, in recent years, party leaders like Nancy Pelosi have advocated against Democrats building bipartisan cosponsorship coalitions[7] (Brownstein 2007, 342). Tea Party groups who have positioned themselves as watchdogs of Republican members have similarly advocated against bipartisanship, halfway measures, or compromise (Skocpol and Williamson 2012, 178). Outside groups compound this pressure. Dick Armey, head of the conservative non-profit Freedom Works, now pressures members not to engage in the same efforts at seeking places

---

[7] This leadership involvement in members' cosponsorship behavior stands in contrast to the typical patterns discussed in Chapter 2.

of common ground that he himself orchestrated a decade earlier as majority leader (Skocpol and Williamson 2012, 174). Contribution patterns to members in the 2010 election indicate that 77 percent of the incoming Republicans in the 112th Congress, including dozens of Tea-Party-backed Republicans, were further to the right than the typical Republican member in the 111th Congress (Bonica 2010; Skocpol and Williamson 2012, 170). As a result of members' own preferences and pressures from leaders, interest groups, and activist segments of the electorate, members have few incentives to craft bipartisan coalitions. With lower levels of bipartisan agreement on legislation, there are more places where partisan differentiation in voting is beneficial for the majority, and thus where a partisan agenda rather than a bipartisan agenda helps to build the party brand.

Second, the costs of failing to produce a record of legislative success may be lower for the majority party than in previous eras. The dominance of partisan pieces of legislation on the agenda, combined with record low levels of productivity, suggest that concerns about governance are not constraining partisan agenda-setting. However, legislative failure alone is not enough to prevent partisan agenda-setting. Failure is only a constraint if the majority party fears the consequences of an unproductive Congress. That is, the valence concerns that drive the majority party's attention to successful enactment of laws require public expectations and electoral pressures to do so. Historically, there is evidence to support this assertion (e.g., Adler and Wilkerson 2013). But governance is only a constraint if voters punish politicians for inaction and partisan gridlock.

Although majorities in the public express support for leaders who are willing to compromise to get the job done (which likely entails pursuing areas of bipartisan agreement during divided government), a growing gap has emerged over the last few years between self-identified Democrats and Republicans. Pew Research Center's Values Survey (2012) reports that while roughly 80 percent of Americans agree with the statement: "I like political leaders who are willing to make compromises in order to get the job done," 90 percent of Democrats but only 68 percent of Republicans agree with the statement (Pew 2012). Although the partisan gap on this question has been growing for the last 15 years, it accelerated during the Obama administration. Moreover, members of the public who identify with the Tea Party movement are even more likely than other Republicans to oppose bipartisanship (Skocpol and Williamson 2012).[8] If Republican voters are increasingly less willing to punish Republican members at the ballot box for legislative inaction resulting from partisan conflict, then there is little reason for the GOP majority to be constrained in its partisan agenda-setting and to be forced to pursue bipartisan options. As a result, public preferences can reinforce partisanship in Congress rather than incentivize bipartisanship.

---

[8] For instance, a 2011 Pew Research Center poll found that in the case of the 2011 budget debates, two-thirds of Tea-Party-identified Republicans favored a shutdown over compromise, while the majority of more moderate Republicans and Independents preferred meeting Democrats part way (Pew Research Center Publications 2011).

Whether or not governance concerns constrain the majority's pursuit of partisan legislation also hinges on how parties view their role in governing. The view of governance used throughout this book focused on the ability of Congress to enact laws, addressing both the routine business of government and new issues confronting the country. If GOP members and their constituents, particularly those who align with the Tea Party movement, believe that the responsibility of members is not to govern in the sense of passing new laws, but instead in reining in the size of government, sticking to "no new taxes" pledges, and aligning government priorities with their interpretation of the constitution, then perhaps "governance" is still of concern – but the definition of governance for Republicans has changed. Rather than meaning legislative action, fulfilling the duties of governance entails limiting, if not eliminating, government activities.[9] In some cases, legislative inaction achieves this goal while simultaneously meeting policy objectives.[10] Well-sorted districts allow GOP leaders to pursue partisan legislation, emphasizing the differences between the two parties without detracting from this alternate goal of governance.

Third, one of the notable features of the 112th and 113th Congresses has been the unwillingness of the members of the Tea Party Caucus to support more centrist or bipartisan options.[11] In previous eras, members' electoral interests constrained their leaders' pursuit of partisan legislation. Cross-pressured members, Blue Dog Democrats, and moderate Republicans risked electoral defeat if they supported a partisan agenda. As a result, members' electoral interests and collective governance goals aligned, both pushing bipartisan legislation onto the agenda. Only policy goals and partisan differentiation pushed leaders to pursue partisan legislation. But with the rise of the Tea Party movement, members' electoral incentives may be driven more by primary rather than general election fears. As a result, the electoral interests of GOP members are yoking them to the right, pushing them toward a partisan, rather than bipartisan, agenda.

---

[9] Even Speaker John Boehner alluded to this definition of governance, suggesting that Congress should be judged on how many laws it repeals, rather than on how many new laws it enacts (O'Brien 2013).

[10] Not only does legislative inaction limit government activities, it also helps the Republicans advance policy aims. On many policies, failure to update legislation to changing socioeconomic conditions undermines the effectiveness of the legislation and the benefits it provides (Hacker 2005). By allowing policies to drift, the GOP can achieve policy objectives without having to repeal or otherwise change the legislation behind these programs.

[11] There is some evidence that bipartisan bills (that receive a roll call vote) are less likely to pass in recent years than in previous periods. Over the period of analysis is this book, the House passages rates for bipartisan legislation did not decline over time (and in fact, have a positive relationship with time when assessed by Congress). Thus, the current political climate appears to be an anomaly rather than reflective of a broader change over time. However, the potentially bigger impact comes from support within the GOP to even bring a bipartisan bill to a vote. Thus, the observed differences in passage rates among bills that reach a vote are likely a lower bound on the extent to which segments of the GOP refuse to support bipartisan options for legislation.

Ultimately, the lack of support for a more bipartisan agenda in the GOP likely comes from Tea Party adherents who are fundamentally opposed to bipartisan legislation on some issues, as their policy aims do not overlap with Democratic members, as well as from mainstream GOP members who fear electoral retribution for compromising or pursuing bipartisan agreement. The behavior of members who self-identify with the Tea Party movement may reflect a belief that they are governing "correctly" and prioritizing principles rather than legislative success (Vogel and Smith 2011). These members may therefore not engage in bipartisanship or support a bipartisan floor agenda. Not surprisingly, an average of 33 percent of cosponsored bills by Republicans in the Tea Party Caucus in the 112th Congress had bipartisan coalitions, compared to 43 percent for non-Tea Party Republicans (p < 0.001). Nonetheless, those Republican members outside of the Tea Party may still be willing to support a partisan floor or roll call agenda, even if they engage in somewhat greater levels of bipartisan cosponsorship. For these members, support of a partisan agenda may provide electoral cover in primary elections, while support for a bipartisan agenda may expose them to risk. This suggests that members' electoral interests continue to affect the agendas that leaders pursue. However, in contrast to Southern Democrats in the 1970s who could not support a *partisan* agenda for fear of electoral harm, mainstream GOP members now may be unable to support a *bipartisan* legislative agenda for fear of electoral retribution in primary elections. In this case, the perceived risk of losing one's seat through a primary loss may be larger than the perceived risk of losing one's seat in the general election, even if the majority does not produce a record of legislative success.

With greater opportunities and potential benefits from differentiation on partisan legislation, fewer costs for inaction among co-partisans in the public, and more electoral risks for members if the party pursues a bipartisan rather than partisan agenda, the leadership's calculus of agenda-setting favors partisan legislation. As a consequence, leaders may pursue partisan Republican initiatives even if they cannot enact them into law. For instance, traditionally bipartisan legislation like the 2013 Farm Bill was stripped of its food stamps provision in order to gain support within the Republican Party[12] (Steinhauer 2013), dooming it in the Senate and with the President. To the extent that legislation is required to meet traditional measures of governance, the GOP leadership may have to count on votes from the minority to overcome objections and electoral concerns by

[12] The first of two farm bills advanced by Republican Representative Frank Lucas (H.R. 1947) was cosponsored by Democrat Collin Peterson and passed through the House Agriculture Committee with bipartisan support (by a vote of 36–10). However, this bill then failed on the House floor (by a vote of 195–234). This bill included cuts to SNAP (Supplemental Nutrition Assistance Program). The cuts were unpopular with Democrats, who disapproved of the cuts altogether, and Republicans, who thought the cuts were not deep enough (Rogers 2013; *Why Did the Farm Bill Fail in the House?* 2013). In 2014, the House passed a farm bill that re-combined food stamps and farm subsidies. Although the passage vote was a party unity vote, it split both parties (Kasperowicz and Wasson 2014).

members in their own party. For instance, votes from the minority party were necessary to pass critical legislation like the 2013 Disaster Relief Supplemental Appropriations Act (providing disaster relief following Hurricane Sandy), the American Taxpayer Relief Act (averting the "fiscal cliff"), and the 2014 debt ceiling increase. All of these bills passed without the support of a majority of Republicans. These points suggest that the insights of the framework outlined in this book continue to ring true in terms of the balance between individual and collective goals, and between governance and differentiation. However, the direction of the individual electoral constraint has changed at the same time as the ability to differentiate and build the party brand has increased and the costs for failing to govern have decreased. Shifts in all three of these areas produced the perfect storm for the majority to pursue a partisan agenda despite the consequences for legislative productivity.

THE FUTURE OF BIPARTISANSHIP

Whether the 112th Congress reflects a new normal, or whether political conditions will shift again in ways that incentivize and constrain party leaders to balance governance and partisan differentiation, remains to be seen. Over the long-term, districts will sort or unsort, the primary election influence of groups like the Tea Party will wax and wane, and public pressures for governance will vary. As a result, leaders' calculations of whether bipartisan or partisan legislation best achieves their objectives will shift across time, moving in response to changing conditions. Yet, even in the short term, there are signs that traditional governance concerns may once again counter-balance the incentives for partisan agenda-setting, and that bipartisanship will again become somewhat more prominent in the House. Consider, for example, the reaction of some GOP supporters in the wake of the October 2013 government shutdown and protracted debt-ceiling fights. Prominent interest groups that have been a mainstay of the Republican Party released harsh words toward the Tea Party wing and promised to support mainstream Republican candidates who would make sure that budgeting legislation passed and that the economic interests of the country were not put at risk by legislative inaction. In his State of American Business address, Tom Donohue, president and CEO of the U.S. Chamber of Commerce, promised that "In primaries and in the general election, we will support candidates who want to work within the legislative process to solve the nation's problems" (Goad and Bogardus 2014).

Combined with "establishment" GOP efforts to influence primaries and weaken the influence of the Tea Party, this reaction points to the possibility that party leaders will need to emphasize legislative action and governance, not just partisan differentiation. And, in fact, there are some recent examples of this shift. In 2014, Speaker John Boehner announced that he would bring legislation to increase the debt ceiling to a vote with no strings attached (in terms of policy concessions on spending or other issues) (Parker and Weisman 2014). Although the bill lacked the support of many members within his own party, some of whom voiced concerns about their primary election interests, the Speaker's decision to bring the bill to a vote demonstrates his recognition of the importance of governance. Likewise, the Farm Bill (H.R. 2642) passed in 2014 once farm subsidies and food stamps were put back into one bill (Kasperowicz and Wasson 2014). Although the House vote was not bipartisan by the metrics used in this book, the vote split both parties: Republicans voted 162–63 (yea-nay) and Democrats voted 89–103. These examples point to the recognition that somewhat more bipartisan legislation may be needed to produce a record of legislative success.

A second sign of shifting political conditions comes from the emergence of groups like "No Labels," a bipartisan group created in 2010 after seeing the Affordable Care Act pass without a single Republican vote. This citizens' movement of Democrats, Republicans, and Independents is focused on the politics of problem solving. The shared belief of the No Labels group is that "politicians in Washington need to find a way to work together again" (*No Labels* 2014). Former Utah Governor Jon Huntsman, one of the founders of No Labels, argues that not only are there still plenty of people in Washington who want to solve problems, but that "common ground in Washington really *does* exist" (Huntsman and Manchin 2014, location 121). They just need a governing process that prioritizes these places of agreement and problem solving.

In January of 2013, No Labels unveiled the "Problem Solvers," a group of House and Senate members committed to meeting regularly, working across the aisle to solve problems, and governing for the future, not just the next election (*No Labels* 2014). As of 2014, seventy-nine House members had joined the Problem Solvers, suggesting that they view governance as an important goal (and potentially one with electoral consequences). No Labels' discussion of members who embrace the politics of problem solving aligns remarkably well with the themes and evidence presented through this book. Their requirements ask that members be "willing to sit down with anyone – especially people from the other party – so long as they are willing to work together to achieve shared success for America. And it means recognizing that having principled and deeply held political beliefs doesn't require an all-or-nothing approach to governance. Especially with divided government, our leaders simply must work together" (*No Labels* 2014). In essence, problem solving entails finding the places of common ground, and pursuing those places on the legislative agenda over partisan policies that limit legislative success. Consistent with the groups' mission to work across the aisle, an average of 45 percent of bills cosponsored by Republican Problem Solvers had bipartisan coalitions in the 112th Congress, compared to 40 percent of the bills cosponsored by other Republican members ($p = 0.043$).

Interestingly, some GOP members who were part of the Tea Party Caucus in the 112th Congress have left the Caucus and aligned themselves with No Labels, citing the tactics of the Tea Party and a lack of focus on governance as part of their reason for leaving. For instance, Mike Coffman (R-CO) joined the Tea Party because of his views about rolling back spending (Riley 2010). He dropped his affiliation after the 112th Congress and joined No Labels as a Problem Solver, citing an interest in governing and working in a bipartisan manner to solve the nation's problems (Coffman 2013). One explanation for Coffman's renewed interest in governance is his electoral concerns. His seat is considered vulnerable in the 2014 general election. This suggests that if members' general election concerns trump primary election concerns, they may support a strategy that balances governance and partisan differentiation rather than one that focuses predominantly on partisanship.

A third sign is that members themselves continue to identify bipartisanship as important in cultivating general election support. For instance, the *Chicago Tribune* invited incumbents in 2012 to answer questionnaires before the editorial board made their endorsements. In addition to asking questions on particular policies, the questionnaires asked members to discuss how Congress can overcome partisan gridlock and to provide examples of when they went against the party leadership on a significant issue. The combination of these questions and answers suggests that perceptions of governance matter and that members seek to cultivate (or at least portray) a record of bipartisan, and not just partisan, accomplishments. Pursuing partisanship may help members curry support among primary constituencies, but demonstrating bipartisanship may be necessary to win over general election constituencies.

In response to the *Tribune*'s questions, members mentioned their voting record, as well as their cosponsorship and other bipartisan efforts. Democrat Daniel Lipinski (D-IL) wrote of how he was "one of five Democrats and four Republicans who joined together to introduce a plan to cut the deficit" (Lipinski 2012). Republican Robert Dold (R-IL), who narrowly lost his reelection bid to Democrat Brad Schneider, also noted that he was a cosponsor of the bipartisan budget resolution based on the Simpson-Bowles Commission (Dold 2012). Other members further elaborated on the meaning of bipartisanship and how their actions reflected real efforts to work across the aisle. For instance, Republican Peter Roskam (R-IL) stated that "True bipartisanship comes when the two parties find an issue of common ground and build support to advance a solution" (Roskam 2012). He offered the example of his legislation to combat Medicare fraud, which was supported by the AARP and the White House and was cosponsored by Democrats in both the House and Senate (Roskam 2012). Combined, these statements suggest that even at the height of partisanship in the 112th Congress, members were engaging in bipartisan activities, and they were cognizant of the ways that bipartisanship was beneficial in the general election. If general election concerns trump primary election concerns, members' support for bipartisan legislative agendas may increase.

Fostering Greater Attention to Governance

The record of the 112th Congress suggests that political conditions in congressional politics may have, at least temporarily, fostered a partisan agenda that is less constrained by the need for legislative success. In previous eras, the electoral interests of cross-pressured members were reinforced by the need to govern; both pushed party leaders to pursue bipartisan legislation on the agenda. In recent years, the electoral interests of GOP members and the need to govern have been at odds; members fear punishment for bipartisanship in primaries, but need bipartisan legislation to govern. Perhaps Mayhew's (2011) case for popular sovereignty and institutional self-correction has changed, at least during the Obama years (Mann and Ornstein 2012, 110). Leaders' incentives to pursue partisan legislation have certainly changed, and there are few political constraints encouraging them to pursue bipartisan legislation. But perhaps, like the GOP after the 104th Congress, congressional parties today will find that they have over-stepped in their partisan aims, at the expense of governance, and will be forced to be more pragmatic down the road. For members, this may mean that general election concerns or interest groups that support more mainstream candidates will need to counter the threats from primaries that pull members toward partisanship. The responses discussed above, by the Chamber of Commerce and groups like No Labels, point to these possibilities.

If the public wants Congress to put a greater emphasis on governance and produce a legislative agenda that balances partisan policy goals with legislative success, what must be done? First, congressional majorities must be held accountable for legislative gridlock. Although scholars have noted the limitations of the idea of "throwing the bums out" as a referendum on the performance of the party in government in times of polarized politics (Mann and Ornstein 2012, 189), punishment for failing to govern is essential for encouraging party leaders and members to balance partisan policy goals against governance. As noted by former House member and Secretary of Agriculture Daniel Glickman, the public must demand bipartisanship if they are to get it (Glickman 2011). Likewise, interest groups and others who support the parties must, like the Chamber of Commerce, make governing a criterion for support in *both* primary and general elections.

Second, individual members must also be held accountable for partisanship in the general election to make members fear not just primary but also general election constituencies. Without this pressure, individual electoral interests may push members to support partisan rather than bipartisan agendas. Although portions of this book pointed to reasons that electoral risks for members have declined over time (as sorting increased), the experiences of the Democrats in the 2010 elections suggest that members in that party were punished for partisanship, particularly if they came from more competitive districts. A comment from a moderate Democrat who lost his seat in that election highlights the effects of the partisan strategy when the national tide swung toward the Republican Party:

And certainly Pelosi was no better than Hastert at relying only upon Democrats to advance her legislation and she did not care at all if basically it was a one-party-only approach even though that proved to be politically catastrophic to people like me. So instead of negotiating with centrist Republicans and getting at least a [small amount] of bipartisanship, she drives it to the left edge of the caucus ... and the center portion of the Democratic caucus that is now being yoked to the left end up becoming increasingly politically exposed. That is why we had the single worst congressional election in my view for House Democrats ever. (Anonymous 2011)

The same consequences must hold true for Republicans if the public can expect elections to rein in partisan agenda-setting. By holding members accountable for partisanship in November, voters can balance out the incentives for partisanship that come from the primary electorate or from collective party goals.

If a strategy of crafting a partisan legislative agenda exposes more moderate contingents of the majority party to defeat, the future trends of partisanship in Congress will depend on who replaces those moderate members. The more homogenous the party, the more willing they are to pursue a partisan agenda, suggesting that if sorted members of one party replace unsorted members of an opposing party, then there may be a potentially vicious cycle of partisanship. However, if members in the most competitive districts become a voice against a partisan legislative strategy, prioritizing their individual general reelection goals above the policy and brand goals of the collective party, party leaders may be forced to pursue more bipartisan legislation on the agenda.

A SHIFT IN AGENDA-SETTING FROM BIPARTISANSHIP BY CONSTRAINT TO PARTISANSHIP BY CHOICE

Over the quarter-century from 1973 to 2004, House majorities shifted the focus of their legislative agendas from prioritizing bipartisan legislation to the inclusion of more and more partisan bills. I argued that early in this period, party leaders pursued bipartisan legislation on the floor and roll call agendas as a result of the constraints of members' electoral interests. Over time, district-party sorting opened the door for members to support a more partisan agenda, but bipartisan legislation was nonetheless propelled forward by governance concerns, particularly during periods with small majorities or divided government. When the majority leaders saw their partisan agenda end in legislative failure in 1995, they shifted their agenda, bringing more bipartisan legislation to the floor in the late 1990s. This pattern changed during the Obama era as Republican House majorities pursued partisan legislation despite legislative defeat during divided government. When the majority party faced few punishments for failing to govern and individual members faced primary election pressures to pursue partisanship rather than bipartisanship, incentives to pursue partisan legislation abounded.

Partisan legislation meets the majority party's policy goals and its interest in pointing out differences with the opposing party, while bipartisan legislation muddles the differences between the two sides. As a result, House majorities have increasingly pursued partisan agenda-setting over time as the electoral interests of members have become better aligned with the collective interests of their party. Representative Jeff Flake (R-AZ) sums up the increasing connection between differentiating the two sides and developing a partisan legislative strategy, in spite of alternative routes that could have fostered bipartisanship:

It seems that over the last couple of years [that] if something can come to the floor and you can pass it with a bipartisan majority, . . . or if you can bring it to the floor in a way that you can just get Republican support and use it as a political issue against the Democrats, we have chosen the latter every time. (Brownstein 2007)

As a consequence, partisan conflict in the House of Representatives has been magnified by the content of the roll call agenda. Bipartisanship in policymaking remains possible, but both parties must have incentives to pursue that route over one of partisanship.

Appendix

In this appendix, I present both robustness checks and complete model specifications for the analyses used throughout this book. Appendices are separated by chapter, with supplemental materials for Chapters 1, 2, 4, 5, 6, and 7.

CHAPTER 1 APPENDIX MATERIALS

The appendix materials for Chapter 1 provide a complete list of the interviews conducted with former members and House staffers as well as a reference table of years and Congresses used in the analyses. These interviews were used to supplement the empirical analyses and to provide examples of the concepts discussed in the book. Former House members interviewed include Michael Castle (R-DE), Artur Davis (D-AL), Daniel Glickman (D-KS), Daniel Maffei (D-NY) (who subsequently regained his seat), Alan Mollohan (D-WV), Earl Pomeroy (D-ND), and Ike Skelton (D-MO). House staffers interviewed include Michael Stephens (former Appropriations staffer), Eric Lausten (Chief of Staff for Daniel Lipinski (D-IL)), two staff members for senior Democrats in the 112th Congress, and two staff members for senior Republicans in the 112th Congress (all of whom asked to remain anonymous).

CHAPTER 2 APPENDIX MATERIALS

The appendix materials for Chapter 2 provide a number of robustness checks of the bipartisanship measures presented in the main text. Combined, they show that: (1) the trend of bipartisan cosponsorship, which declined relatively little between 1973 and 2004, is not an artifact of the threshold for defining bipartisanship, minority-sponsored bills, bills with very few cosponsors, active moderate members or shifts in issue attention over time; (2) bipartisan and partisan cosponsored bills fare differently in subsequent voting patterns (in terms of the

TABLE AI.1 *Reference Table of Years and Congresses*

Years	Congress	House Majority	President
1973–1974	93	Democrats	Nixon
1975–1976	94	Democrats	Ford
1977–1978	95	Democrats	Carter
1979–1980	96	Democrats	Carter
1981–1982	97	Democrats	Reagan
1983–1984	98	Democrats	Reagan
1985–1986	99	Democrats	Reagan
1987–1988	100	Democrats	Reagan
1989–1990	101	Democrats	H.W. Bush
1991–1992	102	Democrats	H.W. Bush
1993–1994	103	Democrats	Clinton
1995–1996	104	Republicans	Clinton
1997–1998	105	Republicans	Clinton
1999–2000	106	Republicans	Clinton
2001–2002	107	Republicans	G.W. Bush
2003–2004	108	Republicans	G.W. Bush

likelihood of a bipartisan vote); and (3) omitting non-cosponsored bills does not bias the analysis toward showing the persistence of bipartisanship over time.

Bipartisan Cosponsorship Persists Between 1973 and 2004

Robustness Check: Are over time patterns of bipartisan cosponsorship sensitive to the threshold for defining bipartisanship?
While the level of bipartisanship varies depending on the threshold for classifying cosponsorship coalitions as bipartisan, the trend over time does not. Figure A2.1 shows the percentage of cosponsored bills that are bipartisan, varying the threshold from 20 percent to 50 percent of the cosponsors being from the party opposite the party of the sponsor.

Robustness Check: Is bipartisan cosponsorship occurring primarily on minority-sponsored bills (that are unlikely to receive further legislative attention)?
The trend of continued bipartisan agreement over time among all cosponsored bills is not driven by cosponsorship of minority-sponsored bills. Rather, the trend of bipartisan cosponsorship among majority-sponsored bills (Figure A2.2) is positive (especially at the end of the time series), suggesting that bipartisan agreement continued to occur frequently on majority-sponsored bills. Since majority-sponsored bills are more likely to gain attention at subsequent legislative stages than minority-sponsored bills, this pattern emphasizes that bipartisan agreement continues on those bills that the leaders would most likely pursue for the floor and roll call agendas.

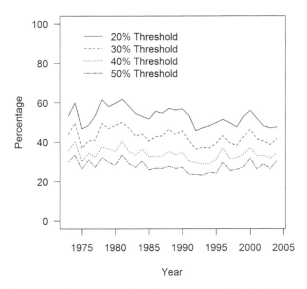

FIGURE A2.1 Bipartisan Cosponsorship with Alternative Thresholds

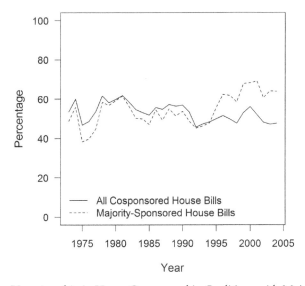

FIGURE A2.2 Bipartisanship in House Cosponsorship Coalitions with Majority Sponsors

Robustness Check: Is the persistence of bipartisan agreement confined to bills with very few cosponsors?

Whether the analysis of bipartisan agreement uses all cosponsored House bills or bills with the median or more cosponsors (by Congress), the patterns are nearly identical. Figure A2.3 provides patterns of bipartisanship for all

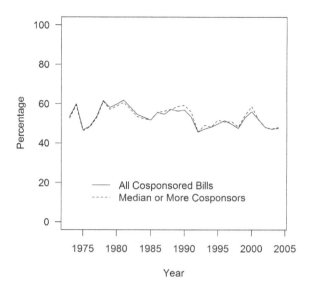

FIGURE A2.3 Bipartisanship in House Cosponsorship Coalitions with More than the Median Number of Cosponsors

cosponsored bills and for cosponsored bills with the median or more cosponsors. The differences between these two groups of bills are slight: they never differ by more than 2.6 percentage points and the correlation between the two is 0.97 ($p < 0.001$). Thus, the inclusion of bills in the analysis with very few cosponsors is not driving the patterns of bipartisan agreement over time.

Robustness Check: Do factors such as the distribution of policies or active moderates drive the observed patterns that bipartisan agreement continued over time in cosponsorship coalitions?
If the distribution of issues that members cosponsor has shifted over time from highly partisan issues to highly bipartisan issues, then the overall pattern of bipartisan cosponsorship may be biased toward finding bipartisan agreement. While there are differences between issues in the likelihood of attracting bipartisan agreement, variation over time in the proportion of the cosponsorship agenda in each of these issue areas across Congresses does not systematically bias the cosponsorship measures toward seeing greater bipartisanship over time. Among the 19 issue areas (defined by the major topic codes of the Congressional Bills Project (Adler and Wilkerson 2008)), 10 have significant correlations with time. However, those with positive correlations include a range of issue types (based on the degree to which the issue attracts bipartisanship), as do those with

negative correlations.[1] Moreover, the size of the change in agenda attention is on the magnitude of only a few percentage points (i.e., an issue was 6 percent of the agenda and is now 3 percent of the agenda). While there is some variation in the distribution of these issues among cosponsored bills over time, there is little evidence that cosponsored bills have gone from occurring disproportionately on the least bipartisan issues to the most bipartisan issues.

A second potential concern is whether bipartisan cosponsorship coalitions are merely the result of active moderates in the chamber. Previous work has found that more ideologically extreme members, rather than moderates, are more active in cosponsoring legislation (Campbell 1982), which offers an initial suggestion that the concern may be unfounded. Certainly, moderate members end up in bipartisan coalitions more often than ideologically extreme members, but, at the bill level, higher frequency of cosponsorship by ideologically extreme members would suggest that partisanship, not bipartisanship, should be overstated in cosponsorship coalitions. To systematically assess whether the composition of coalitions has changed over time, I examine the ideological make-up of cosponsorship coalitions using the DW-NOMINATE scores of the members in the cosponsoring coalition.

Figure A2.4 plots the interquartile range of the cosponsors' DW-NOMINATE score against the median score for both the bills defined as "partisan" and "bipartisan" for selected Congresses.[2] The gray dots represent the ideological distribution of partisan bills, and the black dots represent the ideological distribution of bipartisan bills. The primary change in the distribution of bills over time from the 93rd to the 108th Congresses is an absence of bipartisan bills that include only moderates (i.e., where the interquartile range is small but the median is near 0). Therefore, to the extent that they have changed at all, the nature of bipartisan cosponsorship coalitions has been to become increasingly broad ideologically rather than increasingly made up of moderates, as one might have expected.

Moreover, the percentage of cosponsored bills that are bipartisan and have as a cosponsor at least one member who is among the 10 percent most liberal and at least one member who is among the 10 percent most conservative is stable at roughly 20 percent across the time period.[3] Combined with the previous analysis, these patterns suggest that the legislation classified as bipartisan has not changed over time to be the result of just a handful of active moderates. Rather,

---

[1] Policy areas with a significant positive correlation with time include issues that are the least bipartisan (labor, education), medium bipartisan (health, public lands), and most bipartisan (space and technology, international affairs). Likewise, policy areas with a significant negative correlation with time cross the spectrum as well, with issues that are the least bipartisan (social welfare), medium bipartisan (energy), and most bipartisan (agriculture, transportation).

[2] Bipartisan bills are defined as those in which at least 20 percent of the cosponsors are from the party opposite of the party of the bill's primary sponsor. Results are similar if all Congresses, rather than a subset, are shown.

[3] Note that members are coded as among the 10 percent most liberal or conservative in each Congress but the bill level analysis includes members who were among the 10 percent most liberal/conservative in any Congress.

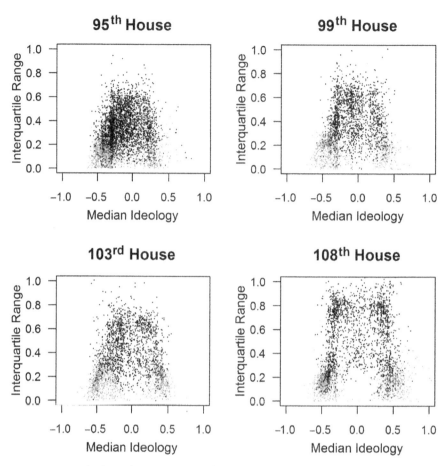

FIGURE A2.4 Ideological Composition of Cosponsorship Coalitions
Note: The x-axis represents the DW-NOMINATE score of the median member of the cosoponsorship coalition. The y-axis represents the interquartile range of the DW-NOMINATE scores of members in the coalition (75–25 percent). Gray points represent partisan bills and black points represent bipartisan bills. The observed pattern holds across Congresses.

bipartisan and partisan cosponsorship coalitions appear to be capturing real variation in the likelihood of garnering support from members of both parties.

Bipartisan Cosponsored Bills are Different from Partisan Cosponsored Bills

Robustness Check: Are bills with bipartisan cosponsorship coalitions more likely to receive bipartisan roll call votes than partisan cosponsored bills?
Using data from the Policy Agendas Project, Rohde's (2004) dataset of House roll call votes, and my bipartisan bill cosponsorship measures, I analyze whether

bipartisan bills received *any* bipartisan votes and whether they received a bipartisan *final passage* vote. The same analysis is done for partisan bills, with the expectation that bills classified as bipartisan in their cosponsorship will be more likely than bills classified as partisan to receive bipartisan roll call votes. Table A2.1 presents the proportion of bipartisan cosponsored bills receiving a bipartisan vote, the proportion of partisan cosponsored bills receiving a bipartisan vote, and the difference between these two measures (as well as the p-value (two-tailed) on the difference in means).[4] The first set of columns considers whether a bill receives any bipartisan votes and the latter set considers whether a bill received a bipartisan final passage vote. In all cases, the difference is positive, and in most cases this reflects a significant difference, which indicates that the cosponsorship measure is capturing differences between bipartisan and partisan bills.

Insights from Cosponsored Bills Versus Non-Cosponsored Bills

Robustness Check: Do differences between cosponsored and non-cosponsored bills limit the ability to infer patterns of early-stage bipartisan agreement more generally from the observed patterns of cosponsored bills?

Cosponsorship coalitions suggest that there continue to be a number of bills where bipartisanship is possible; roll call votes suggest declining agreement over time. The classification of cosponsorship coalitions as bipartisan or partisan, however, requires that we ignore non-cosponsored bills since they are not informative about the supporting coalition. This series of robustness checks considers whether this "missing data" should be of concern when using bipartisan cosponsorship to make inferences about substantive agreement on legislation over time. It does so by, first, exploring possible models of the data-generation process behind cosponsorship and, second, comparing cosponsored and non-cosponsored bills on observable variables related to bipartisan agreement.

As argued by Desposato et al. (2011), using cosponsorship coalitions to measure legislator ideal points can be problematic when we do not know the underlying data-generation process and thus how to treat bills that a member does not cosponsor. In particular, we may not want to assume that a failure to cosponsor a bill is equivalent to a nay vote. Desposato and his co-authors explore four possible data-generation processes: sincere (where failure to cosponsor is a nay vote), random (where members select a random set of bills to consider, then cosponsor or not), neighbor (where members select bills for consideration based on whether the bill was authored by a colleague with similar preferences), and network (where members consider bills that are authored by colleagues with whom they share connections). In the latter three, only subsets of failures to cosponsor are equivalent to nay votes. Do assumptions about which process is at work affect my

---

[4] Note that the values in each column are rounded to two significant digits, meaning that in some instances the difference score differs marginally from the rounded proportion of bipartisan bills minus the rounded proportion of partisan bills.

TABLE A2.1 *Proportion of Bills Receiving a Bipartisan Roll Call Vote*

	Any Bipartisan Roll Call Vote			Final Passage Bipartisan Roll Call Vote		
Congress	Bipartisan Cosponsored Bills	Partisan Cosponsored Bills	Difference (Bipartisan–Partisan)	Bipartisan Cosponsored Bills	Partisan Cosponsored Bills	Difference (Bipartisan–Partisan)
93	0.92	0.81	0.11 (p = 0.13)	0.89	0.69	0.20 (p = 0.024)
94	0.83	0.73	0.09 (p = 0.15)	0.79	0.60	0.19 (p = 0.0079)
95	0.94	0.89	0.05 (p = 0.29)	0.88	0.75	0.13 (p = 0.028)
96	0.90	0.86	0.04 (p = 0.49)	0.71	0.69	0.02 (p = 0.79)
97	0.87	0.67	0.20 (p = 0.052)	0.77	0.56	0.21 (p = 0.056)
98	0.84	0.55	0.29 (p < 0.001)	0.75	0.43	0.31 (p < 0.001)
99	0.84	0.62	0.22 (p = 0.017)	0.76	0.45	0.31 (p = 0.0015)
100	0.87	0.67	0.20 (p = 0.012)	0.75	0.57	0.18 (p = 0.033)
101	0.89	0.72	0.16 (p = 0.034)	0.79	0.57	0.21 (p = 0.017)
102	0.95	0.58	0.36 (p < 0.001)	0.82	0.46	0.36 (p < 0.001)

103	0.90	0.68	0.22 (p = 0.0062)	0.82	0.43	0.38 ($p < 0.001$)
104	0.86	0.63	0.23 (p = 0.0026)	0.78	0.48	0.30 ($p < 0.001$)
105	0.85	0.56	0.29 ($p < 0.001$)	0.77	0.43	0.34 ($p < 0.001$)
106	0.90	0.65	0.25 ($p < 0.001$)	0.85	0.60	0.25 ($p < 0.001$)
107	0.93	0.68	0.25 ($p < 0.001$)	0.92	0.58	0.34 ($p < 0.001$)
108	0.93	0.53	0.41 ($p < 0.001$)	0.91	0.47	0.44 ($p < 0.001$)

measures of bipartisan cosponsorship or the inferences from them? Moreover, if there is a change over time between which data-generation process is at work, does that affect the measurement of bipartisan cosponsorship coalitions and the inferences regarding strategic agenda-setting?

I argue that the answer to both questions is no. Since I am focusing on bills rather than on members, I am agnostic about failures to cosponsor a bill. Looking at the mix of members from the two parties who *do* jointly cosponsor a bill simply tells us that there is substantive agreement between that group of members on that issue/bill. While the issue of how members select bills to cosponsor may affect the degree of noise in the measure (in terms of using cosponsorship coalitions to speak to broader levels of bipartisan agreement on the bill), I suggest that this is a relatively minor concern, for the following reasons.

If members are considering all bills, then assessments of agreement between coalitions from both sides of the aisle would be accurate, but the small number of cosponsors would suggest that only a handful of bills in each Congress could pass (i.e., only those with more than 218 cosponsors) – a pattern that is rejected by the data. If members are considering a random subset of bills, then assessments of bipartisanship with my data are quite informative and patterns of bipartisan cosponsorship are likely to reflect the broader extent of bipartisan agreement. If members are considering only a subset of bills based on social connections, then gauging broader bipartisan or partisan agreement in the chamber would only be restricted if the social connections that lead to members' consideration of the bill for cosponsorship were in some way correlated with support for the bill. If members are considering only bills by like-minded ideologues, this could be more problematic, but it would indicate that bipartisan bills resulted only from moderates sponsoring the bills of other moderates. The previous robustness check indicated that this was not the case. Moreover, if either of the last two data-generation processes were at work to an extent where my metrics of bipartisan cosponsorship did not translate to the likelihood of bipartisan agreement on the floor, we should not have seen the clear differences in rates of bipartisan roll call voting for bills with bipartisan versus partisan cosponsorship coalitions.

Second, if there is a change over time between which data-generation process is at work, does that affect the measurement of bipartisan cosponsorship coalitions and the inferences regarding strategic agenda-setting? Again, I suggest that the answer is no. For instance, if members engaged in a sincere (complete) or random process of selecting which bills to consider for cosponsorship in the 1970s, but moved toward a neighbor or network model in the 1990s (for instance, considering bills sponsored by same-state members), we might be concerned that bipartisan cosponsorship measures reflected broad bipartisan agreement in the 1970s but more narrow agreement in the 1990s. However, if this were the case, the average number of cosponsors on a bill would have likely dropped over time. Table 2.2 in Chapter 2 shows the opposite: the number of cosponsors on bills increased over time. In addition, the analysis of the percentage of bipartisan and partisan cosponsored bills (that received any roll call votes) that received bipartisan votes, indicated, first, that bipartisan bills are always more likely than partisan bills to receive bipartisan votes, and, second, that the correlation with time was positive (not negative, which would be more concerning). Finally, if the data-generation process changed in a way that makes the cosponsorship measure of bipartisanship indicate increasingly narrow or minimal bipartisanship over time, it would again bias the subsequent analyses against finding support for the argument of strategic agenda-setting. That is, if the bills classified as bipartisan are ultimately no different in their prospects for support between the two parties than the bills classified as partisan (minus a few members from the same state or other shared network or ideological grouping), then we would not expect to see any differences in the treatment of these two categories of bills over time in the floor scheduling and voting.

To emphasize that patterns from cosponsored bills translate to patterns of bipartisan agreement on introduced bills more broadly, I examine whether non-cosponsored bills differ on observables from cosponsored bills in ways that would counter (and possibly invalidate) the claim that bipartisanship in the early stages of the legislative process has been remarkably stable over this period of Congressional politics. These analyses make the assumption that had these non-cosponsored bills been cosponsored, the effect of key observable variables on these bills would be similar to the effect of these variables on cosponsored bills. More broadly, this assumes that cosponsored and non-cosponsored bills are not fundamentally different from one another in terms of their propensity for substantive agreement between members of the two parties when controlling for observable variables.

Before considering differences on observables between all cosponsored and non-cosponsored bills, two preliminary points are worth emphasizing. First, the rates of cosponsorship over time indicate that over the period of analysis cosponsorship grew in frequency (from 30 percent of bills in the 93rd Congress to 73 percent of bills in the 108th Congress). Thus, the percentage of all introduced bills that I am capturing with the cosponsorship measure increases over time. Second, among bills that receive roll call votes, the patterns of bipartisan voting are very similar among all votes, votes on bills that were cosponsored, and votes on bills that were not cosponsored.

Figure A2.5 shows the percentage of bipartisan roll call votes in Congress, building from Figure 2.1 and adding non-cosponsored bills as an additional subset of votes. The first subset of votes is what I term "H.R. bills." These are votes where the underlying bill was a House bill (i.e., H.R.) according to the Policy Agendas Project coding.[5] Across the years in the analysis, over 95 percent

---

[5] The cosponsorship analysis omits private bills, since they are rarely cosponsored (only 29 instances across all Congresses in this analysis) but make up a potentially larger pool of non-cosponsored bills. If roll call votes occurred frequently on private bills at any point in the analysis and they were largely bipartisan, we would want to make the same adjustment for the roll call data. Although

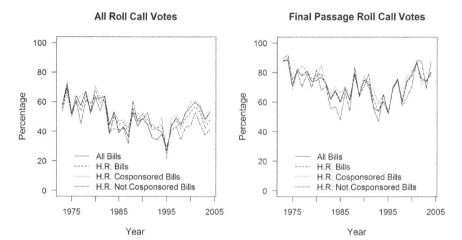

FIGURE A2.5 Bipartisanship in House Roll Call Voting by Type of Bill
Note: Bipartisan votes defined as those where a majority of Democrats vote with a majority of Republicans. H.R. bills designate House bills.

of votes are on House originating bills, including House bills, resolutions, and so forth. Moreover, an average of 66 percent of votes occurred where the underlying bill is a House bill (captured in the "H.R. bills" category). The next subset of votes focuses on those where the underlying bill was a House bill (H.R.) with at least one cosponsor. Across all years, an average of 39 percent of all House votes fall in this category. The final category in the figure is votes where the underlying bill was a House bill (H.R.) but there were no cosponsors on the bill. Across all years, an average of 27 percent of all House votes fall in this category. As seen in Figure A2.5 (left-hand panel), regardless of the subset of votes that are included, the patterns are very similar. In fact, the correlation between cosponsored and non-cosponsored H.R. bills is 0.74 and the correlation increases when cosponsored H.R. bills are compared to either all roll call votes (r = 0.89) or to all H.R. bills (r = 0.95). Figure A2.5 (right-hand panel) provides a similar analysis of final passage votes, comparing H.R. bills, H.R. cosponsored bills, and H.R. non-cosponsored bills. Here, the average yearly percentage of final passage votes that occur on cosponsored House bills is 57 percent, compared to only 31 percent for non-cosponsored bills. As with the full set of votes, the patterns of final passage votes reveal very similar patterns between votes on cosponsored and non-cosponsored bills (r = 0.75) and between votes on cosponsored bills and all House bills (r = 0.94).

69 percent of votes on private bills were bipartisan, a total of only 16 private bills received roll call votes in the period of my analysis (with a maximum of 7 private bills receiving votes in the 94th Congress). Since this small number of votes is unlikely to bias the results of the analyses, I include all House bills, both public and private, in these analyses.

These patterns indicate two important points: first, cosponsored bills are a sizeable component of the roll call agenda; and second, the voting patterns on all bills, cosponsored bills, and non-cosponsored bills are very similar, which provides some mitigation against the concern that cosponsored and non-cosponsored bills are systematically different. In this case, the observable feature is the voting patterns. However, since the larger argument of this book is that the roll call agenda is a non-random sample of legislation, the next analyses focus on observable differences between *all* cosponsored and non-cosponsored bills, not just among those that receive roll call votes.

Non-cosponsored bills can be considered a case of an unknown counter-factual, where we do not know whether the bill would have received a bipartisan or partisan coalition of cosponsors had it been cosponsored.[6] Given this missing information, the most important question for my analyses of cosponsored data and inferences regarding continued substantive agreement in this area is whether non-cosponsored bills changed over time from being overwhelmingly bipartisan (had they been cosponsored) in the 1970s to overwhelmingly partisan (had they been cosponsored) in the 1990s and 2000s. If non-cosponsored bills changed in this way, then the analysis of only cosponsored bills would mask a broader trend of declining bipartisan agreement that would be observed if non-cosponsored bills had, in fact, been cosponsored. I present two sets of analyses that draw on observable features of all introduced bills to allay this concern. The first focuses on the distribution of bill sponsor ideologies and the second focuses on the distribution of policy issues.

The first comparison focuses on the estimated ideology of the bill sponsor. The key pattern here is not whether ideal point estimates show that members are becoming more ideologically extreme, but whether the ideology estimates for bill sponsors are similar for the subsets of cosponsored and non-cosponsored bills *within* a Congress. Assuming that bills sponsored by the more moderate members of the chamber are more likely to be bipartisan than bills sponsored by ideologues, it would be problematic for my argument if non-cosponsored bills had sponsors among the most moderate in the chamber in the 1970s but among the most extreme in the 1990s and 2000s. The first condition of the previous sentence is borne out by the data on cosponsored bills, suggesting that this is an important observable variable on which to compare cosponsored and non-cosponsored bills. Among all cosponsored bills between the 93rd and 108th Congresses, a logistic regression of bipartisanship (using the 20 percent

[6] With the exception of appropriations bills, all other bills have the potential for cosponsors. The restriction on cosponsorship for appropriations bills comes from the rule that the deadline for cosponsoring a bill is when it is reported from committee. Since appropriations bills come to life as an original measure reported out of the committee, there is no opportunity to cosponsor. However, there are only as many bills in this category as there are appropriations bills in each year, which is equivalent to 13 or 14 House bills in the typical year. Thus, the lack of cosponsorship on these bills is not the predominant reason for a lack of cosponsorship. Moreover, among final passage votes on appropriations bills there is not a strong time trend on the percentage of bipartisan votes ($r = -0.12$).

definition) on the absolute value of the bill sponsor's first dimension DW-NOMINATE score yields a significant result ($\beta = -2.84$, $p < 0.001$). This result holds within Congresses as well, by adding dummy variables for each Congress to the model or by running the analysis separately on each Congress. As the extremity of a bill sponsor's DW-NOMINATE score increases (within a Congress), their bill is less likely to receive a bipartisan coalition of cosponsors.[7]

Analyses of the absolute value of the bill sponsor's first dimension DW-NOMINATE score, separated for the subset of bills that are cosponsored and the subset that are not cosponsored, suggest that although there are slight differences between the two sets of bills, there has not been a shift over time toward non-cosponsored bills having more extreme sponsors than cosponsored bills. Figure A2.6 presents a box plot for each subset in each Congress. Although there is a trend over time of increasingly extreme DW-NOMINATE values,

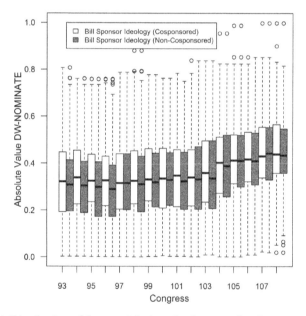

FIGURE A2.6 Distribution of Sponsor Ideology by Congress for Cosponsored and Non-Cosponsored Bills

---

[7] The relationship between bill sponsor ideology and the likelihood of receiving bipartisan cosponsorship coalitions is consistent with multiple views of bill sponsorship. From a spatial perspective, this would be consistent with moderate members introducing more ideologically moderate legislation. However, this need not be the case, as bill cosponsorship may not be mere position taking and committee leadership and majority party status may have a moderating effect on legislation, as found by Woon (2008). Nonetheless, the relationship between sponsor ideology and the type of cosponsorship coalition suggests that this is an important observable variable on which to compare cosponsored and non-cosponsored legislation.

consistent with the ideal point-based measures of polarization, the important comparison for this analysis is between the cosponsored bar plot (in white) and the non-cosponsored bar plot (in gray) *within* a Congress. From the 93rd to 103rd Congresses, the median sponsor ideology on bills that were not cosponsored was marginally more moderate than the bill sponsors of cosponsored bills. By the 104th Congress (and onward) there was essentially no difference in the medians between the two groups. This suggests that while non-cosponsored bills may have had slightly more moderate sponsors than cosponsored bills in the early period of my analysis, there were few differences between the ideologies of the sponsors of the two sets of bills in the more recent period. In no way did the sponsors of non-cosponsored bills become substantially more ideologically extreme than the sponsors of cosponsored bills in these recent years.

Since the number of bills in a given Congress ranges from 4,344 in the 104th Congress to 17,690 in the 93rd Congress, the large N in the analysis allows many of the differences in median or mean values between the cosponsored and non-cosponsored bill populations to be statistically significant. To explore whether these differences are *substantively* important for understanding the potential for bipartisan agreement on cosponsored and non-cosponsored bills within each Congress, I analyze the predicted probability of bipartisan cosponsorship for each mean value of sponsor ideology, with the results shown in Table A2.2.[8] Although the difference in means between the two distributions is significantly different from 0 in 8 of the 16 Congresses ($p < 0.05$), the substantive effect is quite small. The raw difference in means ranges from 0.0 to 0.04 on a 0 to 1 scale, but only three Congresses have a mean difference of 0.03 or larger. Thus, the difference is rarely more than 3 percent of the possible range. Moreover, using these mean values to predict the likelihood of bipartisan cosponsorship coalitions yields similarly small substantive differences (and few statistically significant differences).[9] These findings suggest that while non-cosponsored bills may, on average, have had more moderate sponsors in the early period of my analysis, the substantive impact on the likelihood of bipartisan cosponsorship (compared to cosponsored bills) is slight. Moreover, the trend over time is a shift toward more similar distributions between the two subsets of bills, not a

[8] First, for each Congress, I took the subset of bills that are cosponsored and regressed bipartisan cosponsorship on the absolute value of the sponsor's ideology. Second, for both non-cosponsored and cosponsored bills, I calculated the mean of the absolute value of the sponsor's ideology. Third, I examined the predicted probability of having a bipartisan cosponsorship for each observed mean value (non-cosponsored and cosponsored), basing the predictions on the regression in the first step. Finally, I calculated the 95 percent confidence interval for each predicted probability. If the differences in sponsor ideology between non-cosponsored and cosponsored bills are substantively important, then their predicted probabilities should be significantly different from one another, as shown by non-overlapping confidence intervals. If, however, the confidence intervals in each Congress overlap for the two sets of bills, this suggests that the differences in sponsor ideology between non-cosponsored and cosponsored bills are minor.

[9] For all but the 94th Congress the 95 percent confidence intervals on these predictions intersect for the non-cosponsored and cosponsored mean sponsor ideology.

TABLE A2.2 *Average Extremity of Sponsor Ideology and Predicted Probability of Bipartisan Cosponsorship for Non-Cosponsored and Cosponsored Bills*

Congress	Mean Sponsor Ideology (Non-Cosponsored)	Mean Sponsor Ideology (Cosponsored)	Difference (p-value)	Predicted Probability of Bipartisan Cosponsorship for Non-Cosponsored Mean Ideology (95% CI)	Predicted Probability of Bipartisan Cosponsorship for Cosponsored Mean Ideology (95% CI)
93	0.31	0.32	−0.01 ($p < 0.001$)	0.58 (0.56, 0.59)	0.56 (0.55, 0.58)
94	0.30	0.34	−0.04 ($p < 0.001$)	0.51 (0.49, 0.52)	0.47 (0.46, 0.49)
95	0.30	0.33	−0.03 ($p < 0.001$)	0.59 (0.58, 0.60)	0.57 (0.56, 0.58)
96	0.30	0.33	−0.03 ($p < 0.001$)	0.61 (0.59, 0.63)	0.59 (0.57, 0.61)
97	0.33	0.32	0.01 ($p < 0.1$)	0.61 (0.59, 0.63)	0.62 (0.60, 0.63)
98	0.32	0.34	−0.014 ($p < 0.01$)	0.56 (0.54, 0.57)	0.55 (0.53, 0.56)
99	0.33	0.34	−0.01 ($p < 0.01$)	0.55 (0.53, 0.56)	0.54 (0.52, 0.55)
100	0.34	0.34	0.00 ($p = 0.70$)	0.56 (0.55, 0.58)	0.56 (0.54, 0.58)
101	0.33	0.34	−0.01 ($p < 0.05$)	0.58 (0.56, 0.60)	0.57 (0.56, 0.60)

Congress	Non-cosponsored bills	Cosponsored bills	Difference	Predicted probability	
102	0.34	0.34	0.00 (0=0.31)	0.51 (0.50, 0.53)	0.51 (0.49, 0.53)
103	0.35	0.36	−0.01 (p < 0.01)	0.49 (0.47, 0.51)	0.48 (0.46, 0.50)
104	0.39	0.39	0.00 (p = 0.23)	0.52 (0.50, 0.53)	0.51 (0.49, 0.53)
105	0.41	0.42	−0.01 (p = 0.16)	0.50 (0.48, 0.52)	0.49 (0.48, 0.51)
106	0.43	0.43	0.0 (p = 0.20)	0.55 (0.53, 0.57)	0.55 (0.53, 0.56)
107	0.45	0.45	0.0 (p = 0.78)	0.51 (0.50, 0.53)	0.51 (0.50, 0.53)
108	0.46	0.47	−0.01 (p = 0.29)	0.48 (0.46, 0.49)	0.48 (0.46, 0.49)

Note: For each Congress, the table presents the mean sponsor ideology (as the absolute value of DW-NOMINATE scores), first for non-cosponsored bills and then for cosponsored bills. The difference (and its significance) follows. The last two columns present the predicted probability of bipartisan cosponsorship for the observed mean ideology using the regression results of the relationship between bipartisan cosponsorship and sponsor ideology among cosponsored bills.

change to where non-cosponsored bills were substantially more likely to be proposed by ideologically extreme members. Thus, despite some differences between cosponsored and non-cosponsored bills, the patterns of sponsor ideology and their relationship to bipartisan agreement suggest that the exclusion of non-cosponsored bills does not omit bills that were substantially more bipartisan (if they had been cosponsored) in the early period but more partisan (if they had been cosponsored) in the later period relative to the observed cosponsored bills. As a result, omitting non-cosponsored bills does not invalidate the patterns of bipartisan agreement shown in Chapter 2.

The next comparison of cosponsored and non-cosponsored bills on observable variables focuses on the policy area of each bill since this too may be related to the likelihood of achieving bipartisan support. Drawing on the major topic codes assigned to each bill by the Congressional Bills Project (Adler and Wilkerson 2008), I focus on 19 substantive issue areas. As discussed at length in Chapter 6, there is substantial variation between policy areas in the likelihood of having bipartisan rather than partisan cosponsorship coalitions. This variation matches much of the common understandings of partisan conflict – among the most bipartisan issues are defense, space and technology, and transportation; and among the least bipartisan issues are civil rights, labor, and education. As with the previous analysis of sponsor ideology, the important comparison here is not whether the distribution of issues among non-cosponsored bills changes over time but whether the distribution of issues among non-cosponsored bills changes over time in a way that is substantially different from changes in the distribution of issues among cosponsored bills. That is, we ought to be concerned if non-cosponsored bills change across the period of analysis from being dominated by defense bills to being dominated by civil rights bills, while cosponsored bills change across the same period in the opposite manner, from being dominated by civil rights bills to being dominated by defense bills. If this were the case, then measures of cosponsorship would understate the potential for bipartisan agreement in the early period but overstate the potential for bipartisan agreement in the later period, relative to the full set of introduced bills.

To make the relevant comparison between the two sets of bills – cosponsored and non-cosponsored – I first calculate the proportion of bills within each subset that fall into a particular issue area. For each Congress and each policy, I then calculate the ratio between the proportion of non-cosponsored bills in an issue area and the proportion of cosponsored bills in an issue area. If the ratio is greater than 1, the proportion of non-cosponsored bills on this issue is greater than the proportion of cosponsored bills on this issue. Just having a significant time-trend in the ratio is not necessarily problematic for my claim that bipartisanship has declined relatively little in cosponsorship coalitions. The data will only be biased *toward* finding a persistence of bipartisanship in cosponsorship if, over time, highly bipartisan issues become less likely to fall among non-cosponsored bills while becoming more likely to fall among cosponsored bills (negative slope for the ratio) and highly partisan issues become more likely to fall among non-cosponsored bills relative to cosponsored bills (positive slope for the ratio). For instance, it would be problematic if the slope on the ratio for transportation bills was negative while the slope on the ratio for civil rights was positive (and this pattern held more broadly across issues).

However, the patterns reveal the opposite. Those policy areas with a positive trend (which means that this issue is becoming a larger proportion of non-cosponsored bills than of cosponsored bills) include public lands, transportation, and foreign trade. Both transportation and foreign trade are among the third of all issues that are most bipartisan in terms of cosponsorship patterns. This suggests that, over time, the pool of non-cosponsored bills is increasingly made up of issues that are likely to garner bipartisan support. In contrast, the issues with significant negative trends are social welfare, space and technology, health, labor, law, education and defense. Space and defense are among the third of issues that are most likely to garner bipartisan support; health and law are among the middle third; and social welfare, labor, and education are among the third of issues that are least likely to garner bipartisan support. Thus, those issues that are appearing less frequently over time among non-cosponsored bills include policies of all types, including those that are most likely to be partisan (i.e., those least likely to garner bipartisan support). Combined, these patterns suggest that, if anything, non-cosponsored bills are becoming more common on the issues that are quite likely to garner bipartisan agreement (if they were cosponsored) while those issue areas seeing fewer non-cosponsored bills come from a number of policy areas. Thus, if we assume that the likelihood of bipartisan agreement is similar within a policy area for bills that do and do not receive cosponsors, the data *do not* bias the analysis of only cosponsored bills toward a claim of persisting bipartisanship and may, in fact, bias the analysis against this finding.

In order to take advantage of empirical differences in the likelihood of bipartisan agreement across issue areas, I summarize the patterns across three categories of legislation: those with the least bipartisanship, those with a medium level of bipartisanship, and those with the most bipartisanship.[10] The least bipartisan issues include civil rights, labor, education, social welfare, community, and macroeconomics. The medium bipartisan issues include health, law, energy, government operations, banking, and public lands. The most bipartisan issues include foreign trade, agriculture, international affairs, environment, space and technology, transportation, and defense. For each Congress, I examine what proportion of bills fall into each category (labeled "Least," "Medium," "Most" Bipartisan). I calculate this proportion separately for non-cosponsored bills and for cosponsored bills, and then measure the ratio between the proportion of non-cosponsored bills and the proportion

---

[10] In calculating the level of bipartisanship in each issue area, this measure aggregates across all years and looks at the proportion of bills in each issue area that have bipartisan cosponsorship coalitions, regardless of the year in which it occurred.

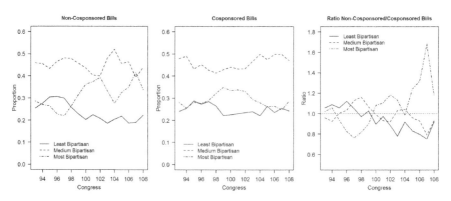

FIGURE A2.7 Distribution of Policy Categories Across Time

of cosponsored bills. As with the previous discussion, when this ratio is greater than 1, bills in this category make up more of the non-cosponsored bills than their share of cosponsored bills.

First, consider non-cosponsored bills in the left panel of Figure A2.7 and the time-trend for each category of bills. Over time, the proportion of bills falling into the category of least bipartisan issues declines, while the proportion of bills in the medium bipartisan category is relatively constant, and the proportion of bills in the most bipartisan category increases. This suggests that, over time, non-cosponsored bills are increasingly made up of bipartisan policy areas. Second, consider cosponsored bills in the center figure. Here, there are no clear time trends for any category of issues, suggesting that the distribution of cosponsored bills among these three categories is relatively similar over time. Finally, consider the ratio between non-cosponsored and cosponsored bills, again for each policy category. The ratio for the least bipartisan issues declines over time, indicating that from the 1970s through 2000s, the proportion of non-cosponsored bills on issues that are unlikely to garner bipartisan support (i.e., partisan issues) dropped. In contrast, the ratio for the most bipartisan issues increases, indicating that, over time, bills in very bipartisan policy areas made up an increasingly large proportion of non-cosponsored bills. The ratio for the medium category fluctuates but does not have a clear trend. Combined, these results confirm the previous analysis. If anything, non-cosponsored bills have become more likely to be made up of bipartisan issues over time. This suggests that there is an even greater potential for bipartisan agreement on legislation in recent Congresses (than seen in just cosponsored bills), despite the decline of bipartisanship in roll call voting.

CHAPTER 4 APPENDIX MATERIALS

The appendix materials for Chapter 4 provide robustness checks of the findings presented in the main text, showing that the shifting patterns of agenda-setting over time are not an artifact of a single measure of bipartisan cosponsorship or agenda attention. The primary finding of Chapter 4 was that, despite relatively little decline in bipartisan cosponsorship between 1973 and 2004, the subset of bills that received roll call and floor attention shifted over time, moving from a bipartisan agenda to a more partisan agenda. Moreover, these patterns of agenda-setting were very highly correlated with patterns of bipartisanship in roll call voting. Figure A4.1 provides a robustness check of Figure 4.1, focusing on the selection of bills to receive roll call votes and showing that the pattern of agenda-setting is nearly identical when the analysis is restricted to bills receiving final passage votes (as opposed to any roll call vote, as in Figure 4.1).

The primary analyses in Chapter 4 utilize a threshold of 20 percent of the cosponsors from the party opposite the sponsor to define bipartisan cosponsorship. Figure A4.2 compares the patterns of bipartisanship among all cosponsored bills and among those cosponsored bills receiving roll call votes (i.e., the roll call agenda) for various definitions of bipartisan cosponsorship. Similar patterns of variation, with a larger decline between the 1970s and 1990s in bipartisanship among bills receiving roll call votes than all cosponsored bills, are seen when using thresholds of 20, 30, 40, and 50 percent to define bipartisan bills. However, the largest changes and the biggest divergence between

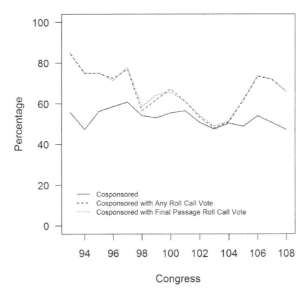

FIGURE A4.1 Bipartisan Agenda-Setting on All Roll Call and Final Passage Roll Call Votes
Note: Y-axis represents the percentage of cosponsored bills with bipartisan coalitions. Bipartisan cosponsorship is measured using the threshold of 20% or more of the cosponsors from the party opposite the bill's sponsor.

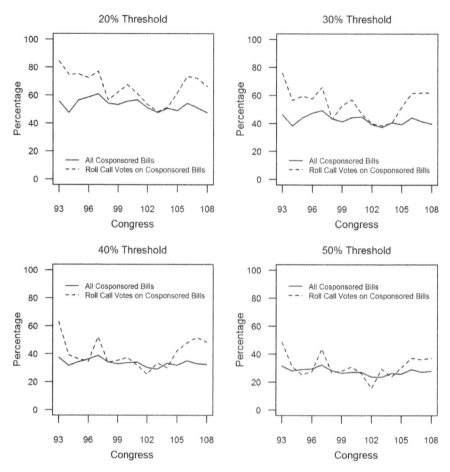

FIGURE A4.2 Bipartisan Agenda-Setting by Threshold of Bipartisan Cosponsorship
Note: Y-axis represents the percentage of cosponsored bills with bipartisan coalitions.

bipartisan cosponsorship and the roll call agenda are most apparent for the 20 percent and 30 percent definitions.

The conditional probability of a roll call vote (or floor attention) given that a bill was bipartisan (or partisan) offered a second metric of agenda-setting over time. To emphasize the importance of agenda-setting in later legislative stages and not just gate-keeping by committees, Figure A4.3 presents the conditional probability of a roll call vote given a bill's coalition *and* that it was reported from committee (among majority-sponsored bills). Even when taking into account the shift in agenda via committee reporting, the roll call agenda has still seen a change toward greater prioritization of partisan legislation.

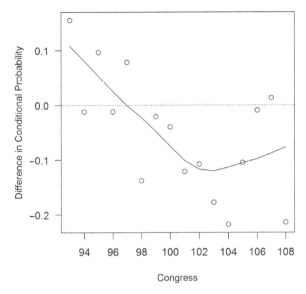

FIGURE A4.3 Difference in Conditional Probability of a Roll Call Vote Given that Bill Was Reported from Committee (Majority-Sponsored Bills)
Note: Y-axis is the difference between the conditional probability of receiving a roll call vote for bipartisan bills that were reported from committee and the conditional probability of receiving a roll call vote for partisan bills that were reported from committee. Raw data is plotted in circles with a loess trend through the data.

CHAPTER 5 APPENDIX MATERIALS

The appendix materials for Chapter 5 provide robustness checks of the estimated effects of bipartisan cosponsorship on subsequent agenda attention. The estimated effects are presented graphically for the addition of random effects by policy area, controlling for committee reporting, variation across forms of divided government, and those without majority seat share in the model. Other key insights of additional robustness checks are discussed as well. These effects, like those in Chapter 5, are based on bootstrapping simulations. For these simulations, the model is estimated on a sample of data drawn from the full dataset of majority-sponsored cosponsored bills with replacement, new data is created from the sample where the values of bipartisan cosponsorship are varied between 0 (partisan) and 1 (bipartisan), and the values of sorted districts (or other contextual variables) are set at the observed value for a particular Congress. Then predicted probabilities of a roll call vote are calculated using the new data and the average difference between the prediction for bipartisan and partisan cosponsored bills is calculated for each observed value of sorted districts. This bootstrapping procedure is done 1,000 times.

The results of Chapter 5 (Table 5.3, Model 1 and Figure 5.1) are similar when plotting the average treatment effects of Model 2 (with random effects by policy area) or Model 3 (controlling for committee reporting). Both sets of results are presented in Figure A5.1. With random effects by policy area, the interaction between the percentage of sorted districts and bipartisan cosponsorship yields nearly identical results to Figure 5.1; the effect of bipartisan cosponsorship varies significantly across district sorting, but insignificantly across divided government and majority seat share (through the latter approaches significance).

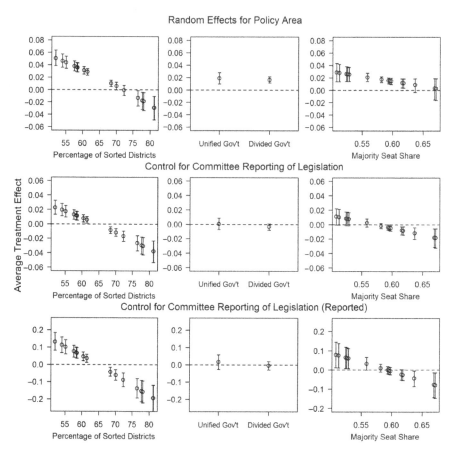

FIGURE A5.1 Additional Model Specifications of Effect of Bipartisan Cosponsorship on Receiving a Roll Call Vote
Note: Average treatment effects based on Table 5.3, models 2 and 3. Based on 1,000 simulated draws of the data. Average treatment effect is the mean difference between the predicted probability of a roll call vote for bipartisan and partisan cosponsored legislation. Analyses restricted to majority-sponsored bills.

When controlling for committee reporting of legislation, estimated average treatment effects depends on whether we assume that bills receiving roll call votes are first reported from committee. If committee reporting is held at observed values, the effect of bipartisanship is positive for sorted levels lower than 65 percent and negative for levels of sorting above that point. At both low and high levels of district sorting, the 90 percent confidence intervals do not overlap zero. The range of the effect is shifted downward from the original model specification, moving from approximately 0.02 to –0.04. A similar pattern of negative and positive treatment effects across the range of sorted districts is found when we assume that all bills receiving votes were first reported from committee, but the magnitude of the effect increases substantially since bills that are reported from committee are much more likely than the average bill to receive a roll call vote. Here, the average treatment effect of bipartisan cosponsorship ranges from 0.15 to –0.2. Although the average treatment effects for bipartisan cosponsorship are insignificant for divided government, the differences between the effects for small and large majority seat shares are significant. Whereas leaders significantly advantage bipartisan legislation when there are small seat shares, they significantly advantage partisan legislation at the highest seat shares. Combined, these results show that district sorting is strongly associated with a change in whether bipartisan or partisan bills are favored in roll call votes and that small majority seat shares may also lead to the prioritization of bipartisan legislation.

Robustness checks with broader floor attention as the dependent variable (Figure A5.2) also yield similar results to those presented in the main text (although there are fewer systematic differences in attention to bipartisan legislation after committee reporting as should be expected given the high correlation between committee reporting and floor attention). In both specifications, the average treatment effect of bipartisan cosponsorship is always positive and significantly different from zero. As in Figure 5.2, the effects are not significantly different from one another across the range of the percentage of sorted districts and majority seat share. In all specifications, the estimated effect of bipartisan cosponsorship is larger in divided government than in unified government, and the results approach significant differences. Across the models, bipartisan legislation is always favored over partisan legislation on the broader floor agenda.

The relationships between bipartisan cosponsorship and divided government in Chapter 5 are largely similar across the possible configurations of divided government. Figure A5.3 presents the estimated effect of bipartisan cosponsorship on roll call attention (left-hand panel) and floor attention (right-hand panel) for each possible configuration of unified and divided government. When I vary the type of divided government, there is a positive effect of bipartisan cosponsorship on roll call attention in all institutional arrangements and no significant differences between the arrangements. However, compared to unified

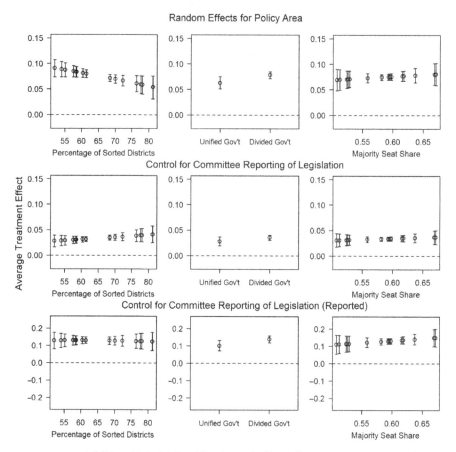

FIGURE A5.2 Additional Model Specifications of Effect of Bipartisan Cosponsorship on Receiving Floor Attention

Note: Average treatment effects based on Table 5.3, models 5 and 6. Based on 1,000 simulated draws of the data. Average treatment effect is the mean difference between the predicted probability of floor attention for bipartisan and partisan cosponsored legislation. Analyses restricted to majority-sponsored bills.

government, the average treatment effect of bipartisan cosponsorship is largest when the House and President are of one party and the Senate is from the opposing party. In contrast, in both other forms of divided government, the effect of bipartisan cosponsorship is lower than in unified government. Though not significant, these patterns are suggestive that some forms of divided government may be more likely to encourage bipartisanship than others. When the dependent variable is attention on the broader floor agenda, the average treatment effect of bipartisan cosponsorship is similar in all configurations of divided government.

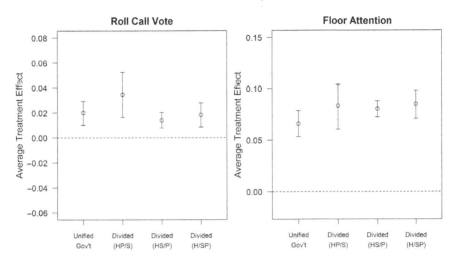

FIGURE A5.3 Effect of Bipartisan Cosponsorship on Legislative Attention Across Forms of Divided Government
Note: Average treatment effects of bipartisan cosponsorship. Based on 1,000 simulated draws of the data. Average treatment effect is the mean difference between the predicted probability of legislative attention for bipartisan and partisan cosponsored legislation. Analyses restricted to majority-sponsored bills.

As further robustness checks of the primary findings in the chapter, I re-ran the primary model specifications for both roll call and floor attention as the dependent variable across a number of variable specifications and modeling assumptions. These models include the percentage of sorted districts in the majority party (rather than the full chamber), the normalized presidential vote to assess the percentage of sorted districts,[11] measures of district sorting that provide various adjustments for redistricting, 30 percent and 40 percent thresholds for bipartisan cosponsorship, a continuous measure of bipartisan cosponsorship based on the absolute value of the difference in party support score (from

---

[11] The normalized presidential vote first calculates the difference between the observed Democratic presidential vote in the district and the average Democratic presidential vote in that election across all districts. I then follow the same process as I did in calculating the normal presidential vote, taking the two-election cycle average of the Democratic presidential vote in the district and then using this for Democratic members and this value multiplied by –1 for Republican members. The resulting distribution of normalized presidential votes ranges from –0.21 to 0.51, with a mean of 0.06. Here, sorted districts are defined as those where the normalized presidential vote is greater than or equal to zero, indicating those districts where presidential candidates of the member's party do better than the national average. Unsorted districts are defined as those where presidential candidates do worse than the national average. By Congress, the correlation between the percentage of sorted districts for the normal and normalized vote is 0.83.

Chapter 2),[12] and a specification that drops the majority seat share variable from the model since it is correlated with the percentage of sorted districts. All models were also replicated using standard logistic models, estimating the effects of all interacted terms by bootstrapping the results with sampling proportional to the number of the bills in each Congress to yield results similar to clustered standard errors by Congress. In these models, I also analyzed all cosponsored bills by adding majority sponsorship to each interaction (creating three-way interactions for each contextual variable). Here, I summarize the findings for the multi-level models, though effects are similar when using standard logistic models.

When the dependent variable is a roll call vote, the relationship between sorted districts and decreasing roll call attention for bipartisan legislation is strong and robust across specifications. For all specifications except the continuous measure of bipartisan cosponsorship, the effect of bipartisan cosponsorship shifts from positive (and significant) to negative (and significant) over the percentage of sorted districts. That is, party leaders shift from disproportionately favoring bipartisan legislation to favoring partisan legislation. In the model with a continuous measure of bipartisanship, the agenda shifts from significantly favoring bipartisan bills to treating bipartisan and partisan bills similarly. As in the models discussed in the main text and above, bipartisan legislation is typically advantaged in both unified and divided government (with the exception being models using the 30 percent and 40 percent thresholds for bipartisan cosponsorship) but there are no significant differences between the two effects. Thus, divided government does not appear to constrain partisanship on the roll call agenda. For majority seat share, the trend of the results across model specification is that leaders significantly advantage bipartisan legislation at low seat shares but either treat bipartisan and partisan bills similarly or benefit partisan bills with large seat shares. Those models that capture significant differences in the effect of bipartisan cosponsorship across the range of majority seat shares include the normalized vote for measuring sorting, and the 30 percent and 40 percent thresholds for bipartisan agreement.

When the dependent variable is floor attention through either roll call votes or passage by voice votes, the effect of bipartisan legislation is always positive across the percentage of sorted districts. However, the attention to bipartisan bills changes significantly across the percentage of sorted districts for model specifications using the 30 percent threshold of bipartisan cosponsorship, the continuous measure of bipartisan cosponsorship, the normalized presidential vote to measure sorted districts, and when omitting majority seat share from the model. Although the robustness checks do not generally show significant differences in how the agenda treats bipartisan bills during unified versus divided government, the trend

---

[12] Using the difference in party support score from Chapter 2, the continuous measure of bipartisan agreement leverages the absolute value of this score, ranging from 0 to 100. The estimated effect of bipartisan cosponsorship leverages the difference in the predicted attention for bills with a score one standard deviation below the mean and one standard deviation above the mean.

is always consistent with the hypothesis that divided government constrains partisanship and promotes bipartisanship in agenda-setting. Moreover, many of the effects approach statistical significance. Similarly, the effect of bipartisan cosponsorship is positive across majority seat shares but differences between the effects are generally not significant. Both of these patterns are consistent with the effects found in the primary model specifications presented in Chapter 5.

Since the percentage of sorted districts is negatively correlated with the majority seat share, Figure A5.4 presents the estimated effect of bipartisan cosponsorship for model specifications that omit the majority seat share. With this variable removed, the confidence intervals shrink in size, yielding significant differences in agenda attention across the percentage of sorted districts for both the roll call and broader floor agenda.

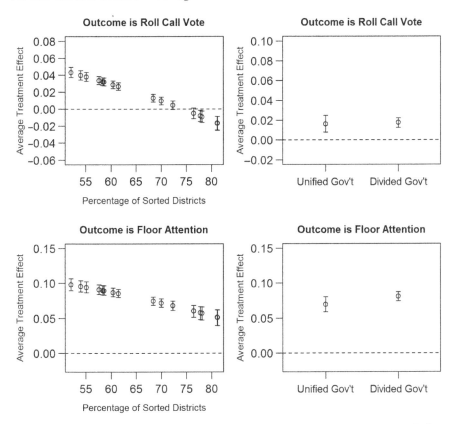

FIGURE A5.4 Effect of Bipartisan Cosponsorship on Legislative Attention (Excluding Majority Seat Share)
Note: Average treatment effects of bipartisan cosponsorship. Based on 1,000 simulated draws of the data. Average treatment effect is the mean difference between the predicted probability of legislative attention for bipartisan and partisan cosponsored legislation. Analyses restricted to majority-sponsored bills.

CHAPTER 6 APPENDIX MATERIALS

The appendix materials for Chapter 6 include information on the policy codes used in the main analyses as well as the complete regression results behind the estimated effects of agenda-setting. The focus of Chapter 6 was on differences in bipartisan cosponsorship and agenda-setting across issue areas. Policy issue coding comes from the Congressional Bills Project (Adler and Wilkerson 2008). The issue coding scheme, also used by the Policy Agendas Project, assigns each bill to one of 19 major topic areas and to one of over 200 subtopic codes. Table A6.1 summarizes the major topic areas, along with the abbreviations used in the figures of Chapter 6.

Figures 6.2 and 6.3 in the main text plotted the predicted difference in conditional probability of a roll call vote (and broader floor attention) across the observed values of each of the three independent variables of interest. These estimates are based on multi-level linear models with random effects by Congress and by policy. The estimates from these models are presented in Table A6.2. The dependent variable in both models is the difference in the conditional probability of legislative attention for bipartisan and partisan bills, where legislative attention is defined as a roll call vote in Model 1 and as floor attention (either a roll call vote or passage by voice vote) in Model 2. These differences are calculated separately for each issue-area Congress.

TABLE A6.1 *Major Topic Codes in the Congressional Bills Project*

Major Topic	Abbreviation
1 = Macroeconomics	*Macroeconomics*
2 = Civil Rights, Minority Issues, and Civil Liberties	*Civil Rights*
3 = Health	*Health*
4 = Agriculture	*Agriculture*
5 = Labor, Employment, and Immigration	*Labor*
6 = Education	*Education*
7 = Environment	*Environment*
8 = Energy	*Energy*
10 = Transportation	*Transportation*
12 = Law, Crime, and Family Issues	*Law*
13 = Social Welfare	*Social Welfare*
14 = Community Development and Housing Issues	*Community*
15 = Banking, Finance, and Domestic Commerce	*Banking*
16 = Defense	*Defense*
17 = Space, Science, Technology, and Communications	*Space*
18 = Foreign Trade	*Foreign*
19 = International Affairs and Foreign Aid	*International*
20 = Government Operations	*Government*
21 = Public Lands and Water Management	*Public Lands*

TABLE A6.2 *Difference in Conditional Probability of Legislative Attention*

	Model 1 (Roll Call Vote)	Model 2 (Floor Attention)
Intercept	0.344	0.154
	(0.236)	(0.217)
Percent Sorted Districts	−0.00293**	−0.00183
	(0.00128)	(0.00118)
Divided Government	−0.00974	0.00508
	(0.0152)	(0.0141)
Majority Seat Share	−0.226	−0.00244
	(0.259)	(0.239)
Proportion of Cosponsored Bills	0.390**	0.546***
Receiving Legislative Attention	(0.162)	(0.101)
$\sigma^2_{Congress}$	0.000309	0.0000429
σ^2_{Policy}	0.000216	0.000728
N	303	303
Log Likelihood	391	292

Standard errors in parentheses. ^ $p < 0.1$, * $p < 0.05$, ** $p < 0.01$, *** $p < 0.001$.
Note: Estimates and standard errors from multi-level linear regressions examining the effects of contextual variables on the difference in the conditional probability legislative attention for bipartisan and partisan cosponsored bills.

If I include random effects in the model to allow the intercept, percentage of sorted districts, divided government, and majority seat share to vary by policy category, the results provide preliminary support for the hypothesis that strategic partisan agenda-setting will be most apparent among the least bipartisan issues while attention to bipartisan legislation will persist among the most bipartisan legislation. When the dependent variable is the difference in conditional probability of a roll call vote, the effect of moving from one standard deviation below the mean of sorted districts to one standard deviation above the mean has a large and significant effect for policies in the least bipartisan category, with the estimated effect declining in the medium and most bipartisan categories (although not significantly so given large confidence intervals). When the dependent variable is the difference in conditional probability of floor attention, the effect of moving from one standard deviation below the mean to one standard deviation above the mean for the percentage of sorted districts is significant for the least bipartisan issues, but insignificant for the medium and most bipartisan issues. No significant effects were found for divided government or majority seat share.

Table A6.3 presents the complete regression results behind Figures 6.5 and 6.6. Both figures estimated the effect of bipartisan cosponsorship on legislative attention for bills in the least, medium, and most bipartisan categories of policies. These categories are based on the average percentage of bipartisan

TABLE A6.3 *Legislative Attention for Cosponsored Bills with Majority Sponsors by Policy Category*

	Model 1 Roll Call Vote Least Bipartisan	Model 2 Roll Call Vote Medium Bipartisan	Model 3 Roll Call Vote Most Bipartisan	Model 4 Floor Least Bipartisan	Model 5 Floor Medium Bipartisan	Model 6 Floor Most Bipartisan
Intercept	-9.25*	-5.44*	-8.23*	-6.94^	-1.49	-3.32
	(3.93)	(2.55)	(4.17)	(3.82)	(3.62)	(4.01)
Bipartisan Cosponsorship	7.91	2.67	5.28	6.90	-1.79	0.440
	(6.39)	(4.88)	(3.78)	(4.50)	(2.50)	(3.63)
Number of Cosponsors	0.0106***	0.00557***	0.00699***	0.00616***	0.00254***	0.00454***
	(0.000887)	(0.000664)	(0.000863)	(0.000793)	(0.000512)	(0.000732)
Member of Committee	1.49***	0.739***	0.922***	1.39***	0.551***	0.935***
	(0.128)	(0.0804)	(0.0981)	(0.0998)	(0.0514)	(0.0697)
Chair of Committee	1.31***	1.06***	0.830***	1.40***	1.01***	0.876***
	(0.124)	(0.0905)	(0.0874)	(0.105)	(0.0675)	(0.0675)
Subcommittee Chair of Committee	0.495***	0.538***	0.539***	0.707***	0.654***	0.822***
	(0.142)	(0.103)	(0.117)	(0.105)	(0.0707)	(0.0791)
Second Session	0.184^	-0.0244	0.0704	0.364***	0.276***	0.229***
	(0.102)	(0.0705)	(0.0767)	(0.0805)	(0.0455)	(0.0562)
Percent Sorted Districts	0.0517*	0.0336*	0.0269	0.0416*	0.0100	0.000841
	(0.0215)	(0.0140)	(0.0230)	(0.0208)	(0.0196)	(0.0218)
Divided Government	0.119	-0.177	-0.078	0.0464	-0.174	-0.175
	(0.249)	(0.159)	(0.270)	(0.243)	(0.233)	(0.259)

Majority Seat Share	2.09	−0.590	4.19	0.158	−3.10	0.000539
	(4.29)	(2.76)	(4.55)	(4.19)	(3.98)	(4.41)
Bipartisan x Percent Sorted	−0.0851*	−0.0403	−0.0328	−0.0671**	−0.000145	−0.000501
	(0.0350)	(0.0266)	(0.0210)	(0.0245)	(0.0135)	(0.0198)
Bipartisan x Divided Government	−0.159	0.123	−0.118	−0.110	0.315*	0.119
	(0.409)	(0.312)	(0.242)	(0.284)	(0.160)	(0.233)
Bipartisan x Majority Seat Share	−3.61	0.129	−4.09	−2.93	3.88	0.653
	(6.98)	(5.34)	(4.10)	(4.92)	(2.74)	(2.99)
$\sigma^2_{Congress}$	0.0669	0.00985	0.0745	0.0751	0.0964	0.0965
$\sigma^2_{Bipartisan\ Cospon\ (by\ Congress)}$	0.226	0.138	0.0187	0.0841	0.0214	0.0547
N	9484	18073	11989	9484	18073	11989
Log Likelihood	−1714	−3647	−2842	−2418	−6926	−4507

Standard errors in parentheses. ^ $p < 0.1$, * $p < 0.05$, ** $p < 0.01$, *** $p < 0.001$.

Note: Estimates and standard errors from multi-level logistic regressions examining the effect of bipartisan cosponsorship and contextual variables on legislative attention.

cosponsorship coalitions in a policy area. The least bipartisan issues include civil rights, labor, education, social welfare, community development, and macroeconomics. The medium bipartisan issues include health, law, energy, government operations, banking, and public lands. The most bipartisan issues include foreign trade, agriculture, international affairs, environment, space and technology, transportation, and defense. Each of the models presented in Table A6.3 focuses on one subset of these categories and on legislative attention as either a roll call vote or broader floor action. The unit of analysis is a bill, but since bills are nested within Congresses and the contextual variables of interest vary only by Congress, a multi-level logistic regression is used with random effects included by Congress for both the intercept and the effect of bipartisan cosponsorship. As in Chapter 5, the analyses are restricted to majority-sponsored bills.

CHAPTER 7 APPENDIX MATERIALS

These materials supplement the analyses in Chapter 7, providing additional details about the variables of interest, and full model specifications behind the figures presented in the text. Table A7.1 presents summary statistics about the frequency of cosponsorship at a member level (rather than bill level, as in Chapter 2). Here, the frequencies reflect all cosponsorship coalitions, both partisan and bipartisan. As in Chapter 2, where the percentage of bills with cosponsors increased over time, the average frequency of cosponsorship by members increased over time as well. However, given the full number of House bills in each Congress, the percentage of bills that the average member cosponsors ranges from 0.62 percent in the 93rd Congress to 4.24 percent in the 108th Congress.

FULL MODEL SPECIFICATIONS FOR FIGURES IN CHAPTER 7

Figure 7.1 in the text is based on predictions from models of legislative behavior as a function of district preferences and other control variables. Table A7.2 presents the full model specification used for predicting legislative behavior. I model legislative behavior using a binomial model, which accounts for the likelihood that a member engages in partisan (or bipartisan) behavior relative to the number of times they do not.[13] This model, rather than an OLS model, is used in order to include the number of votes or total cosponsorships in our

---

[13] The model specification presented here uses a quasi-binomial model, which allows for over-dispersion in the data. Over-dispersion refers to data where there is more variation than is explained by the model, and is common when logistic regression is applied to count data, as is the case here. Without adjusting for over-dispersion, confidence intervals would be too narrow and estimates would be overconfident (Gelman and Hill 2007, 116–17). The quasi-binomial adjustment multiplies the standard error of coefficient estimates by the square root of the estimated over-dispersion, thus widening the confidence intervals.

TABLE A7.1 *Summary Statistics on the Frequency of Cosponsorship by Members*

Congress	Min	Mean	Median	Max	SD
93	0	104	79	561	87.3
94	1	115	83	632	98.5
95	5	125	98	476	91.2
96	0	125	110	434	78.1
97	4	128	115	496	72.0
98	3	153	130	581	92.5
99	13	162	137	713	102
100	9	189	163	666	110
101	16	216	192	790	117
102	0	211	190	677	109
103	0	168	158	513	76.0
104	0	141	136	415	63.5
105	4	186	173	686	85.9
106	28	235	218	771	103
107	22	230	204	804	127
108	20	227	200	878	124

analysis, so that we have less confidence in our estimates when members engage in very few votes or cosponsorships. The dependent variable in this model is made up of two components – the number of "successes" and the number of "failures." In the case of party unity support scores, "successes" in the model are votes with the party and "failures" are votes against the majority of the party. In contrast, in the case of bipartisan cosponsorship, "successes" in the model are bipartisan cosponsorship coalitions and "failures" are partisan cosponsorship coalitions. Since my aim is to explicitly model the coefficients in each Congress, a factor variable for Congress is interacted with the normal vote.

Table A7.3 presents the full regression results behind Figure 7.2 in the text. These regressions model legislative behavior as a function of district preferences, the percentage of party unity votes in Congress, an interaction between these two variables, and other control variables. Since this interaction is between a member-Congress-level variable (normal presidential vote) and a Congress-level variable (percentage of party unity votes), a multi-level model is appropriate, allowing both the intercept of the model and the slope of the normal vote to vary by Congress. To capture the nested structure of the data, random effects on the intercept and the normal presidential vote are included by Congress.

Figure 7.4 in the text presented the estimated effects of increasing the partisanship of members' legislative behavior on their vote share. These estimates were based on bootstrapped simulations from the models presented in Table A7.4. The analyses pool together all contested House elections from 1974–2004,

TABLE A7.2 *Models of Voting and Cosponsorship Behavior (1973–2004)*

	Cosponsorship	Party Unity
Intercept	1.54***	−2.23***
	(0.143)	(0.211)
Majority Party Member	−0.556***	0.849***
	(0.0134)	(0.0258)
Normal Presidential Vote in District (%)	−0.0143***	0.0597***
	(0.00246)	(0.00379)
Female	−0.215***	−0.059
	(0.0195)	(0.042)
Age	0.00209**	−0.00637***
	(0.00075)	(0.00134)
Number of Congresses Served	−0.00372^	−0.0132***
	(0.00209)	(0.0035)
House Leadership	−0.425***	0.908***
	(0.0738)	(0.144)
94th *Congress*	−0.974***	−0.113
	(0.184)	(0.252)
95th *Congress*	−0.219	−0.59*
	(0.187)	(0.262)
96th *Congress*	0.449*	−0.453^
	(0.192)	(0.273)
97th *Congress*	0.884***	0.928*
	(0.208)	(0.374)
98th *Congress*	−0.352^	1.08***
	(0.188)	(0.325)
99th *Congress*	−0.201	1.86***
	(0.172)	(0.272)
100th *Congress*	−0.274	2.08***
	(0.168)	(0.276)
101st *Congress*	0.175	1.79***
	(0.165)	(0.275)
102nd *Congress*	0.0577	1.47***
	(0.165)	(0.268)
103rd *Congress*	0.749***	0.563^
	(0.198)	(0.33)
104th *Congress*	0.349^	0.446
	(0.212)	(0.316)
105th *Congress*	0.944***	0.765*
	(0.181)	(0.326)
106th *Congress*	1.35***	0.249
	(0.175)	(0.356)
107th *Congress*	0.99***	1.16**
	(0.172)	(0.399)
108th *Congress*	0.877***	0.966*
	(0.176)	(0.388)

TABLE A7.2 *(cont.)*

	Cosponsorship	Party Unity
94th *Congress x Normal Vote*	0.00635^	0.00525
	(0.00334)	(0.00489)
95th *Congress x Normal Vote*	0.00278	0.0122*
	(0.00338)	(0.00506)
96th *Congress x Normal Vote*	−0.00461	0.0129*
	(0.00346)	(0.00527)
97th *Congress x Normal Vote*	−0.0043	−0.0147*
	(0.00367)	(0.00695)
98th *Congress x Normal Vote*	0.00481	−0.015*
	(0.00336)	(0.00606)
99th *Congress x Normal Vote*	0.00227	−0.0263***
	(0.00305)	(0.00504)
100th *Congress x Normal Vote*	0.00469	−0.0279***
	(0.00299)	(0.00511)
101st *Congress x Normal Vote*	−0.00226	−0.0245***
	(0.00294)	(0.00513)
102nd *Congress x Normal Vote*	−0.00423	−0.0153**
	(0.00294)	(0.00508)
103rd *Congress x Normal Vote*	−0.0187***	0.00684
	(0.00349)	(0.00624)
104th *Congress x Normal Vote*	−0.0109**	0.009
	(0.00371)	(0.00592)
105th *Congress x Normal Vote*	−0.0212***	0.000344
	(0.00313)	(0.00599)
106th *Congress x Normal Vote*	−0.0255***	0.0107
	(0.00302)	(0.00655)
107th *Congress x Normal Vote*	−0.021***	−0.000423
	(0.00296)	(0.00728)
108th *Congress x Normal Vote*	−0.0216***	0.00691
	(0.00303)	(0.00712)
N	6991	6997

Standard errors in parentheses. ^ $p < 0.1$, * $p < 0.05$, ** $p < 0.01$, *** $p < 0.001$.

excluding those races where redistricting dramatically changed the district boundaries or moved incumbents into new districts (as well as those with missing spending data). The analyses are restricted to contested elections between two major party candidates with an incumbent from one party running. The dependent variable is the incumbent's two-party vote share. The primary independent variables are vote-based measures of ideological or partisan extremity, an indicator for whether the district is sorted, and an interaction between voting extremity and sorted districts. Four different measures of voting

TABLE A7.3 *Member Responsiveness in Voting and Cosponsorship (1973–2004)*

	Model 1 (Party Unity Support)	Model 2 (Bipartisan Cosponsorship)
Intercept	−5.54***	2.56***
	(0.114)	(0.120)
Majority Party Member	0.850***	−0.519***
	(0.00368)	(0.00435)
Normal Presidential Vote in District (%)	0.107***	−0.0282***
	(0.00214)	(0.00217)
Percent of Party Unity Votes in Congress	0.0741***	−0.0128***
	0.00223)	(0.00235)
Normal Vote x % Party Unity Votes	−0.00104***	0.000191***
	(0.0000419)	(0.0000427)
Female	0.0840***	−0.296***
	0.00625)	(0.00633)
Age	−0.00247***	0.00139***
	(0.000193)	(0.000244)
Number of Congresses Served	−0.0154***	−0.00542***
	(0.000503)	(0.000679)
House Leadership	0.885***	−0.416***
	(0.0204)	(0.0240)
$\sigma^2_{Congress}$	0.00610	0.00610
$\sigma^2_{Normal\ Vote\ (by\ Congress)}$	0.0000215	0.00000207
N	6991	6991
Log Likelihood	−161513	−34458

Standard errors in parentheses. ^ $p < 0.1$, * $p < 0.05$, ** $p < 0.01$, *** $p < 0.001$.
Note: Table presents fixed effect estimates and standard errors from a multi-level binomial (logistic) model. The dependent variable captures the number of "successes" relative to the number of "successes" and "failures."

behavior are used – the extremity of the member's ADA score (as done in the original Canes-Wrone et al. (2002) analysis), the absolute value of the member's first dimension DW-NOMINATE score, the member's party unity support score, and the member's party unity support score weighted by the percentage of party unity votes in the Congress. Sorted districts are defined as those where the normal presidential vote is greater than or equal to 50 percent and unsorted districts as those where it is less than 50 percent. Following the original Canes-Wrone et al. (2002) analysis, additional control variables include the normal presidential vote in the district; differences in challenger and incumbent spending; indicators for quality challengers, freshman members, and whether or not the member is in the president's party; and interactions between the president's party and the variables capturing change in real income per capita in the year prior to the election, presidential popularity, and midterm election years. In

TABLE A7.4 *Impact of Legislative Behavior on Members' Vote Share (1974–2004)*

	Model 1 Extremity of ADA Score	Model 2 Extremity of DW-NOMINATE	Model 3 Party Unity Support Score	Model 4 Party Unity Support Score Weighted	Model 5 Bipartisan Cosponsorship
Intercept	42.7***	37.2***	46.6***	45.5***	28.1***
	(5.30)	(6.01)	(6.00)	(7.07)	(6.12)
MC Behavior (varies by model)	-0.0873***	-16.0***	-0.148***	-0.282***	0.138***
	(0.00654)	(1.09)	(0.00961)	(0.0172)	(0.0129)
Sorted District (normal vote > 50%)	-3.03***	-3.67***	-5.65***	-5.12***	4.16***
	(0.711)	(0.487)	(1.08)	(0.790)	(0.974)
MC Behavior x Sorted District	0.0224**	6.98***	0.0495***	0.0845***	-0.0946***
	(0.00888)	(1.27)	(0.0127)	(0.0175)	(0.0149)
Normal Presidential Vote (%)	0.517***	0.554***	0.528***	0.526***	0.493***
	(0.0137)	(0.0144)	(0.0137)	(0.0137)	(0.0143)
Quality Challenger	-2.69***	-2.82***	-2.63***	-2.67***	-2.79***
	(0.230)	(0.228)	(0.229)	(0.229)	(0.233)
Logged Challenger – Incumbent Spending	-2.12***	-2.12***	-2.13***	-2.14***	-2.14***
	(0.0549)	(0.0545)	(0.0545)	(0.0545)	(0.0556)
Freshman	-0.975***	-1.01***	-0.931***	-0.904***	-1.01***
	(0.236)	(0.234)	(0.234)	(0.234)	(0.239)
President's Party	-1.35	2.74	1.46	1.45	2.31
	(9.05)	(10.8)	(10.5)	(10.3)	(10.4)
Change in Income	-0.0101	-0.119	-0.0825	0.117	-0.0772
	(0.361)	(0.410)	(0.408)	(0.483)	(0.4=0)
Presidential Popularity	-0.0121	0.0288	0.0121	0.0313	0.00270
	(0.108)	(0.123)	(0.122)	(0.145)	(0.1=3)

(continued)

TABLE A7.4 (cont.)

	Model 1 Extremity of ADA Score	Model 2 Extremity of DW-NOMINATE	Model 3 Party Unity Support Score	Model 4 Party Unity Support Score Weighted	Model 5 Bipartisan Cosponsorship
Midterm Election Year	1.58	1.74	1.62	0.752	1.71
	(1.87)	(2.13)	(2.12)	(2.51)	(2.13)
President's Party x Change in Income	0.676	0.881	0.849	0.803	0.993
	(0.622)	(0.743)	(0.722)	(0.707)	(0.717)
President's Party x Pres. Pop.	−0.0211	−0.101	−0.0834	−0.0864	−0.0947
	(0.187)	(0.223)	(0.217)	(0.212)	(0.215)
President's Party x Midterm Election	−3.69	−3.88	−3.71	−3.52	−3.73
	(3.23)	(3.86)	(3.75)	(3.67)	(3.72)
σ^2_{Year}	11.3	14.7	14.5	20.4	14.6
$\sigma^2_{President's\ Party\ (by\ Year)}$	33.8	48.7	45.9	43.9	45.2
N	4761	4761	4761	4761	4761
Log Likelihood	−15418	−15376	−15383	−15390	−15479

Standard errors in parentheses. ^ $p < 0.1$, * $p < 0.05$, ** $p < 0.01$, *** $p < 0.001$.

order to account for the nested structure of the data, the analysis leverages a multi-level model with random effects by year for both the intercept and the indicator for the president's party (since it is interacted with Congress-level variables).

Figure 7.5 in the text is based on models that interact an indicator for competitive districts with the percentage of bipartisan cosponsorship coalitions by each member. The remainder of the model specification is like that in Canes-Wrone et al. (2002). The tables below (A7.5 and A7.6) present the full results of the linear regression model for each election year between 1974 and 2004. The analyses are restricted to contested elections between two major party candidates with an incumbent from one party running. Cases of major redistricting that affected the incumbent status of a member or moved a member into a new district were dropped from the analysis. Also omitted are those districts without information on campaign spending or the other key variables of interest. Competitive districts are defined as those where the normal presidential vote in the district is less than the median (by election year). It should be noted that because of missing data and the need to exclude uncontested elections (or those without an incumbent), the number of competitive and non-competitive districts are not equal in all years. Nonetheless, all substantive patterns are similar if missing challenger or incumbent spending is replaced with \$5000, thus increasing the number of observations.

Figure 7.6 in the text presented the effect of bipartisan cosponsorship on members' vote share, first for all members in competitive districts and then for majority party members in competitive districts. The effects in Figure 7.6 are based on bootstrap simulations that vary bipartisan cosponsorship and the percentage of party unity votes across the observed values, with all other variables held at their observed simulation values. These simulations are based on the following model and results (Table A7.7), pooling contested election results from 1974 to 2004. As in previous models, the dependent variable is the two-party vote share. The key independent variables of interest are the percentage of cosponsorship coalitions by a member in the previous Congress that are bipartisan, the percentage of party unity votes in the previous Congress, and an interaction between bipartisan cosponsorship and the percentage of party unity votes. Other control variables from the pooled models above are included, with the addition of a variable for the member's own party unity support score. I estimate a linear multi-level model with random effects by year for the intercept, bipartisan cosponsorship, and the indicator for members in the president's party (since each is interacted with year-level variables). The model focuses on members in competitive seats (defined by election year), in contested elections between the two parties, and without substantial redistricting that affected the alignment of incumbents with their previous district. Because the majority of competitive districts fall within the majority party, the analysis of all competitive districts is similar to that for only majority party members.

TABLE A7.5 *Impact of Bipartisan Cosponsorship on Members' Vote Share (1974–88)*

	1974	1976	1978	1980	1982	1984	1986	1988
Intercept	66.1***	36.3***	32.1***	40.3***	42.8***	40***	45.4***	28.4***
	(6.86)	(6.35)	(7.14)	(6.1)	(7.31)	(4.24)	(5.29)	(4.58)
Percent Bipartisan Cosponsors	−0.0926	−0.0545	0.0473	−0.0427	0.0516	0.0135	−0.0248	0.105*
	(0.0637)	(0.0541)	(0.0588)	(0.0423)	(0.0522)	(0.0464)	(0.0506)	(0.0455)
Competitive District	−9.12^	−7.40*	−12.3**	−7.59^	−1.72	−3.8	−6.93^	1.08
	(4.94)	(3.06)	(4.37)	(4.13)	(5.76)	(3.05)	(3.72)	(3.25)
Normal Presidential Vote (%)	0.158*	0.497***	0.463***	0.438***	0.395***	0.422***	0.409***	0.541***
	(0.0756)	(0.0707)	(0.0767)	(0.0669)	(0.0809)	(0.0505)	(0.0575)	(0.0506)
Quality Challenger	−4.09***	−2.79**	−5.02***	−2.25*	−2.05*	−2.79***	−4.03***	−0.143
	(1.05)	(0.898)	(1.11)	(0.961)	(0.985)	(0.825)	(0.904)	(0.948)
Logged Challenger – Incumbent Spending	−3.17***	−1.62***	−2.55***	−3.97***	−1.11***	−2.76***	−2.86***	−2.51***
	(0.339)	(0.197)	(0.277)	(0.307)	(0.131)	(0.228)	(0.241)	(0.22)
Freshman	0.864	−1.02	−1.41	0.142	−2.62*	−1.25^	−3.81**	−1.91*
	(1.1)	(0.948)	(1.09)	(0.953)	(1.07)	(0.73)	(1.12)	(0.956)
President's Party	−12.2***	4.94*	6.8**	0.0613	−9.80***	−3.62*	−7.92***	−7.77***
	(2.03)	(2.40)	(2.19)	(1.02)	(1.14)	(1.84)	(1.59)	(1.36)
Pct Bipartisan Cospon x Competitive	0.123^	0.238***	0.218**	0.109*	0.0132	0.0514	0.152**	0.0409
	(0.0729)	(0.0649)	(0.0765)	(0.0541)	(0.0693)	(0.0533)	(0.058)	(0.0518)
N	288	328	309	334	246	339	317	325
R^2	0.618	0.496	0.515	0.612	0.614	0.674	0.608	0.590
Adjusted R^2	0.607	0.483	0.502	0.602	0.601	0.666	0.598	0.579

Standard errors in parentheses. ^ $p < 0.1$, * $p < 0.05$, ** $p < 0.01$, *** $p < 0.001$.

TABLE A7.6 *Impact of Bipartisan Cosponsorship on Members' Vote Share (1990–2004)*

	1990	1992	1994	1996	1998	2000	2002	2004
Intercept	41.0***	37.5***	48.5***	19.5***	16.5***	27.2***	29.0*^*	27.6***
	(6.01)	(6.37)	(5.26)	(3.62)	(4.67)	(4.75)	(5.31)	(3.66)
Percent Bipartisan Cosponsors	-0.0486	-0.00559	-0.0875*	0.0679^	0.106*	0.0768	-0.0304	0.109**
	(0.0639)	(0.0475)	(0.0402)	(0.0359)	(0.0453)	(0.0479)	(0.0539)	(0.0363)
Competitive District	-15.5***	-6.29	-11.4***	-1.44	-2.29	-5.59	-12.6*^	-4.33^
	(4.49)	(4.41)	(3.06)	(2.64)	(3.62)	(3.61)	(4.15)	(2.48)
Normal Presidential Vote (%)	0.416***	0.397***	0.358***	0.647***	0.667***	0.500***	0.537*^*	0.563***
	(0.0616)	(0.0841)	(0.0634)	(0.0407)	(0.0502)	(0.0490)	(0.0546)	(0.0410)
Quality Challenger	-2.78*	-3.29**	-2.84**	-1.78**	-1.86*	-1.10^	0.151	-0.665
	(1.11)	(1.17)	(0.908)	(0.634)	(0.747)	(0.626)	(0.866)	(0.627)
Logged Challenger – Incumbent Spending	-2.07***	-2.53***	-3.04***	-2.81***	-2.28***	-2.44***	-2.21*^*	-1.18***
	(0.221)	(0.343)	(0.243)	(0.195)	(0.212)	(0.176)	(0.232)	(0.145)
Freshman	0.526	2.72*	-0.567	-2.91***	-0.898	-1.40^	-0.978	-1.31^
	(1.2)	(1.38)	(0.733)	(0.625)	(0.746)	(0.794)	(0.98)	(0.665)
President's Party	-6.49***	-1.58	-7.23***	-2.14**	-0.777	0.704	1.93*	-5.11***
	(1.60)	(1.12)	(0.746)	(0.666)	(0.735)	(0.553)	(0.747)	(0.535)
Pct Bipartisan Cospon x Competitive	0.291***	0.120^	0.185***	0.0638	0.0843	0.0923	0.241*^*	0.0677
	(0.0737)	(0.0675)	(0.052)	(0.0432)	(0.0592)	(0.0581)	(0.0677)	(0.0427)
N	315	220	320	349	297	273	185	316
R^2	0.484	0.453	0.679	0.822	0.740	0.739	0.70	0.735
Adjusted R^2	0.471	0.432	0.671	0.818	0.732	0.731	0.686	0.728

Standard errors in parentheses. ^ $p < 0.1$, * $p < 0.05$, ** $p < 0.01$, *** $p < 0.001$.

TABLE A7.7 *Impact of Bipartisan Cosponsorship on Members' Vote Share as Risk of Being Out-of-Step Increases (Competitive Districts Only) (1974–2004)*

	Model 1 (Majority and Minority Incumbents)	Model 2 (Majority Party Incumbents)
Intercept	63.4***	62.7***
	(7.31)	(13.1)
Percent Bipartisan Cosponsorship	−0.0922	−0.0380
	(0.0748)	(0.102)
% Party Unity Votes in Congress	−0.280***	−0.355*
	(0.0997)	(0.157)
% Bipartisan Cospon x % Party Unity Votes	0.00270^	0.00205
	(0.00143)	(0.00197)
Party Unity Support Score	−0.117***	−0.102***
	(0.0110)	(0.0137)
Normal Presidential Vote (%)	0.401***	0.428***
	(0.0260)	(0.0302)
Quality Challenger	−2.30***	−2.32***
	(0.297)	(0.348)
Logged Challenger – Incumbent Spending	−2.40***	−2.37***
	(0.0776)	(0.0867)
Freshman	−6.40*	−0.531
	(0.313)	(0.362)
President's Party	−1.10	−2.55
	(5.27)	(12.8)
Change in Income	0.408	0.320
	(0.378)	(0.787)
Presidential Popularity	−0.0499	−0.0174
	(0.102)	(0.211)
Midterm Election Year	2.86	2.40
	(1.78)	(3.56)
President's Party x Change in Income	0.109	0.333
	(0.393)	(0.915)
President's Party x Pres. Pop.	−0.00899	0.0218
	(0.108)	(0.279)
President's Party x Midterm Election	−4.68	−4.72
	(1.85)	(4.66)
σ^2_{Year}	44.4	38.9
$\sigma^2_{President's\ Party\ (by\ Year)}$	21.5	6.25
$\sigma^2_{\%\ Bipart\ Cospon\ (by\ Year)}$	0.00369	0.00333
N	2148	1943
Log Likelihood	−7793	−6308

Standard errors in parentheses. ^ $p < 0.1$, * $p < 0.05$, ** $p < 0.01$, *** $p < 0.001$.

References

Abramowitz, Alan I. 2010. *The Disappearing Center*. New Haven: Yale University Press.

Abramowitz, Alan I., and Kyle L. Saunders. 1998. "Ideological Realignment in the U.S. Electorate." *Journal of Politics* 60 (3):634–52.

——2008. "Is Polarization a Myth?" *Journal of Politics* 70 (2):542–55.

Achen, Christopher H. 1978. "Measuring Representation." *American Journal of Political Science* 22 (3):475–510.

Adler, E. Scott, and John Wilkerson. 2008. "Congressional Bills Project: 1973–2002." NSF 00880066 and 00880061.

——2013. *Congress and the Politics of Problem Solving*. New York: Cambridge University Press.

Albert, Carl. 1973. "Political Situation and Democratic Party Prospects." In *Speaker's Legislative Office: Carl Albert Center Archive Box 178*, F1.

——1979. "Interview between Carl Albert and Ronald Peters for Book on American Speakership." Carl Albert Center Archive.

Aldrich, John H. 1995. *Why Parties? The Origin and Transformation of Party Politics in America*. Chicago: University of Chicago Press.

Aldrich, John H., and David W. Rohde. 2000. "The Republican Revolution and the House Appropriations Committee." *Journal of Politics* 62 (1):1–33.

——2001. "The Logic of Conditional Party Government: Revisiting the Electoral Connection." In *Congress Reconsidered*, ed. L. C. Dodd and B. I. Oppenheimer. Washington D.C.: CQ Press, 269–92.

Aleman, Eduardo, Ernesto Calvo, Mark P. Jones, and Noah Kaplan. 2009. "Comparing Cosponsorship with Roll-Call Ideal Points." *Legislative Studies Quarterly* XXXIV (1):87–116.

Anonymous. 2011. Interview with Former Blue-Dog Democrat in House of Representatives. Evanston, IL, August 25.

Anselmo, Joseph C. 2003. "Energy Omnibus: What's in, What's out." In *CQ Weekly*. Washington D.C.: Congressional Quarterly.

Ansolabehere, Stephen, James M. Snyder, and Charles Stewart III. 2000. "Old Voters, New Voters, and the Personal Vote: Using Redistricting to Measure the Incumbency Advantage." *American Journal of Political Science* 44 (1):17–34.

———2001. "Candidate Positioning in U.S. House Elections." *American Journal of Political Science* 45 (1):136–59.

APSA. 1950. "Toward a More Responsible Two-Party System: A Report of the Committee on Political Parties." *American Political Science Review* 44 (3):v–99.

Armey, Richard. 1997. "Outline of Speech by Richard Armey at Williamsburg Congress of Tomorrow." *in Richard Armey Collection:* Carl Albert Center Archive Box 55, F13.

Arnold, R. Douglas. 1990. *The Logic of Congressional Action.* New Haven: Yale University Press.

———2004. *Congress, The Press, and Political Accountability.* Princeton: Princeton University Press.

Arrow, Kenneth. 1951. *Social Choice and Individual Values.* New York: Wiley.

Babington, Charles. 2010. "Despite all the Nice Talk, Partisanship Reigns." February, 9. *Associated Press.* Available from http://www.cleveland.com/nation/index.ssf/2010/02/despite_all_the_nice_talk_part.html.

Bach, Stanley. 1990. "Suspension of the Rules, the Order of Business, and the Development of Congressional Procedure." *Legislative Studies Quarterly* 15 (1):49–63.

Bach, Stanley, and Steven S. Smith. 1998. *Managing Uncertainty in the House of Representatives: Adoption and Innovation in Special Rules.* Washington D.C.: Brookings Institution Press.

Badger, Emily. 2009. "There Is No Common Ground Anymore." *Pacific Standard Magazine*, October 13, 2009 [accessed February 12, 2013]. Available from http://www.psmag.com/politics/there-is-no-common-ground-anymore-3412/.

Barriere, John E. 1973. "Memo to Honorable Carl Albert. Subject: Wage-Price Control Bill (H.R. 6168)." In *Speaker's Legislative, John Barriere Memos* Carl Albert Center Archive Box 238, F11.

———1975. "Memo to Honorable Carl Albert. Subject: Accomplishments of the House (and its Leadership) in the 94th Congress." In *Speaker's Legislative, John Barriere Memos.* Carl Albert Center Archive Box 238, F15.

Baumgartner, Frank R., and Bryan D. Jones. 2000. "Congressional Roll Call Votes." Policy Agendas Project with the support of National Science Foundation grant number SBR 9320922.

Bean, Melissa. 2010. "Editorial Board Questionnaires." In *Chicago Tribune* [accessed October 27, 2010]. Chicago. Available from http://elections.chicagotribune.com/editorial/melissa-bean/.

Beinart, Peter. 2008. "When Politics No Longer Stops at the Water's Edge: Partisan Polarization and Foreign Policy." In *Red and Blue Nation? Consequences and Correction of America's Polarized Politics*, ed. P. S. Nivola and D. W. Brady. Washington D.C.: Brookings Institution Press, 151–67.

Benenson, Bob. 1993. "ENVIRONMENT: House Easily Passes Overhaul of 1872 Mining Law." *Congressional Quarterly Weekly* (November 20, 1993). Washington D.C.: Congressional Quarterly, 3191–92.

Bernhard, William, and Tracy Sulkin. 2013. "Commitment and Consequences: Reneging on Cosponsorship Pledges in the U.S. House." *Legislative Studies Quarterly* 38(4):61–87.

Berry, Christopher R., Barry C. Burden, and William G. Howell. 2010. "After Enactment: The Lives and Deaths of Federal Programs." *American Journal of Political Science* 54 (1):1–17.

Bessette, Joseph M. 1994. *The Mild Voice of Reason: Deliberative Democracy and American National Government*. Chicago: University of Chicago Press.

Binder, Sarah. 2003. *Stalemate: Causes and Consequences of Legislative Gridlock*. Washington D.C.: Brookings Institution Press.

Black, Duncan. 1958. *The Theory of Committees and Elections*. Cambridge: Cambridge University Press.

Bonica, Adam. 2010. *Introducing the 112th Congress* [accessed March 4, 2014]. Available from http://ideologicalcartography.com/2010/11/05/introducing-the-112th-congress/.

Brady, David W., John Ferejohn, and Laurel Harbridge. 2008. "Polarization and Public Policy: A General Assessment." In *Red and Blue Nation? Consequences and Correction of America's Polarized Politics*, ed. P. S. Nivola and D. W. Brady. Washington D.C.: Brookings Institution Press, 185–216.

Brady, David W., and Hahrie C. Han. 2006. "Polarization Then and Now." In *Red and Blue Nation? Characteristics and Causes of America's Polarized Politics*, ed. P. S. Nivola and D. W. Brady.

Brady, David W., Hahrie Han, and Jeremy C. Pope. 2007. "Primary Elections and Candidate Ideology: Out-of-Step with the Primary Electorate?" *Legislative Studies Quarterly* 32 (1):79–105.

Brownstein, Ronald. 2007. *The Second Civil War: How Extreme Partisanship Has Paralyzed Washington and Polarized America*. New York: Penguin Press HC.

Burden, Barry C. 2001. "The Polarizing Effects of Congressional Primaries." In *Congressional Primaries and the Politics of Representation*, ed. P. F. Galderisi, M. Ezra, and M. Lyons. Lanham: Rowman & Littlefield, 95–115.

——2004. "Candidate Positioning in US Congressional Elections." *British Journal of Political Science* 34:211–27.

——2005. "Institutions and Policy Representation in the States." *State Politics & Policy Quarterly* 5 (4):373–93.

——2007. *Personal Roots of Representation*. Princeton: Princeton University Press.

Butler, Daniel M., and David E. Broockman. 2011. "Do Politicians Discriminate Against Constituents? A Field Experiment on State Legislators." *American Journal of Political Science* 55 (3):463–67.

Butler, Daniel M., and Eleanor Neff Powell. 2014. "Understanding the Party Brand: Experimental Evidence on the Role of Valence." *The Journal of Politics* 76 (02): 492–505.

Campbell, James E. 1982. "Cosponsoring Legislation in the U.S. Congress." *Legislative Studies Quarterly* 7 (3):415–22.

Canes-Wrone, Brandice, David W. Brady, and John F. Cogan. 2002. "Out of Step, Out of Office: Electoral Accountability and House Members' Voting." *American Political Science Review* 96 (1):127–40.

Capehart, Jonathan. 2010. "America Really Hates Congress." *The Washington Post*, March 17, 2010 [accessed July 26, 2012]. Available from http://voices.washington post.com/postpartisan/2010/03/post_2.html.

Carroll, Royce, and Jason Eichorst. 2013. "The Role of Party: The Legislative Consequences of Partisan Electoral Competition." *Legislative Studies Quarterly* 38 (1):83–109.

Carrubba, Clifford, Matthew Gabel, and Simon Hug. 2008. "Legislative Voting Behavior, Seen and Unseen: A Theory of Roll Call Vote Selection." *Legislative Studies Quarterly* XXXII (4):543–72.

Carson, Jamie L., Charles J. Finocchiaro, and David W. Rohde. 2010a. "Consensus, Conflict, and Partisanship in House Decision Making: A Bill-Level Examination of Committee and Floor Behavior." *Congress and the Presidency* 37 (3):231–53.

Carson, Jamie L., Gregory Koger, Matthew J. Lebo, and Everett Young. 2010b. "The Electoral Costs of Party Loyalty in Congress." *American Journal of Political Science* 54 (3):598–616.

Castle, Michael. 2011. Interview. Washington D.C., August 17, 2011.

Clausen, Aage R. 1973. *How Congressmen Decide: A Policy Focus*. New York: St. Martin's Press.

Clinton, Joshua D. 2006. "Representation in Congress: Constituents and Roll Calls in the 106th House." *Journal of Politics* 68 (2):397–409.

——2007. "Lawmaking and Roll Calls." *Journal of Politics* 69 (2):355–467.

——2012. "Using Roll Call Estimates to Test Models of Politics." *Annual Review of Political Science* 15:79–99.

Coffman, Mike. 2013. *Rep. Mike Coffman: How to Get Things Done*, July 15, 2013 [accessed February 11, 2014]. Available from http://www.nolabels.org/blog/rep-mike-coffman-how-get-things-done.

Cogan, John F., David W. Brady, and Douglas Rivers. 1997. "The 1996 House Elections: Reaffirming the Conservative Trend." Stanford University: Hoover Institution.

Coleman, John J. 1996. *Party Decline in America: Policy, Politics, and the Fiscal State*. Princeton: Princeton University Press.

"Compromise Highway Bill Completed After Two-Year Clash." 2006. In *Congressional Quarterly Almanac* [accessed January 14, 2009]. Washington D.C.: Congressional Quarterly. Available from http://library.cqpress.com/cqalmanac/cqal05-766-20103-1042223

"Congress Grants Nation's Capital Limited Home Rule." 1973. In *Congressional Quarterly Almanac*. Washington D.C.: Congressional Quarterly.

"Congressional Record." 1967. Washington D.C.

"Congressional Record." 1995. Washington D.C.

"Congressional Record." 2002. Washington D.C.

"Congressional Record." 2006. Washington D.C.

Conlon, Richard P. 1961. "House Democrats and Responsible Party Government." ed. Responsible Party Model Study Democratic Caucus: Library of Congress Democratic Study Group Archive Folder 12, Box II: 2.

Converse, Phillip E. 1964. "The Nature of Belief Systems in Mass Publics." In *Ideology and Discontent*, ed. D. E. Apter. New York: Free Press, 206–31.

Converse, Phillip E., and Roy Pierce. 1986. *Political Representation in France*. Cambridge: Harvard University Press.

Cooper, Joseph, and David W. Brady. 1981. "Institutional Context and Leadership Style: The House From Cannon to Rayburn." *American Political Science Review* 75 (2):411–25.

Cooper, Joseph, and Garry Young. 1997. "Partisanship, Bipartisanship, and Cross-partisanship in Congress Since the New Deal." In *Congress Reconsidered*, ed. L. C. Dodd and B. I. Oppenheimer. Washington D.C.: CQ Press, 246–73.

"Corporate Tax Breaks Enacted." 2005. In *Congressional Quarterly Almanac* [accessed January 13 2009]. Washington D.C.: Congressional Quarterly. Available from http://library.cqpress.com/cqalmanac/cqal04-836-24355-1084697.

Cosgrove-Mather, Bootie. 2005. "Congress Approves Big Highway Bill." *CBS News*, July 29, 2005 [accessed January 14, 2009]. Available from http://www.cbsnews.com/stories/2005/07/29/politics/main712780.shtml.

Cox, Gary, and Jonathan N. Katz. 2002. *Elbridge Gerry's Salamander: The Electoral Consequences of the Reapportionment Revolution*. Cambridge: Cambridge University Press.

Cox, Gary, and Mathew D. McCubbins. 1993. *Legislative Leviathan*. Berkeley: University of California Press.

——2002. "Agenda Power in the U.S. House of Representatives, 1877–1986." In *Party, Process, and Political Change in Congress: New Perspectives on the History of Congress*, ed. D. W. Brady and M. D. McCubbins. Stanford: Stanford University Press, 107–45.

——2005. *Setting the Agenda: Responsible Party Government in the U.S. House of Representatives*. New York: Cambridge University Press.

"CQ Fact Sheet Bipartisan Voting." 1963. In *Congressional Quarterly Almanac*. Washington D.C.: Congressional Quarterly.

"CQ Fact Sheet Bipartisan Voting." 1970. In *Congressional Quarterly Almanac*. Washington D.C.: Congressional Quarterly.

Crespin, Michael H., David W. Rohde, and Ryan J. Vander Wielen. 2013. "Measuring Variation in Party Unity Voting: An Assessment of Agenda Effects." *Party Politics* 19 (3):432–57.

Dahl, Robert A. 2003. *How Democratic Is the American Constitution?* 2nd ed. New Haven: Yale University Press.

David. 1997. "Memo from David to Kerry. Subject: Criteria for Considering Legislation on the Floor." In *Richard Armey Collection*: Carl Albert Center Archive Box 55, F13.

DeLay, Tom, and Stephen Mansfield. 2007. *No Retreat, No Surrender*. New York: Sentinel.

Democratic Senatorial Campaign Committee. 2008. *Elizabeth Dole: Rocking Chairs* [accessed June 27, 2012]. Available from http://www.youtube.com/watch?v=LLkazmjpcIs.

Democratic Staffer. 2011. Interview. Washington D.C., August 2011.

Democratic Study Group. 1961. "Congressional Report Vol. 10 No. 1." In *Academic Studies and History*, ed. N. C. f. a. E. Congress: Library of Congress Democratic Study Group Archive Folder 2, Box II: 1.

Den Hartog, Chris, and Nathan W. Monroe. 2011. *Agenda Setting in the U.S. Senate: Costly Consideration and Majority Party Advantage*. New York: Cambridge University Press.

Desposato, Scott W., Matthew C. Kearney, and Brian F. Crisp. 2011. "Using Cosponsorship to Estimate Ideal Points." *Legislative Studies Quarterly* XXXVI (4):531–65.

Diermeier, Daniel, and Razvan Vlaicu. 2011. "Parties, Coalitions, and the Internal Organization of Legislatures." *American Political Science Review* 105 (2):359–80.

Dinan, Stephen. 2013. "Capitol Hill Least Productive Congress Ever: 112th Fought 'About Everything'." *The Washington Times*, January 9, 2013 [accessed January 9, 2013]. Available from http://www.washingtontimes.com/news/2013/jan/9/capitol-hill-least-productive-congress-ever-112th-/?page=all.

Dodd, Lawrence C., and Bruce I. Oppenheimer. 2004. "A Decade of Republican Control: The House of Representatives, 1995–2005." In *Congress Reconsidered*, ed. L. C. Dodd and B. I. Oppenheimer. Washington D.C.: CQ Press, 23–54.

———2012. "Congress at the Precipee: The 2012 Elections and the Fiscal Cliff." In *Congress Reconsidered*, ed. L. C. Dodd and B. I. Oppenheimer. Washington D.C.: CQ Press, 465–94.

Doherty, David. 2013. "To Whom Do People Think Representatives Should Respond: Their District or the Country?" *Public Opinion Quarterly* 77 (1):237–55.

Dold, Robert. 2012. "Editorial Board Questionnaires." In *Chicago Tribune* [accessed October 11, 2012]. Chicago. Previously available from http://elections.chicagotri bune.com/editorial/robert-dold/ [no longer available at date of publication].

Druckman, James N, Martin J Kifer, and Michael Parkin. 2009. "Campaign communications in US congressional elections." *American Political Science Review* 103 (3):343–66.

Egan, Patrick J. 2013. *Partisan Priorities: How Issue Ownership Drives and Distorts American Politics*. New York: Cambridge University Press.

Ehrlich, Andy, Mark Strand, and Paul Morrell. 1999. "Memo to Majority Leader Richard Armey and Assisstant Majority Leaders Rick Lazio and Jim Talent. Subject: The 55 Percent Caucus Project." In *Richard Armey Collection*: Carl Albert Center Archive Box 55, F7.

Eilperin, Juliet. 2006. *Fight Club Politics: How Partisanship is Poisoning the House of Representatives*. Edited by P. Berkowitz and T. Lindberg. Lanham: Rowman and Littlefield.

Erikson, Robert S., and Gerald C. Jr. Wright. 1980. "Policy Representation of Constituency Interests." *Political Behavior* 2 (1):91–106.

———2005. "Voters, Candidates, and Issues in Congressional Elections." In *Congress Reconsidered*, ed. L. C. Dodd and B. I. Oppenheimer. Washington D.C.: CQ Press, 77–106.

Eulau, Heinz, and Paul D. Karps. 1977. "The Puzzle of Representation: Specifying Components of Responsiveness." *Legislative Studies Quarterly* 2 (3):233–54.

Eulau, Heinz, John C. Wahlke, William Buchanan, and Leroy C. Ferguson. 1959. "The Role of the Representative: Some Empirical Oberservations on the Theory of Edmund Burke." *American Political Science Review* 53:742–56.

FEC. 2009. *Number of Federal PACs Increases* [Report]. Federal Election Commission, March 9, 2009 [accessed October 24, 2011]. Available from http://www.fec.gov/ press/press2009/20090309PACcount.shtml.

Fenno, Richard F. Jr. 1978. *Home Style: Home Members in Their Districts*. Boston: Little, Brown.

———1997. *Learning to Govern: An Institutional View of the 104th Congress*. Washington D.C.: Brookings Institution.

Fiorina, Morris P., and Samuel A. Abrams. 2008. "Political Polarization in the American Public." *Annual Review of Political Science* 11:563–88.

———2009. *Disconnect: The Breakdown of Representation in American Politics*. Norman, OK: University of Oklahoma Press.

Fiorina, Morris P., Samuel Abrams, and Jeremy Pope. 2005. *Culture War? The Myth of a Polarized America*. New York: Pearson Longman.

Fiorina, Morris P., and David W. Brady. 2008. *Cooperative Congressional Election Study, 2008: Stanford Content* (Data Release 1) [Computer File] 2008 [accessed February 2009]. Available from projects.iq.harvard.edu/cces/data.

Fowler, James. 2006a. "Connecting the Congress: A Study of Cosponsorship Networks." *Political Analysis* 14 (4):456–87.

——2006b. "Legislative Cosponsorship Networks in the U.S. House and Senate." *Social Networks* 28:454–65.

Fram, Alan. 2012. "Dems, GOP Using Popular Bills to Hurt Other Party." *Associated Press*.

Franzese, Robert J., and Cindy Kam. 2007. *Modeling and Interpretting Interactive Hypotheses in Regression Analysis*. Ann Arbor: University of Michigan Press.

Galston, William A., and Pietro S. Nivola. 2006. "Delineating the Problem." In *Red and Blue Nation? Characteristics and Causes of America's Polarized Politics*, ed. P. S. Nivola and D. W. Brady. Washington D.C., 1–48.

Geiger, Kim. 2013. "Gun Trafficking Bill Carrying Hadiya Pendleton's Name Clears Senate Panel." *Chicago Tribune, March* 7, 2013.

Gelman, Andrew, and Jennifer Hill. 2007. *Data Analysis Using Regression and Multilevel/Hierarchical Models*. New York: Cambridge University Press.

Gilligan, Thomas, and Keith Krehbiel. 1987. "Collective Decision-Making and Standing Committees: An Informational Rational for Restrictive Amendment Procedures." *Journal of Law, Economics, and Organization* 3:287–335.

Gilmour, John B. 1995. *Strategic Disagreement*. Pittsburgh: University of Pittsburgh Press.

Glickman, Daniel. 2011. Interview. Washington D.C., August 22, 2011.

Goad, Ben, and Kevin Bogardus. 2014. "Chamber Chief Promises Midterm Blitz." *The Hill*, January 8, 2014 [accessed January 30, 2014]. Available from http://thehill.com/business-a-lobbying/business-a-lobbying/194841-chamber-chief-vows-vigorous-defense-of-pro-business.

Goldman, Joe. 2013. "Our Approach to Polarization and Gridlock." *Democracy Fund*, February 4, 2013 [accessed February 11, 2013]. Available from http://www.democracyfund.org/blog/entry/our-approach-to-polarization-and-gridlock.

Goldreich, Samuel. 2003a. "Flash Points in Energy Bill Versions Threaten Another Fatal Conference." In *Congressional Quarterly Weekly*, April 12, 2003. Washington D.C.: Congressional Quarterly, 376–78.

——2003b. "Hard-Fought Utility Deals Power Omnibus Energy Bill." In *Congressional Quarterly Weekly*, April 5, 2003. Washington D.C.: Congressional Quarterly: 818–22.

Grandy, Fred. 1995. "Under Newt Management – Bipartisan Leadership in Congress." *Washington Monthly*, January 1 1995.

Green, Matthew N. 2010. *The Speaker of the House: A Study of Leadership*. New Haven: Yale University Press.

Groeling, Tim, and Samuel Kernell. 2000. "Congress, the President, and Party Competition via Network News." In *Polarized Politics: Congress and the President in a Partisan Era*, ed. J. R. Bond and R. Fleisher. Washington D.C.: CQ Press, 73–95.

Groseclose, Tim, and Nolan McCarty. 2001. "The Politics of Blame: Bargaining before an Audience." *American Journal of Political Science* 45 (1):100–19.

Grynaviski, Jeffrey D. 2010. *Partisan Bonds*. New York: Cambridge University Press.

Gugliotta, Guy. 1996. "They Flat Do Not Care." *Washington Post Weekly*, January 1–7, 1996.

Gutmann, Amy, and Dennis Thompson. 2012. *The Spirit of Compromise: Why Governing Demands It and Campaigning Undermines It*. Princeton: Princeton University Press.

Hacker, Jacob S. 2005. "Policy Drift: The Hidden Politics of US Welfare State Retrenchment." In *Beyond Continuity: Institutional Change in Advanced Economies*, ed. W. Streeck and K. Thelen. Oxford: Oxford University Press, 40–82.

Hacker, Jacob S., and Paul Pierson. 2005. *Off Center: The Republican Revolution and the Erosion of American Democracy*. New Haven: Yale University Press.

Hall, Richard L. 1996. *Participation in Congress*. New Haven: Yale University Press.

Han, Hahrie, and David W. Brady. 2007. "A Delayed Return to Historical Norms: Congressional Party Polarization after the Second World War." *British Journal of Political Science* 37 (3):505–31.

Harbridge, Laurel, and Neil Malhotra. 2011. "Electoral Incentives and Partisan Conflict in Congress: Evidence from Survey Experiments." *American Journal of Political Science* 55 (3):1–17.

Hayes, Danny. 2005. "Candidate Qualities Through a Partisan Lens: A Theory of Trait Ownership." *American Journal of Political Science* 49 (4):908–23.

Heller, William B., and Carol Mershon. 2008. "Dealing in Discipline: Party Switching and Legislative Voting in the Italian Chamber of Deputies, 1988–2000." *American Journal of Political Science* 52 (4):910–25.

Herger, Wally Jr., and Pete Stark. 2011. "Stark, Herger Reintroduce Bipartisan Bill to Fight Medicare Fraud." Washington D.C.: Project Vote Smart.

Hetherington, Marc J. 2001. "Resurgent Mass Partisanship: The Role of Elite Polarization." *American Political Science Review* 95 (3):619–31.

Hibbing, John R., and Elizabeth Theiss-Morse. 1995. *Congress as Public Enemy: Public Attitudes Toward American Political Institutions*. New York: Cambridge University Press.

—— 2001. "Process Preferences and American Politics: What the People Want Government to Be." *American Political Science Review* 95 (1):145–53.

—— 2002. *Stealth Democracy*. New York: Cambridge University Press.

Holian, David B. 2006. "Trust the Party Line." *American Politics Research* 34 (6):777–802.

"House Advances Education Reform Bill." 1993. In *Congressional Quarterly Almanac*. Washington D.C.: Congressional Quarterly. Washington D.C.: Congressional Quarterly: 404–7.

"House of Representatives Casts Historic Vote To Impeach Clinton." 1999. In *Congressional Quarterly Almanac 1998*. Washington D.C.: Congressional Quarterly. Available from http://library.cqpress.com/cqalmanac/cqal98-17-24538-1087774 [accessed October 7, 2011].

House Report 108-067 Energy Tax Policy Act of 2003. 2003. House Committee on Ways and Means 2003 [accessed August 27, 2013]. Available from http://thomas.loc.gov/cgi-bin/cpquery/R?cp108:FLD010:@1%28hr067%29:.

Hulse, Carl. 2009. "Democrats Eye Maine Senator for a G.O.P. Vote on Health." *The New York Times, August* 29, 2009, 11.

Huntsman, Jon, and Joe Manchin, eds. 2014. *No Labels: A Shared Vision for a Stronger America*. New York: Diversion Books.

Hurwitz, Mark S., Roger J. Moiles, and David W. Rohde. 2001. "Distributive and Partisan Issues in Agriculture Policy in the 104th House." *American Political Science Review* 94 (4):911–22.

Jacobson, Gary. 2010. "House Election Data 1946–2010."

Jochim, Ashley E., and Bryan D. Jones. 2013. "Issue Politics in a Polarized Congress." *Political Research Quarterly* 66 (2):352–69.

Jones, David R. 2010. "Partisan Polarization and Congressional Accountability in House Elections." *American Journal of Political Science* 54 (2):323–37.

Jones, David R., and Monika L. McDermott. 2010. *Americans, Congress, and Democratic Responsiveness: Public Evaluations of Congress and Electoral Consequences.* Ann Arbor: University of Michigan Press.

Kanthak, Kristin, Brian F. Crisp, and Santiago Olivella. 2010. "... And Keeping Your Enemies Closer: Cosponsorship Patterns as a Means of Challenger Deterrence." Paper read at the Annual Meeting of the Midwest Political Science Association. Chicago, IL.

Kasperowicz, Pete, and Erik Wasson. 2014. "House passes $956B farm bill." *The Hill*, January 29, 2014 [accessed February 11, 2014]. Available from http://thehill.com/blogs/floor-action/house/196819-house-passes-956b-farm-bill.

Kernell, Georgia. 2009. "Giving Order to Districts: Estimating Voter Distributions with National Election Returns." *Political Analysis* 17 (3):215–35.

Kessler, Daniel, and Keith Krehbiel. 1996. "Dynamics of Cosponsorship." *American Political Science Review* 90 (3):555–66.

Kiewiet, D. Roderick, and Mathew D. McCubbins. 1991. *The Logic of Delegation.* Chicago: University of Chicago Press.

Killian, Linda. 1998. *The Freshmen: What Happened to the Republican Revolution?* Boulder: Westview Press.

Kingdon, John W. 1973. *Congressmen's Voting Decisions.* New York: Harper and Row.

——1995. *Agendas, Alternatives, and Public Policies.* 2nd ed. New York: Longman.

Kline, John. 2004. "Creating Jobs and Growing Minnesota's Rural Economy: A Report from Congressman John Kline." U.S. House of Representatives.

Koger, Gregory. 2003. "Position Taking and Cosponsorship in the U.S. House." *Legislative Studies Quarterly* 28 (2):225–46.

Koger, Gregory, and Matthew J. Lebo. 2012. "Strategic Party Government and the 2010 Elections." *American Politics Research* 40 (5):927–45.

Koszczuk, Jackie. 1995. "'Train Wreck' Engineered by GOP Batters Party and House Speaker." *Congressional Quarterly Weekly Report*, November 18, 1995. Washington D.C.: Congressional Quarterly, 3506.

Krehbiel, Keith. 1993. "Where's the Party?" *British Journal of Political Science* 23 (2):235–66.

——1995. "Cosponsors and Wafflers from A to Z." *American Journal of Political Science* 39 (4):906–23.

——1998. *Pivotal Politics.* Chicago: University of Chicago Press.

——2006. "Partisan Roll Rates in a Nonpartisan Legislature." *Journal of Law, Economics, and Organization* 23 (1):1–23.

Lausten, Eric. 2011. Interview. Washington D.C., August 16, 2011.

Lawler, Andrew. 1997. "1998 Budget: Bipartisan Mood in Congress Opens Door for Pork." *Science* 277 (5330):1195–1196.

Lawrence, Eric D., Forrest Maltzman, and Steven S. Smith. 2006. "Who Wins? Party Effects in Legislative Voting." *Legislative Studies Quarterly* 31 (1):33–69.

Lebo, Matthew J., Adam J. McGlynn, and Gregory Koger. 2007. "Strategic Party Government: Party Influence in Congress, 1789–2000." *American Journal of Political Science* 51 (3):464–81.

Lee, Frances E. 2009. *Beyond Ideology: Politics, Principles, and Partisanship in the U.S. Senate*. Chicago: University of Chicago Press.

Levendusky, Matthew. 2009. *The Partisan Sort: How Liberals Became Democrats and Conservatives Became Republicans*. Chicago: University of Chicago Press.

——2013. *How Partisan Media Polarize America*. Chicago: University of Chicago Press.

Levendusky, Matthew S., Jeremy C. Pope, and Simon D. Jackman. 2008. "Measuring District-Level Partisanship with Implications for the Analysis of U.S. Elections." *The Journal of Politics* 70 (3):736–53.

Lipinski, Daniel. 2004. *Congressional Communication: Content and Consequences*. Ann Arbor: University of Michigan Press.

——2010. "Editorial Board Questionnaires." In *Chicago Tribune* [accessed October 27, 2010]. Chicago. Previously available from http://elections.chicagotribune.com/editorial/daniel-lipinski/ [no longer available at date of publication].

——2012. "Editorial Board Questionnaires." In *Chicago Tribune* [accessed October 11, 2012]. Chicago. Previously available from http://elections.chicagotribune.com/editorial/daniel-william-lipinski/ [no longer available at date of publication].

Library Of Congress. 2000. *House and Senate Rules* 2000 [accessed June 1, 2012]. Available from http://permanent.access.gpo.gov/lps3373/rules.html#house.

Loewenberg, Gerhard. 2008. "The Contribution of Comparative Research to Measuring the Policy Preferences of Legislators." *Legislative Studies Quarterly* XXXIII (4):501–10.

Lynch, Michael S., and Anthony J. Madonna. 2008. Viva Voce: Implications from the Disappearing Voice Vote, 1807–1990. Paper read at Annual Meetings of the Midwest Political Science Association, at Chicago, IL.

Madison, James. 1787. "Federalist No. 10." In *The Federalist Papers*, ed. Clinton Roositer. New York: New American Library.

Maltzman, Forrest, and Charles R. Shipan. 2008. "Change, Continuity, and Evolution of the Law." *American Journal of Political Science* 52 (2):252–67.

Mann, Thomas E., and Norman J. Ornstein. 2006. *The Broken Branch: How Congress is Failing America and How to Get it Back on Track*. New York: Oxford University Press.

——2012. *It's Even Worse Than it Looks: How the American Constitutional System Collided With the Politics of Extremism*. New York: Basic Books.

Mansbridge, Jane. 2003. "Rethinking Representation." *American Political Science Review* 97 (04):515–28.

Manzullo, Donald. 2010. "Editorial Board Questionnaires." In *Chicago Tribune* [accessed October 27, 2010]. Chicago. Available from http://elections.chicagotribune.com/editorial/donald-manzullo/.

Martin, Andrew. 2001. "Congressional Decision Making and the Separation of Powers." *American Political Science Review* 95 (2):361–78.

Mayhew, David R. 1974. *Congress: The Electoral Connection*. New Haven: Yale University Press.

——1991. *Divided We Govern*. New Haven: Yale University Press.

——2002. *Electoral Realignments: A Critique of an American Genre*. New Haven: Yale University Press.

——2011. *Partisan Balance: Why Political Parties Don't Kill the U.S. Constitutional System*. Princeton: Princeton University Press.

McCarty, Nolan, Keith T. Poole, and Howard Rosenthal. 2006. *Polarized America: The Dance of Ideology and Unequal Riches*. Cambridge: Massachusetts Institute of Technology Press.

——2009. "Does Gerrymandering Cause Polarization?" *American Journal of Political Science* 53 (3):666–80.

Miller, Warren R., and Donald E. Stokes. 1963. "Constituency Influence in Congress." *American Political Science Review* 57 (1):45–56.

Minta, Michael D. 2009. "Legislative Oversight and the Substantive Representation of Black and Latino Interests in Congress." *Legislative Studies Quarterly* 34 (2):193–218.

Morgan, Dan. 1995. "Spending Cuts Near Approval; House GOP Leaders Offer Concessions to Win Supporters." *The Washington Post, March 16*, 1995.

Muirhead, Russell. 2006. "A Defense of Party Spirit." *Perspectives on Politics* 4 (4):713–27.

National Democratic Institute. 2013. *Democratic Governance* [accessed March 5, 2013]. Available from http://www.ndi.org/governance.

Neiheisel, Jacob R., and Sarah Niebler. 2013. "The Use of Party Brand Labels in Congressional Election Campaigns." *Legislative Studies Quarterly* 38 (3):377–403.

No Labels. 2014 [accessed January 30, 2014]. Available from http://www.nolabels.org/.

Noel, Hans. 2013. *Political Parties and Political Ideologies in America*. New York: Cambridge University Press.

O'Brien, Michael. 2013 *Boehner: Judge Congress by How Many Laws It Repals, Not Passes*. NBC News, July 21, 2013 [accessed June 17, 2014]. Available from http://www.nbcnews.com/news/other/boehner-judge-congress-how-many-laws-it-repeals-not-passes-f6C10699088.

O'Donnell, Norah. 2013. "Obama's New Congress Includes Record Number of Women." *CBS This Morning, January 22*, 2013.

Oppenheimer, Bruce I. 1977. "The Rules Committee: New Arm of Leadership in a Decentralized House." In *Congress Reconsidered*, ed. L. C. Dodd and B. I. Oppenheimer. New York: Praeger Publishers, 96–116.

Ornstein, Norman J. 2011. "Worst. Congress. Ever." In *Foreign Policy*, July 19, 2011 [accessed July 19, 2012]. Available from http://www.foreignpolicy.com/articles/2011/07/19/worst_congress_ever?page=0,0.

Orton, Bill. 1993. "*Congressional Record*." Washington D.C., 7718–19.

Ostrowidski, Vic. 1995. "As Contact with America Aged, Its Importance Grew." *The Times Union*, A13.

Page, Benjamin I., and Lawrence R. Jacobs. 2009. *Class War? What Americans Really Think about Economic Inequality*. Chicago: University of Chicago Press.

Parker, Ashley, and Jonathan Weisman. 2014. "Boehner to Bring Debt Ceiling to Vote Without Policy Attachments." *The New York Times*, February 11, 2014.

Patty, John W. 2008. "Equilibrium Party Government." *American Journal of Political Science* 52 (3):636–55.

"Pension Security Bills Falter." 2002. In *Congressional Quarterly Almanac*. Washington D.C.: Congressional Quarterly, 12/3–12/6.

Petrocik, John R. 1996. "Issue Ownership in Presidential Elections, with a 1980 Case Study." *American Journal of Political Science* 40 (3):825–50.

Petrocik, John R., William L. Benoit, and Glenn J. Hansen. 2003. "Issue Ownership and Presidential Campaigning, 1952–2000." *Political Science Quarterly* 118 (4):599–626.

Pew. 2012. *Trends in American Values: 1987–2012*. The Pew Research Center for People and the Press 2012 [accessed July 9, 2012]. Available from http://www.people-press. org/files/legacy-pdf/06–04-12%20Values%20Release.pdf.

Pew Research Center Publications. 2011. "Most Want Budget Compromise but Split on Who's to Blame for Shutdown." Available at http://www.pewresearch.org/2011/04/ 04/most-want-budget-compromise-but-split-on-whos-to-blame-for-a-shutdown/ [accessed October 8, 2014].

Pitkin, Hanna. 1967. *The Concept of Representation*. Berkeley: University of California Press.

"A Polarized Nation?" 2004. *The Washington Post*, November 14, 2004.

Poole, Isaiah J. 2004. "Party Unity Vote Study: Votes Echo Electoral Themes." In *Congressional Quarterly Weekly Online*, December 11, 2004 [accessed October 20, 2008]. Washington D.C.: Congressional Quarterly, 2906–08. Available at http:// library.cqpress.com/cqweekly/weeklyreport108-000001453590.

Poole, Keith T., and Howard Rosenthal. 1984. "The Polarization of American Politics." *Journal of Politics* 46 (4):1061–79.

——1997. *Congress: A Political-Economic History of Roll Call Voting*. New York: Oxford University Press.

Pope, Jeremy C., and Jonathan Woon. 2009. "Measuring Changes in American Party Reputations, 1939–2004." *Political Research Quarterly* 62 (4):653–61.

Post, James. 2014. "Congressional Report Card: Reed's record mixed in 2013." *The Leader* February 2, 2014 [accessed February 4, 2014]. Available from http://www. the-leader.com/article/20140202/NEWS/140209936.

Preston, Julia. 2013. "Senators Offer a Bipartisan Blueprint for Immigration." *The New York Times, January* 28, 2013.

Prior, Marcus. 2007. *Post-Broadcast Democracy*. New York: Cambridge University Press.

Rae, Nicol C. 2007. "Be Careful What You Wish For: The Rise of Responsible Parties in American National Politics." *Annual Review of Political Science* 10 (169–91).

Ramirez, Mark D. 2009. "The Dynamics of Partisan Conflict on Congressional Approval." *American Journal of Political Science* 53 (3):681–94.

Rice, Stuart A. 1925. "The Behavior of Legislative Groups: A Method of Measurement." *Political Research Quarterly* 40 (1):60–72.

Riker, William H. 1961. "Voting and the Summation of Preferences: An Interpretive Bibliographic Review of Selected Developments during the Last Decade." *The American Political Science Review* 55 (4):900–11.

Riley, Michael. 2010. "Lamborn, Coffman join Tea Party Caucus." *The Denver Post, August* 9, 2010.

Roberts, Jason M. 2007. "The Statistical Analysis of Roll-Call Data: A Cautionary Tale." *Legislative Studies Quarterly* XXXII (3):341–60.

Roberts, Jason, and Steven Smith. 2003. "Procedural Contexts, Party Strategy, and Conditional Voting in the U.S. House of Representatives, 1971–2000." *American Journal of Political Science* 47 (2):305–17.

Rogers, David. 2013. *Farm Bill 2013: House narrowly passes pared-back version* (July 11, 2013). Politico 2013 [cited August 27, 2013]. Available from http://www. politico.com/story/2013/07/farm-bill-2013-house-passes-94031.html.

Rohde, David W. 1991. *Parties and Leaders in the Post-Reform House*. Chicago: University of Chicago Press.

——2004. "Roll Call Data for the United States House of Representatives, 1953–2004." East Lansing, MI: Compiled by the Political Institutions and Public Choice Program, Michigan State University.

Rosas, Guillermo, and Yael Shomer. 2008. "Models of Nonresponse in Legislative Politics." *Legislative Studies Quarterly XXXIII* (4):573–602.

Rosenblum, Nancy L. 2008. *On the Side of the Angels*. Princeton: Princeton University Press.

Roskam, Peter J. 2012. "Editorial Board Questionnaires." In *Chicago Tribune* [accessed October 11, 2012]. Chicago. Previously available from http://elections.chicagotribune.com/editorial/peter-j-roskam/ [no longer available at time of publication].

Schattschneider, E. E. 1942. *Party Government*. New York: Rinehart.

Schickler, Eric. 2001. *Disjointed Pluralism: Institutional Innovation and the Development of the U.S. Congress*. Princeton: Princeton University Press.

Schiller, Wendy. 1995. "Senators as Political Entrepreneurs: Using Bill Sponsorship to Shape Legislative Agendas." *American Journal of Political Science* 39:186–203.

"Senate-House Energy Bills Compared." 2003. In *Congressional Quarterly Weekly*. August 2, 2003. Washington D.C.: Congressional Quarterly: 1967.

Shepsle, Kenneth S., and Barry R. Weingast. 1987. "The Institutional Foundations of Committee Power." *American Political Science Review* 81 (1):85–104.

Shor, Boris, and Nolan McCarty. 2011. "The Ideological Mapping of American Legislatures." *American Political Science Review* 104 (3):530–51.

Sinclair, Barbara. 1983. *Majority Leadership in the U.S. House*. Baltimore: Johns Hopkins University Press.

——1994. "House Special Rules and the Institutional Design Controversy." *Legislative Studies Quarterly* 19 (4):477–94.

——1995. *Legislators, Leaders, and Lawmaking*. Baltimore: Johns Hopkins University Press.

——2006. *Party Wars: Polarization and the Politics of National Policy Making*. Norman: University of Oklahoma Press.

Skocpol, Theda, and Vanessa Williamson. 2012. *The Tea Party and the Remaking of Republican Conservatism*. New York: Oxford Univesity Press.

Smith, S. 1989. *Call to Order*. Washington D.C.: Brookings Institution.

Smith, Steven S. 2007. *Party Influence in Congress*. New York: Cambridge University Press.

Snyder, James M. 1992. "Artificial Extremism in Interest Group Ratings." *Legislative Studies Quarterly* 36:319–45.

Snyder, James M., Jr., and Michael M. Ting. 2002. "An Informational Rationale for Political Parties." *American Journal of Political Science* 46 (1):90–110.

"Social Security Rescue Plan Swiftly Approved." 1983. In *Congressional Quarterly Almanac*. Washington D.C.: Congressional Quarterly: 216–226.

Steinhauer, Jennifer. 2013. "A Day of Friction Notable Even for a Fractious Congress." *The New York Times*, July 12, 2013, A12.

Stephens, Michael. 2011. Interview. Washington D.C., August 15, 2011.

Stiglitz, Edward H., and Barry R. Weingast. 2011. "Endogenous Bias in Ideal Point Estimates." Paper read at the Annual Meeting of the American Political Science Association. Seattle, WA.

Stokes, Donald E. 1963. "Spatial Models of Party Competition." *The American Political Science Review* 57 (2):368–77.

Sulkin, Tracy. 2005. *Issue Politics in Congress*. New York: Cambridge University Press.

———2011. *The Legislative Legacy of Congressional Campaigns*. New York: Cambridge University Press.

Swers, Michele L. 2002. *The Difference Women Make: The Policy Impact of Women in Congress*. Chicago: University of Chicago Press.

Swindell, Bill. 2002. "Quick Resolution of Pension Protection Appears Unlikely as House Chairmen Square Off on Jurisdiction, Enforcement." In *Congressional Quarterly Weekly*, April 6, 2002. Washington D.C.: Congressional Quarterly, 910.

Talbert, Jeffrey, and Matthew Potoski. 2002. "Setting the Legislative Agenda: The Dimensional Structure of Bill Cosponsoring and Floor Voting." *Journal of Politics* 64 (3):841–91.

Theriault, Sean M. 2006. Procedural Polarization in the U.S. Congress. Paper read at the Annual Meeting of the Midwest Political Science Association Meeting, at Chicago, IL.

———2008. *Party Polarization in Congress*. New York: Cambridge University Press.

Thomas, Scott, and Bernard Grofman. 1993. "The Effects of Congressional Rules About Bill Cosponsorship on Duplicate Bills: Changing Incentives for Credit Claiming." *Public Choice* 75:93–8.

Tsebelis, George. 2002. *Veto Players: How Political Institutions Work*. Princeton: Princeton University Press.

Trubowitz, Peter, and Nicole Mellow. 2005. " 'Going Bipartisan': Politics by Other Means." *Political Science Quarterly* 120 (3):433–53.

Van Houweling, Robert. 2012. "Parties as Enablers: Individual Incentives for Partisan Legislative Organization." Manuscript.

Vandoren, Peter M. 1990. "Can We Learn the Causes of Congressional Decisions from Roll-Call Data?" *Legislative Studies Quarterly* 15 (3):311–40.

Vogel, Kennth P., and Ben Smith. 2011. "Kochs' Plan for 2012: Raise $88M." *Politico*, February 11, 2011, 1.

Volden, Craig, and Alan E. Wiseman. 2014. The Lawmakers: Legislative Effectiveness in the United States Congress. New York: Cambridge University Press.

Wawro, Gregory. 2000. *Legislative Entrepreneurship in the U.S. House of Representatives*. Ann Arbor: University of Michigan Press.

Weiner, Rachel, and Ed O'Keefe. 2013. "Judging the (un)productivity of the 113th Congress." *The Washington Post*, August 2, 2013.

Weingast, Barry R. 1996. "Political Institutions: Rational Choice Perspective." In *A New Handbook of Political Science*, ed. R. E. Goodin and H.-D. Klingemann. New York: Oxford University Press.

Weinger, Mackenzie. 2012. "Richard Mourdock Dismisses Dick Lugar Attack." *Politico*, May 9, 2012.

Weissberg, Robert. 1978. "Collective vs. Dyadic Representation in Congress." *The American Political Science Review* 72 (2):535–47.

Westphal, David. 2004. "Moderates Lament Partisan Divide in Congress." *Scripps Howard News Service*, October 15, 2004.

"Why Did the Farm Bill Fail in the House?" 2013. June 26, 2013 [accessed August 27, 2013]. Available from http://sustainableagriculture.net/blog/why-farm-bill-faied/.

Wilkerson, John D. 1990. "Reelection and Representation in Conflict: The Case of Agenda Manipulation." *Legislative Studies Quarterly* 15 (2):263–82.

Wilson, Rick K., and Cheryl D. Young. 1997. "Cosponsorship in the U.S. Congress." *Legislative Studies Quarterly* 22 (1):25–43.

Wilson, Woodrow. 1900. *Congressional Government: A Study in American Politics.* Boston: Houghton Mifflin.

Wolack, Jenifer. 2010. "Why Do People Support Political Compromise?" Paper read at the Annual Meeting the American Political Science Association. Washington D.C.

Woon, Jonathan. 2008. "Bill Sponsorship in Congress: The Moderating Effect of Agenda Positions on Legislative Proposals." *Journal of Politics* 70 (1):201–16.

Wright, Gerald C. 2007. "Do Term Limits Affect Legislative Roll Call Voting? Representation, Polarization, and Participation." *State Politics and Policy Quarterly* 7 (3):256–80.

Zaller, John. 1992. *The Nature and Origin of Mass Opinion.* New York: Cambridge University Press.

Zhang, Yan, A. J. Friend, Amanda L. Traud, Mason A. Porter, James H. Fowler, and Peter J. Mucha. 2008. "Community Structure in Congressional Cosponsorship Networks." *Physica A* 387 (7):1705–12.

Index